The BIG Book of Engagement Strategies

A Continuation of the Book
Engagement is Not a Unicorn
(It's a Narwhal)

Heather Lyon

Copyright © 2021 by Heather Lyon
Published by EduMatch®
PO Box 150324, Alexandria, VA 22315
www.edumatchpublishing.com

All rights reserved. No portion of this book may be reproduced in any form without permission from the publisher, except as permitted by U.S. copyright law. For permissions contact sarah@edumatch.org.

These books are available at special discounts when purchased in quantities of 10 or more for use as premiums, promotions fundraising, and educational use. For inquiries and details, contact the publisher: sarah@edumatch.org.

ISBN: 978-1-953852-42-7

Again and always…
To you Howard, Nolan, Lilia, & Oliver

Also, to all the educators who strive for engagement…
May your progress be all the perfection you need

Praise for *The BIG Book of Engagement Strategies*

"This is the book I desperately needed in year one, and it's the book I still desperately need at year twenty-six. A brilliant mix of both the magical and the practical, Heather has offered the right recipe for teachers to prepare our practice to meet the engagement tastes for each of our hungry humans. A brilliant book that will be at my table for the rest of my career." ~ *Monte Syrie, English Teacher*

"Heather links practical strategies with the concepts associated with meaningfully engaging students in learning. You will find these strategies organized in such a way as to quickly identify which one(s) to use with which student(s) to maximize engagement." ~ *Chad Dumas, Educational Consultant and Author*

"A must-have resource for teachers who want to grow and learn how to move students toward real engagement. You'll find a strategy for every subject and situation while challenging your beliefs about why, how, and what you teach."
~ *Lisa Davidson, K-12 Science Instructional Specialist, National Association of Biology Teachers*

"The BIG Book of Engagement Strategies is a must read for educators. Its supportive tone, thought-provoking rationales, and straightforward explanations for creative classroom implementation make this book a tremendous resource. With over fifty detailed strategies covering compliance, interest, and absorption, Heather Lyon and her contributors have provided teachers with a wonderful gift!" ~ *Julia Borgisi, English Teacher and Technology Integrator*

"This book by Heather Lyon transformed my thinking about engagement strategies. This is a timely must-have for educators to assist them with meeting needs of their diverse learners by zeroing in on just the right strategies to catapult learner engagement." ~ *Kelley Key, Instructional Coach*

"My favorite was Chapter 9 because there were so many practical applications and lots of, 'Oh I loved doing that when I was in the classroom...' and 'Oh, I wish I would have read this book when I was about three years in...' and lots of things I could relate to as a parent (which so many of our teachers are). This is the kind of book that could be read and re-read! Buy it for your teachers as a, 'Congratulations on your tenure appointment' present!'" ~ *Jill Heck, Director of Curriculum, Instruction, Assessment and Technology*

"If we know what engagement in today's classrooms should look like, *The BIG Book of Engagement Strategies* shows us how. Lyon's grab-and-go strategies are easy to make sense of and can be put into practice right away. If you're looking for ways to help students become absorbed in their learning, look no further. No matter what grade or content you teach, dreams of seeing a unicorn become reality, as Lyon's comprehensive list of strategies will help you to discover narwhals in your classroom each and every day." ~ *Diana Maskell, K-16 Educator*

"This book is a must-have follow-up to *Engagement is not a Unicorn* with ready-to-implement strategies for your classroom along with personal stories from Heather" ~ *Dr. Dana Goodier, Podcast Host, Blogger, and Middle School Leader*

"I have had the pleasure of knowing and working with Dr. Heather Lyon while serving on the school board at Lewiston Porter. She not only believes in the work she is doing, she is more than willing to share it with those outside her own district through her writing. Her book is filled with engagement strategies that any teacher can use right now. It should be on every teacher's desk as a reference to what engagement should look like in the classroom." ~ *Matt Mariglia, Social Studies Teacher, Technology Integrator, Google for Education Certified Trainer*

About the Author

Heather Lyon is author of *Engagement is not a Unicorn (It's a Narwhal)* and *The BIG Book of Engagement Strategies*. Heather is a former English teacher and has a Ph.D. in Educational Administration and an Ed.M. in Reading from the University at Buffalo. She is an Assistant Superintendent of Curriculum, Instruction, and Technology for Lewiston-Porter Central School District in Western New York. Heather has been a staff developer and held various administrative titles, but the professional title she likes best is learner. She is also a proud wife and mother who struggles with but values the importance of boundaries and balance—which are so critical for all of us. Heather lives with her husband and three children, who make her smile and teach her the importance of kindness, respect, and patience.

Please follow Heather on Twitter @LyonsLetters and visit her website www.LyonsLetters.com.

You can find Heather Lyon's first book, *Engagement is Not a Unicorn (It's a Narwhal)* at:
- www. edumatch-publishing.myshopify.com/
- www.Amazon.com
- www.BarnesandNoble.com

Contributors

I have learned two very important truths in the process of writing *The BIG Book of Engagement Strategies*. First I've learned that everyone has at least one strategy to increase engagement. That means if you are ever stuck, all you need to do is talk with people you already know and trust. They will be able to give you the inspiration you need. The second is that it feels amazing to share the great work that others are doing! With respect to both of these points, I have the tremendous privilege to share the work of some amazing people that I have met along this journey. I have no doubt that you will enjoy their work as much I do!

In Alphabetical Order

Dana Britt

Strategy: Goals
Dana Britt is an Associate Partner with Education Elements, a national education consultancy provider. At Education Elements, Dana has supported over 100 schools in sixteen states to design personalized learning experiences for all learners, develop and implement strategic plans, and lead high quality professional development. Dana currently leads the organization's work in the state of New York. Prior to joining Education Elements, Dana worked in the District of Columbia Public Schools, first as a high school English teacher, then in the district office as the Manager of Educational Technology. Dana holds a B.A. in English from Wellesley College and an Ed.M. in Technology, Innovation, and Education from Harvard University. When not thinking about personalized learning or strategic planning, Dana enjoys rock climbing and training for her next marathon in Washington, DC.

Strategy: Notice and Wonder
Elizabeth (Liz) Buck has been teaching both earth science and general science at the middle school level for over twenty-one years. The majority of her career has been spent teaching at Lewiston-Porter Middle School in Youngstown, NY. Her approach to teaching has always been a hands-on, experiential method where students engage in the world around them through science. She creates opportunities for her students to consider multiple perspectives and challenges them to ask thought-provoking questions as a way to deepen their thinking.

Elizabeth Buck

Nina Calarco

Strategy: Notice and Wonder
Nina Calarco has been fortunate to be teaching at Lewiston-Porter Middle School for over fifteen years. For the majority of her career, Nina taught mathematics to 8th grade students. In 2016, she also started teaching a course that she co-created called "Innovation Experience." The course became her passion and inspired her to make impactful changes to her mathematics instruction based on what she learned from her Innovation students. Her non-traditional approach focuses on student discourse and a model where students explore and discover mathematics before formal instruction.

Strategy: Standards-Based Grading

Jessica Colavecchia

Jessica Colavecchia has been an educator in the East Irondequoit Central School District for over a decade, where she has been a high school math teacher and is currently the K-12 Math, Science, Technology Coordinator for the district. She also holds her Educational Leadership certification from the University of Rochester. She takes pride in her career knowing that she is helping to shape the lives of future generations by providing students with a deep-rooted, digitally rich, standards-based education. She has proudly shared her passion for educational technology, standards-based curricula and grading systems at various conferences throughout the country. Jessica lives with her husband Greg and their three children. When she is not sharing her enthusiasm for mathematics, she enjoys exercising, camping, sports, puzzles, and traveling.

Susan Cyrulik

Strategy: Modeling

Susan Cyrulik (M.S.Ed.) is a Professional Development Coordinator for Erie 1 BOCES where she shares her passion for science with everyone she meets. Her work is focused on supporting K-12 teachers of science while integrating the use of phenomena and the science and engineering practices, from the New York State P-12 Science Learning Standards. Susan is on the Board of the Western Section Science Teachers Association and the New York State Science Consortium. Prior to working at Erie 1 BOCES, Susan enjoyed her career as a middle school teacher, at the Charter School for Applied Technologies in Buffalo, New York, and in Westport, Connecticut, at Bedford Middle School. Susan is supported at home by her husband and three young men, who she strives to help understand the importance of caring for the planet. Susan is always accessible by email (scyrulik@e1b.org) and welcomes your communication.

Strategies: Peer-To-Peer Mentoring, Targeted Assistance, Community Building Circles, and Service Learning Projects

Lori DeCarlo

Lori DeCarlo retired from the position of Superintendent at Randolph Academy UFSD where the implementation of Restorative Practices began in 2015. As a certified Restorative Justice (RJ) trainer, she has studied under internationally renowned experts in the field. She serves as a trainer for New York State Education Department and New York State Division of Criminal Justice Services sponsored RJ projects. Ms. DeCarlo presents on the topic of RJ and school climate and culture at state, regional, and local conferences. She also practices the art of "circle keeping" by facilitating circles for community organizations. Follow her on Twitter @ldecarlo23.

Molly DiPerro

Strategies: Esti-Mysteries, Which One Doesn't Belong, Can You Make It, and Strategy Share

Molly DiPirro is a math coach and teacher in the Sweet Home School District in western New York. She is also a professional developer for all things related to math routines and number sense development. You can follow Molly on Twitter @mollydip.

Strategy: Golden Lasso Moments
Michael Fisher is an author and instructional coach who works with schools to design contemporary curriculum and modernize instruction with an array of technologies. Michael is the author of several books published by ASCD, Solution Tree, and Times10 publications, most recently *Hacking Instructional Design*. For more information, visit The Digigogy Collaborative (digigogy.com) or find Michael on Twitter @fisher1000.

Michael Fisher

Rebecca Gibboney

Strategy: Be The Tiebreaker
Rebecca Gibboney is currently a Curriculum Specialist but started her career in education in 2010 as a Spanish teacher and Instructional Coach in Williamsport, Pennsylvania. She is passionate about two things in life: sports and education. As a women's assistant college basketball coach and a passionate educational change agent, she lives the best of both worlds. She continues to provide fun and engaging avenues for adult learning while challenging the traditional mindset of professional learning. There is no reason why professional learning experiences cannot add some fun to the workplace! For more information on *The Tiebreaker,* you can follow Rebecca Gibboney on Twitter and Instagram @GibboneyRebecca or visit her website www.rebeccagibboney.com. You can find her book on Amazon https://bit.ly/theTIEBREAKER.

Strategy: Story-Based Learning
Drew Kahn is a State University of New York (SUNY) Distinguished Service Professor in the Department of Theater at SUNY Buffalo State where he teaches acting (President's Award for Excellence in Teaching/SUNY) and has directed over 20 productions (Kennedy Center Award). In addition to his work in higher education, he has taught K-12 populations for over three decades. He is the Founding Director of the Anne Frank Project. He presents and teaches internationally on the use of story as a tool for conflict resolution, community building and identity exploration—most recently in Rwanda, Kenya, Switzerland, DR Congo, Turkey, Burma and Viet Nam (Toby Ticktin Back Award for Holocaust Education and the National Federation for Just Communities-Community Leader Award,). His book, *Story Building: A Practical Guide for Bringing the Power of Stories into the Classroom* is used by teachers and organizations around the world. His favorite roles are husband to his wife Maria and dad to his children Sam and Nate.

Drew Kahn

Melissa Laun

Strategy: Playlists
With her undergraduate degree in in Special and Elementary Education and a master's in Adolescent Education, Melissa Laun worked in various classroom settings ranging from kindergarten through middle school and taught graduate courses for Buffalo State College in the Exceptional Education department. In 2013, Melissa graduated with an advanced certificate in Educational Leadership from the University at Buffalo LIFTS program. In 2018, she became a certified CliftonStrengths coach. Currently Melissa serves as the Director of Special Education and Grant Writing in Lewiston-Porter Central School District. She most enjoys her role in evaluation and coaching teachers, administrators, and related service providers in all areas of growth.

Strategy: Reel Them In

Andrew Marotta

Andrew Marotta is an energetic and enthusiastic leader who has put his positive imprint on his beloved Port Jervis HS, in Port Jervis, NY. With the release of his first book, *The Principal: Surviving and Thriving*, Andrew is expanding his impact on the educational leadership community. His second book, *The Partnership, Surviving & Thriving* is a guide for parents to better assist their children in school by working closely together with schools. In his personal life, Andrew is a loving husband to his wife, Jennifer, and supportive father to their three young children. In his professional life, Andrew has been at Port Jervis HS for over sixteen years, serving as Assistant Principal for seven years and Principal thereafter. Learn more at www.andrewmarotta.com and through his #ELBlog and #ELB podcast, *Education Leadership & Beyond*, found on Facebook, LinkedIn, Twitter @andrewmarotta21, and Instagram.

Angela Messenger

Strategy: Standards-Based Grading

Angela Messenger has been in education for over fifteen years and is currently a high school math teacher in the East Irondequoit Central School District located in Rochester, NY. In 2019, she presented at the NYSCATE Annual Conference about how she uses a standards-based grading approach to engage her students in learning mathematics. Angela is also a Noyce Digitally Rich Master Teaching Fellow at the Warner School of Education at the University of Rochester and is in the process of earning her Educational Leadership certification. Angela lives with her husband Jason and their three daughters. She enjoys camping, running, and decorating cookies when she is not shaping the mathematical minds of the future.

Strategy: Standards-Based Grading

Nicole Mucica

Dr. Nicole Mucica is an Instructional Technology Specialist/Special Education/Math teacher in the East Irondequoit Central School District located in Rochester, New York. She is also an adjunct professor for Inclusive Education Studies at SUNY Brockport. Dr. Mucica completed her Doctoral studies in Teaching and Curriculum at the University of Rochester. She has spent over seventeen years working in the field of education, and is passionate about sharing her experiences and triumphs with standards-based grading. Nicole has presented at numerous conferences around the country about digital engagement, differentiation and equity. Nicole resides with her husband Scott and two children. Please follow Nicole on Twitter @nicolemquick1.

Michael Neumire

Strategy: Student Gamification

Mike Neumire is an instructional technology coach in Rochester, NY. You can keep track of his gamification efforts at libguides.monroe2boces.org/gamify or follow him on Twitter @MNeumire.

Strategy: Room to Breathe

Erin Quinn and Tara Vandertoorn are Grade 8 Humanities teachers at Griffith Woods School in Calgary, Alberta, Canada. They embrace an approach to teaching where their students are co-creators of curriculum. This philosophy has informed their personalized Language Arts program, Room to Breathe and the game-based learning they embrace in Social Studies. Learn more at http://www.creativitycollective.ca/. You can find them on Twitter at @luckybydesign (Erin Quinn) and @bestcircus (Tara Vandertoorn).

Erin Quinn & Tara Vandertoorn

Acknowledgments

How do I put words to the gratitude I feel for the people and opportunities life has blessed me with? The task feels so daunting that what you see here is my feeble attempt; no matter how genuine and strong these words are, the words pale in comparison to the feelings they represent.

First, I want to thank the entire EduMatch Team led by the energetic and empowering Sarah-Jane Thomas. Though you are one-of-a-kind, I wish there were more people like you. Mandy Froehlich, you are one of the most supportive and warm people I know. You make me feel like I not only have something to say, but that my voice is important to the conversation. Thank you. Judy Arzt, thank you once again for your eyes and edits. Finally, I hope that any educator who is considering writing a book has the chance to work with the EduMatch family.

I teach aspiring administrators and I tell my students that if someone says, "It's lonely at the top," they're doing it wrong. If leaders are lonely, they cannot be a leader since being a leader requires a team, a community, and colleagues. I adore being a part of the Lewiston-Porter Central School District community and having the chance to work with so many inspiring and talented teachers, leaders, students, and partners. The opportunities to learn and lead in WNY are possible thanks to the tremendous leadership within the region that I call home.

I am also living proof of the power of a Professional Learning Network who answered my call to action when I was looking for contributors and reviewers for this book. Thank you again to all of the contributors named already and to the reviewers including (alphabetically): Lisa Davidson, Chad Dumas, Kara Dymond, Dana Goodier, Jill Heck, Kelley Key, Mariah Kramer, Melissa Laun, Erin Lawrence, Matt Mariglia, Diana Maskell, Melissa Rivers, and Monte Syrie.

I am who I am because of my family including my mom, dad, brother and two sisters. A special shout out to Emily Schultheis for being not just my sister, but my life-long friend. More importantly, thanks for being the best aunt (A.K.A. Emmy) for "the crazies." XOXO

Nolan, Lil, and Oliver, thank you for your inspiration. Being your mom is the greatest gift and my biggest challenge. You are all exactly who you are supposed to be and I love you.

People always ask me how I could find the time to write one book, let alone two. For me, the answer is easy—it's because of the unwavering love and support from my husband, Howard. Though neither of us is perfect, we are perfect for each other. Without you, I can't be me.

Contents

Chapter 1   1

Section I: Compliance Strategies   25

  Chapter 2: Relationship Building Strategies   27
    Strategy 1: Being Seen   31
    Strategy 2: Check In/Check Out   34
    Strategy 3: Peer-To-Peer Mentoring   36
    Strategy 4: Targeted Assistance   37
    Strategy 5: Community Building Circles   38

  Chapter 3: Communication Strategies   51
    Strategy 6: Getting to Know You Survey   53
    Strategy 7: Catch of the Week   58
    Strategy 8: Positive Communication   60
    Strategy 9: Creating Norms   63
    Strategy 10: Building Interdependence with Story Based Learning   66

  Chpater 4: Consequence Strategies   77
    Strategy 11: Wheel of Fortune   81
    Strategy 12: stickK Contracts   83
    Strategy 13: Everyone Gets an A   84

Section II: Interest Strategies   89

  Chapter 5: Choice and Voice Strategies   91
    Strategy 14: Directed Volunteers   96
    Strategy 15: Coalition of the Willing   98
    Strategy 16: All, Most, Some Learning Targets   102
    Strategy 17: Earn a Badge   105
    Strategy 18: Playlist   108
    Strategy 19: Audiobooks   112

  Chapter 6: Change the Task Strategies   119
    Strategy 20: Peer Feedback   124
    Strategy 21: But Why Does This Matter   129
    Strategy 22: Don't Kill the Wonder   133
    Strategy 23: Talk Moves   137
    Strategy 24: Notice and Wonder   140
    Strategy 25: Math Accountable Talk   145
    Strategy 26: Esti-Mysteries   146
    Strategy 27: Which One Doesn't Belong   148
    Strategy 28: Can You Make It   149
    Strategy 29: Strategy Share   150

Strategy 30: Modeling 153
Strategy 31: Spaced Repetition 157
Strategy 32: 4DX 161
Strategy 33: Read for Speed 167

Chapter 7: Scheduling Strategies **175**
Strategy 34: Intervention Block 178
Strategy 35: Change the Start/End Times 181
Strategy 36: Flipped Classroom 182
Strategy 37: Workshop 185
Strategy 38: Brain Breaks 188

Section III: Absorption Strategies **195**

Chapter 8: Culture, Values, and Belief Strategies **197**
Strategy 39: Who Do You Want to Be 202
Strategy 40: The Learning Pit 203
Strategy 41: Morning T.E.A.M. Time 207

Chapter 9: Grading Strategies **213**
Strategy 42: Focus on the Learning 217
Strategy 43: Goals 222
Strategy 44: Standards-Based Grading 227
Strategy 45: Withholding Scores 244

Chapter 10: Exposure Strategies **249**
Strategy 46: Field Trips 252
Strategy 47: Clubs 255
Strategy 48: Internships 256

Chapter 11: Hook Strategies **263**
Strategy 49: Reel Them In 265
Strategy 50: Be The Tiebreaker 270
Strategy 51: Student Gamification 276

Chapter 12: Project Strategies **285**
Strategy 52: Service Learning Projects 289
Strategy 53: Problem-Based Learning 292
Strategy 54: Golden Lasso Moments 295
Strategy 55: FedEx Day 302
Strategy 56: Room to Breathe 305

Section V: Conclusion **325**
   Chapter 13: Do It **327**

References **331**

Chapter 1

Setting the Stage

*"Your future hasn't been written yet. No one's has.
Your future is whatever you make it. So make it a good one."*
~Doc Brown

Recognizing Your Thinking Before You Read…

1. What are you hoping to learn as a result of reading this book?

   _____

   _____

   _____

2. When you read books, how do you share your learning with others and/or take what you're reading about and put it into practice?

   _____

   _____

   _____

3. Write down an example of when you were engaged as a learner.

   _____

   _____

   _____

Let's Start at the Very Beginning

If you are a student-teacher, teaching assistant, teacher, coach, staff developer, and/or administrator and you're looking for a strategy book to build engagement, *The BIG Book of Engagement Strategies* was designed for you! This book has over fifty strategies that you can use tomorrow with students (alright—some of them will require a little more prep, but you get the gist). What's more, though many of the strategies in this book use a specific content area or grade level for an example, most can be easily modified no matter the age or ability of the students you work with or the content area that you teach. Since there are many books available with strategies that promise to engage students, that's not what makes this book different. *The BIG Book of Engagement Strategies* is unique because it categorizes strategies according to The Engagement Framework I first laid out in the book *Engagement is Not a Unicorn (It's a Narwhal)*.

Of course, I would hope that you have read *Engagement is Not a Unicorn (It's a Narwhal)* before reading this book. However, I know that some people reading this book have not. No worries! I've got you covered. Chapter 1 is written as a refresher for those who have read it and as a summary for those who haven't (yet).

Back to the Future

When I wrote *Engagement is Not a Unicorn (It's a Narwhal)*, my goal was to create a common understanding regarding the term "engagement"—this over-used, under-understood word that is thrown around in education (and certainly other professions). I wanted to ensure that if we were going to say that we needed students to be engaged or teachers to create engaging lessons that we knew both what we were saying and what we were aiming for. There were plenty of strategy books out there already that say they will help you create engagement—that was not the problem. The problem was that there wasn't clarity about what engagement actually was. In other words, I didn't want my book to be another strategy book. I wanted my book to be a resource for understanding how to select a strategy to achieve engagement.

I knew I wanted to have sections that communicated (1) what engagement was, (2) why engagement mattered, and (3) how to take that information and use it. After that initial explanation of what I call The Engagement Framework, the book was divided into three sections: What, So What, and Now What. Using this structure, I provided readers with understanding of the four different levels of engagement in the What and So What sections and then included some example strategies in the Now What section. As I embarked on actually writing the book, I realized that I had so many strategies in my first draft that the book was over 400 pages. Even if there were 200 pages of strategies, I didn't think that people would have the stamina or desire to get through them. Thus, I thought it might be better to streamline the first book and have a companion book (the one you're reading right now) of just strategies.

Narwhals are REAL

Let me start by explaining the title. I have nothing against unicorns. They're beautiful and well-known. However, even though we all know what unicorns are, unicorns are mythical. Engagement can feel that way too at times because even though so much is written about engagement, it can feel like it's not real—something that we all talk about or know in our collective imaginations, but in a classroom is as hard to find as a real unicorn. In fact, while in the middle of writing the first book I feared that this might be true. Upon continued research, reflection, and thinking back to all of the great examples of engagement I really have seen in classrooms, I realized that engagement is not a unicorn, it's a narwhal—a very real animal that is found in the wild even though most people haven't seen them in real life and some people do not even know what they are. In case you don't know what a narwhal is, it looks like a dolphin with a unicorn horn coming out of its head. In figure 1.1 you can see a side-by-side comparison of what engagement in schools would look like as a unicorn and what it looks like as a narwhal.

Figure 1.1: Examples of Engagement as a Unicorn Versus Engagement as a Narwhal[1]

Engagement as a Unicorn	Engagement as a Narwhal
Students applaud and thank the teacher for the fantastic lesson	Students feel proud of their own work and learning
Teachers have endless amounts of resources to add bells and whistles to the lesson to entice students into learning	Teachers have some resources, but the students seek out and provide their own resources as part of the learning process
There is an infinite amount of learning time so the teachers can dig into the things they believe the students are interested in the most	Students make time outside of the classroom to continue digging into the things that they want to know more about
Students fall in love with what the teachers are having them study	Students are empowered to use what they know and care about to drive what they are studying
Parameters like standards, curriculum, and assessments are determined by the teacher	The teacher and students leverage the dictated parameters so that even if the teacher has boundaries, the students have high levels of freedom
Differentiation means that the teacher has created individualization for all students	Differentiation means that the students are trusted to create ways to personalize the task
Teachers can set aside the learning to get to know students	Everyone in the learning environment creates relationships through teaching and learning
All students always do their homework	Homework is learning practice meaning only those who need the practice need to do it
All students get perfect scores on all tests	Students who do not do well on assignments take advantage of the chance to re-do their work because they are focused on the learning
All students do what they're told	Students have a say in what they do
All students find even hard work easy	Students persevere even when the work is hard and seek out challenge

What you need to know is that this book and its predecessor are premised on the idea that it is possible to achieve the highest levels of engagement in schools but doing so, is not common. It does exist, but many people have never seen it, some don't even believe it's possible because they can't even imagine it, and still others think they've achieved it even when they haven't. In schools, absorption (the highest form of engagement) would look like student-driven environments where students initiate the learning and are intrinsically *compelled* to learn. They want to keep at it after the bell rings. After the lesson is over. After the unit is done. Even if they weren't getting graded. It's out there, but it's a narwhal. My previous book aimed to shine a light on the mysterious educational narwhal by explaining what engagement is and is not in order to spawn as many narwhals in your school as possible. The aim of this book is to provide you with even more strategies to achieve that same outcome.

In *Engagement is Not a Unicorn (It's a Narwhal)*, I shared that the reason I started thinking about engagement was due to the fact that two people can watch the same lesson and yet one can walk away saying "Boy those students were engaged" and the other can say, "I don't know what you're talking about. Those students weren't engaged at all." How can it be that they both saw the same lesson and walked away with two different impressions? The answer is easy. This happens because there is not agreement on what engagement is (and isn't) so even though both people are using the same word, the word has different meanings for each person.

So, what is engagement really? To define it, I created an Engagement Continuum (see Figure 1.2).

Figure 1.2: The Engagement Continuum

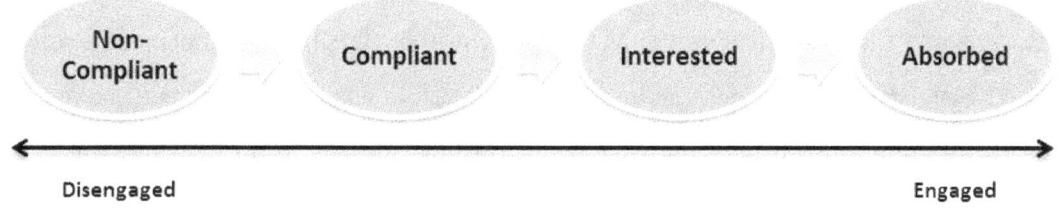

While the terms, "non-compliant" and "compliant" are likely self-evident, for the sake of explanation, below are brief definitions for the purposes of The Engagement Continuum.

- **Non-Compliant:** Actively or passively refusing to do what was expected; insubordinate.
- **Compliant**: Doing the minimum of what was expected but only because there is a consequence[i] (positive or negative) if it wasn't completed.
- **Interested**: Going beyond the minimum expectations because the task is stimulating and has momentary value. Generally speaking, the task is enjoyable but not something that would be done unless it was required and there was a positive or negative consequence doing it.
- **Absorbed**: Getting so involved in a challenging task that the person doing it intrinsically wants to continue even when given the option or direction to stop.

With The Engagement Continuum, as people increase their level of engagement, they move to the right. Conversely, if their engagement decreases, they move to the left. It's important to note that it is not until people move from compliance to interested that they become truly engaged; non-compliance and compliance are both forms of disengagement. While this representation shows movement, it fails to identify what conditions are linked with the progression or regression.

Upon continued reflection, I came to see The Engagement Continuum as bending with both of the poles coming to the middle so that The Engagement Continuum morphs into the 2x2 Engagement Matrix shown in Figure 1.3. The horizontal rows in The Engagement Matrix demonstrate a person's relationship with the task; the left side has a low relationship with the task and the right side has a high relationship. The vertical columns in The Engagement Matrix demonstrate a person's relationship with the person assigning the task or the consequence for (not) completing the task, the

---

[i] With regard to the Engagement Framework, the term "consequence" is a neutral term that can be seen as either positive (like a reward) or negative (like a penalty).

bottom row has a low or irrelevant relationship with the person or consequence and the top row has a high relationship.

Figure I.3: The Engagement Matrix

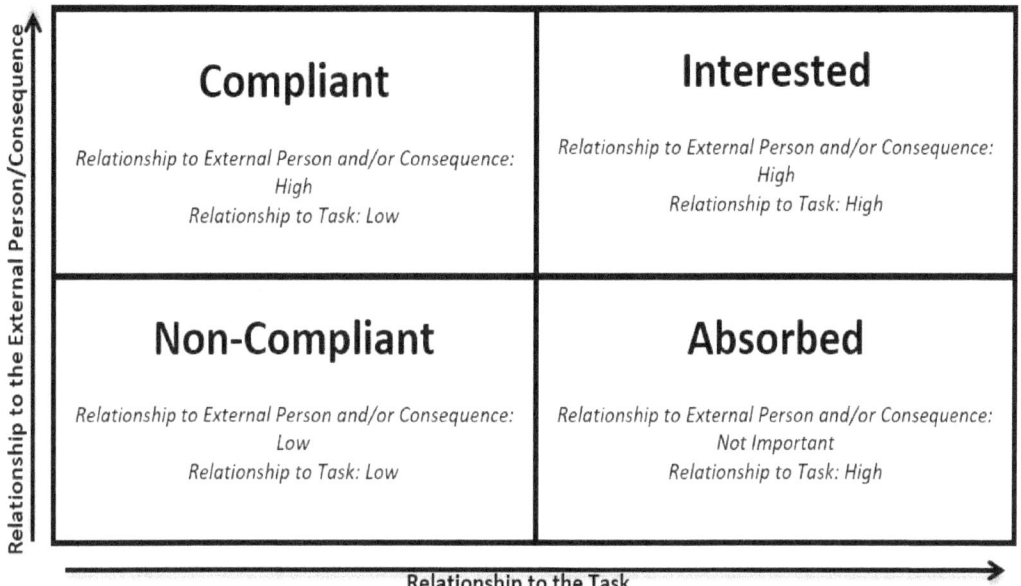

The Engagement Matrix shows that there are two common features between each of the markers on The Engagement Continuum. These features are (1) the relationship you have with the external person and/or consequence and (2) the relationship you have with the task you are doing. In short, The Engagement Continuum shows the linear progression of engagement and The Engagement Matrix shows the variables that impact the levels of engagement. Ultimately, I encapsulate The Engagement Continuum and The Engagement Matrix under the comprehensive umbrella I refer to as The Engagement Framework.

Intrinsic and extrinsic motivation are associated with engagement. However, there are strategic moves that can be made on the part of the person doing the work and/or the person assigning the work to increase someone's engagement in that work. Thus, The Engagement Framework is about more than just intrinsic or extrinsic motivation. Indeed, it is about the source of the motivation. Some people are motivated by a relationship, others are motivated by a reward. Still others are motivated by a punitive consequence. Depending on the source of the motivation, the location on The Engagement Continuum will be different.

The strategies included in this book are designed to help you move someone from one level of engagement to another. As a result, you could be helping someone go from non-compliant to compliant, from compliant to interested, and from interested to absorbed. The following ten highlights provide a general foundation to serve as a reminder to those who did read *Engagement is Not a Unicorn (It's a Narwhal)* and as a springboard for those who have not (yet). They will also provide a foundation on which to read any strategy that promises to lead to engagement. After all, if the strategy is about how to keep students in their seats, as an example, someone familiar with The Engagement Framework will say, "That strategy might help get students to be compliant, but will likely not achieve true engagement." In this way, The Engagement Framework becomes a filter through which you can view what is happening—be it in a classroom with students or in a faculty meeting with adults, a kitchen with your own children or the reason you're struggling to achieve a task you need to do.

Highlight 1: Remember Goldilocks.

Where to Look in *Engagement is Not a Unicorn*: Chapter 4

The first question we need to ask when someone is being non-compliant is whether or not the task they're supposed to be doing is within their Zone of Proximal Development (ZPD). If the task is too easy, the person will refuse due to disinterest. If the task is too hard, the person will refuse to complete the task due to discouragement.

Highlight 2: Though the variables that would create the shift to higher or lower levels of engagement are the same for everyone, not everyone responds the same way to those variables.

Where to Look in *Engagement is Not a Unicorn*: Chapter 2 and 8

It's easy to say that to go from non-compliant to compliant would require a change in someone's relationship with the consequence or the person assigning the task. However, what it takes to change the relationship will vary from person to person.

That's what's hard—trying to identify and respond to the variables needed to engage someone else.

 Highlight 3: Each level of engagement has a variety of ways in which that level manifests.

Where to Look in *Engagement is Not a Unicorn*: Chapter 4, 5, 6, and 7

In the book *Engagement is Not a Unicorn (It's a Narwhal),* I describe how each level of engagement has at least three different ways that level can manifest itself.

Manifestations of Engagement by Engagement Level	
Compliant	**Interested**
First-Timer	Willing Participant
People-Pleaser	Professional
Rule-Follower	Strategist
Non-Compliant	**Absorbed**
Rebel	Novice
Normalizer	Enthusiast
Activist	Addict

Understanding the manifestation can assist you in understanding the motivation behind the behavior and what might be needed in order to shift to a different level of engagement. *Engagement is Not a Unicorn (It's a Narwhal)* describes each level on the Engagement Continuum in great detail, gives examples of what each looks like in action, and provides strategies to help move from the left- to the right-side of The Continuum.

As a preview, here I'll focus on the manifestations of compliance. Compliant people are those who do not want to do the task but will do it because they have the right combination of extrinsic motivators via the impact to the relationship with the person assigning the task or the consequences for doing the task. Compliant people who are the closest to wanting to do the task are what I call "first-timers." These are people who have not done the task before and so they may be nervous and have a high desire to please. Examples of first-timers are student teachers or new hires at a job. These are people who wanted the job even if they did not realize all of the intricacies or requirements of the job. First-timers generally *want* to be told what to do and how to do it because they have not done it before.

People-pleasers are the second type of compliant people. People-pleasers are very concerned about the relationship and would do anything to avoid negatively impacting the relationship between themselves and the person(s) assigning the task. People-pleasers, in fact, may be interested in or even absorbed with the *person* assigning the task making it hard to recognize that they are only compliant with the task itself (i.e., I care about you and our relationship but not about this task). As well, people-pleasers may want to avoid conflict with the person assigning the task because they do not like that person.

Finally, compliance can appear as rule-followers who just want to do what they need to do to get the job done. The goal for rule-followers is task completion. This robotic obedience doesn't mean that they enjoy what they're doing, just that they've done it.

At the start of each new section in this book I will discuss the various manifestations of each quadrant in The Engagement Framework. Understanding what engagement at each level can look like helps to understand what might be needed to make a shift from one level to another.

Highlight 4: Compliance can feel like a victory (and it is) if someone was previously non-compliant. Nevertheless, compliance should not be the stopping point since compliant people are still disengaged.

Where to Look in *Engagement is Not a Unicorn*: Chapter 5 and 9

Since working with someone who is behaving non-compliantly can feel so defeating, it's not surprising that it feels good to have a previously non-compliant person become compliant. That shift is certainly worth celebrating because it is growth. There is a difference, however, between growth and attainment. Growth means you're on your way whereas attainment means you've arrived. Never mistake compliant behavior for engagement. It is not. Compliance is simply a disengaged person who is extrinsically motivated to do the task.

Setting the Stage   11

Highlight 5: Be on the lookout for people who are compliant with behaviors but are non-compliant with the learning.

Where to Look in *Engagement is Not a Unicorn*: Chapter 5 and 12

In far too many classrooms, as long as students are compliant with the behavioral expectations (think *stay in your seat, do not shout out,* etc.) they can be non-compliant with the learning expectations (think *read silently, work with a partner*, etc). Why? Students who are quiet and do not disrupt the learning of others can fall through the learning cracks passively or actively because they do not draw negative attention to themselves. If you only (or mostly) call on students who raise their hands, for example, students learn that they will not be called on if they do not raise their hands or that they should only raise their hand if they *know* the answer. A better approach would be to randomly call on students (see the strategy, "Equity Sticks" in the book *Engagement is Not a Unicorn [It's a Narwhal])*. Keeping students on their toes and ready to answer any question based on chance makes learning required (rather than voluntary) and will lead to more students being engaged.

Highlight 6: The easiest way to bolster engagement is to change the task.

Where to Look in *Engagement is Not a Unicorn*: Chapter 6, 10, and 13

If you are with people who are compliant, meaning they will do the task but they don't really want to do it, then they need to make a shift towards the right of the Engagement Matrix to become truly engaged. The way to move right is by changing the task. For example, let's say the task is to write an essay that identifies three factors that contributed to the American Civil War. Most students will certainly do that task, but few will cross the threshold into interested. If you reflect on what you are trying to ascertain in the writing of the essay, you will acknowledge that the purpose of the task is to have students demonstrate their knowledge of factors that contributed to the American Civil War. If this is the outcome, the task *could* be to write an essay, but it doesn't have to be. If given even two minutes to brainstorm alternative possibilities in how students could demonstrate their knowledge, I would guess any one person (teacher or not) could create a list of at least ten different possibilities. While changing the task might seem a little self-evident at first, classrooms often default to the tried and true, the known and familiar. Essays, end-of-chapter questions, worksheets, etc. are common compliance pitfalls and teachers accept that though boring, these products get the job done. The goal of engagement is more than getting the job done—it's about enjoying the job. And, who doesn't want to enjoy their work?

Highlight 7: If you can't change the task, at least offer choice and/or voice.

Where to Look in *Engagement is Not a Unicorn*: Chapter 6 and 10

I know it sounds simplistic to say, "Change the task and you will have more engagement." Some people reading this will roll their eyes and get defensive, retorting, "What if I can't change the task?!" It is true there are times when a task cannot be changed. Even for adults, there are mundane and unpleasant tasks that are unavoidable. We all have to pay our taxes, do laundry, and mow the grass. If given the opportunity to opt-out of these tasks, many of us would. Our students have to take tests, do homework, and pass certain courses to go on to the next grade and, ultimately, graduate. Like I said, there are times when a task cannot be changed.

Read my blog post, "Three Little Words" to learn more about choice and voice here: https://www.lyonsletters.com/post/three-little-words

The academic goal of the work in schools is for students to achieve the standards. While we have little to no control over the standards, we have a great deal of control over what students can do to demonstrate their achievement of the standards. Going back to the idea of paying taxes, the government does not care how you do your taxes—if you hire an accountant or if you do them yourself, if you do them on paper or electronically. There are many choices available to you regarding *how* you do your taxes even if you don't have a choice about doing them (assuming you're at least compliant). Now apply this thinking to schools. We need to think about how we can provide as much choice and voice to students in *how* they are doing their work even if we cannot provide choice or voice about doing it.

- **Choice refers to options.** Do I want the chicken or the fish? Do I want to do problem set one or problem set two? Would I prefer the fall, winter, or spring date for the training? These are all the options that I can select.
- **Voice is the ability to give input regarding decisions.** This input might be on the design, implementation, or the product. It is allowing people to contribute their ideas and have a say in the design of the task.

In short, the more the authority controls the creation of the task for those who are doing the task, the more likely the feelings towards that task will be at the compliant level (at most). The more voice and choice those doing the task have in the creation and/or selection of the task, the more likely the feelings towards that task will be at the interested level (at least).

So, going back to the test example for a moment, here are some possible ways to infuse choice and voice.

1. While students have to take tests, is there a way to allow students to choose five of seven short answer problems on the test—in other words, they don't have to do all the parts?
2. Rather than having the test be paper/pencil, could the students be given the choice to take the traditional test or do a summative project?
3. Could you have the students design some of the test questions or give voice to name which components of what they learned should be emphasized on the test?

These are just three ways in which choice and voice can be infused into tasks that cannot be changed.

Highlight 8: Interested people enjoy what they are doing temporarily and they still need extrinsic motivation to maintain their interest.

Where to Look in *Engagement is Not a Unicorn*: Chapter 6

Good news! The level of interested has been achieved! The people who are doing the assigned task, when asked, say that they are enjoying what they're doing and what they're doing is appropriately challenging. During group work, everyone is participating—perhaps some of them even have their "butts in the air" as they are leaning in so they can interact with the work that is being created. There is probably a great deal of noise as people talk with each other about the work they are doing. With any luck, they are even asking each other questions to challenge the answers they heard from their peers.

More than likely, when people are interested, they have been doing much of the work and the teacher/facilitator did most of the heavy-lifting during the planning/design portion, which is to say they did their work to prepare for their time with the students or adults. This means that during the time with the students or adults, the ones who are doing the heavy-lifting are the students or adults, not the teacher/facilitator who is probably circulating to give feedback, taking notes to remember things to change or do for the next session, and/or conferring with groups/individuals on their progress. If given the opportunity to present their work, interested people will be proud of it since they put in effort to do a good job. They are excited about the grade/evaluation they will earn because they are confident that it will be good and they feel like they have earned it.

Here's the "bad" news—or at least the aha news—interested people will stop doing interesting work when given the chance to stop. For example, when the bell rings, how do the students react? Interested students pack-up and leave *even if they were enjoying the work they were doing before the bell rang.* Is the project that they have been working on for weeks now over? Interested people will move on to the next assignment—they will not continue learning more about the project even if there is much more that could be learned. Interested people will do their homework, classwork, etc. but if you allow them to stop doing it, they will stop.

But wait, there's more. Interested people need the extrinsic consequences to do the task. Sure, they will do the task to please you (relationship) or get the grade (consequence) but if you said, "You are not going to disappoint me if you don't do this" or "This task is ungraded," what would happen? If they're only interested, they will stop. *I might as well do the task that is graded* or *Are you sure you won't mind if I stop? It's not that I don't like doing this, but I would prefer to do X...* Interested people are temporarily willing to do the task but only as long as they are rewarded for their efforts.

Highlight 9: No one is capable of being absorbed in everything all the time.

Where to Look in *Engagement is Not a Unicorn*: Chapter 7 and 11

Where interested people will stop, absorbed people persist. You have to tell absorbed people to put away their work because you've moved on. Take away the extrinsic motivator for the absorbed person and they may not even notice because they were never doing it for that anyway—they are intrinsically motivated. When people are absorbed, time passes differently. An hour can feel like ten minutes and it still feels like you want more time. The work you're doing is challenging but you are in-the-zone and feel fueled by the task. This is what Mihaly Csikszentmihalyi calls "flow" as described in the book by the same name.

With adults, the things we tend to find absorbing are the things we pay to do, i.e., our hobbies. In fact, it is not uncommon for people to be interested in their profession (that is, they enjoy their work but need to get paid to do it) but they are absorbed in things that they cannot get paid to do. During the COVID-19 quarantine, *CBS Sunday Morning* ran a segment called, "Baking Bread at Home: A Knead for Comfort" where reporter Martha Teichner interviewed people whose day jobs were not bakers but who found baking bread to be cathartic and rewarding. Bridgid Bibbens, a professional violinist, was forced to go home after her tour with a band was cut short. At home, she started to bake bread out of necessity since the grocery store had sold out. Though she'd never baked bread before, Bibbens became so absorbed in baking bread that she gave her sourdough starter a name. Dr. Craig Spencer, a NYC emergency room doctor, also professed his love of baking.

> "It's hard to take care of patients all day," Spencer said. "It's even harder to do so when you're afraid you're gonna [sic] get infected, and even harder to do so when you're doing it in goggles and in masks and in gloves. That is tough. What's even harder is the mental exhaustion that comes." Which is why the bread Dr. Spencer bakes for his family to eat nourishes him more.[2]

Neither Bibbens nor Spencer are getting paid to bake—they are doing it because at this point, they gain intrinsic payment for their efforts. Each would be disappointed if they were told to stop.

What does that look like in school? Absorbed students come into class and tell the teacher the things they learned on their own because they went home and looked it up. Absorbed students are still talking about the lesson days after it is over. Absorbed students may seek out others who are like them or hide in the background because they feel like they are in the margins. In schools, much of what students find absorbing happens outside of the general content—it's the clubs, the extra-curriculars, the activities that take place before- or after-school that are never graded. It's the tasks that students have to raise money for or earn in some way. That doesn't mean that the classroom isn't a prime location for absorption, but it does mean that it's not the only place.

Here is what is important: I have yet to find someone who doesn't demonstrate absorption in at least one thing. It could be reading, playing a sport, hiking, some type of art or craft, cooking, playing a video game, playing an instrument, gardening, posting on social media, searching Pinterest, learning a new language, etc. The list is truly endless. And, while I have yet to find someone who isn't absorbed in something, I also have yet to find someone who is absorbed in *everything*. Humans are not wired to feel this level of intrigue and investment in everything. It's rewarding to find "our people" who get us and enjoy what we enjoy. It's just as rewarding to encounter people who are different from us and enjoy the things we don't. Life would be very boring if we all liked and did the same things. So, what one person is absorbed in, another may only rise to the level of compliance. That's not just okay, that's to be expected.

Highlight 10: Being absorbed doesn't mean the task is easy, it means the task has the appropriate level of challenge and reward—both for failure and success.

Where to Look in *Engagement is Not a Unicorn*: Chapter 7

Remember, to be absorbed means that you are willing to do the task beyond the point that you are able to stop; it is not limited to a timeframe. As well, tasks that are absorbing are those that require persistence because we cannot achieve the highest levels of success the first time we attempt that task. If we did, the task would be too easy and we would lose interest. Tasks that are absorbing are those that require us to be gritty for the very fact that we will need to (a) devote a great deal of time and effort to it before we achieve the end goal and (b) because we will need to be resilient since we will experience failure along the way.

The best example I have of this is when people play videogames. Videogames are designed to work within one's Zone of Proximal Development. The first level is often very easy so you can see the basics of what you will need to do. Then, the game really starts. With that, you will almost certainly lose a few times before you progress to the next level. However, when you lose, you realize something about the game and that fuels your desire to apply that learning immediately. It is that feedback loop of failure and learning that we find absorbing. We do not want to give up because we feel like we are just about to do what we haven't been able to do yet. As we are learning what will make us successful at this level, we are also being primed for skills that will be needed at the next level so that when we "level-up" we are sufficiently able to enter that level but insufficiently prepared to master that level. Indeed, we would not want to play a game where we could breeze through the levels the first time we played it; that would be too easy and we would give up. No adult would want to play an alphabet game, but neither would a child who already knew the alphabet.

> **As we are learning what will make us successful at this level, we are also being primed for skills that will be needed at the next level so that when we "level-up" we are sufficiently able to enter that level but insufficiently prepared to master that level.**

Thinking Ahead

As you read this book, remember that it is non-fiction and you do not have to read it from cover-to-cover in order. Think of it more like a recipe book than a novel. Do you need an appetizer? Turn to this page. Want to make a dessert? Here are some options to consider. This approach is why I have sections according to the quadrants in The Engagement Framework and grouped the chapters to align with the influences within each quadrant. At the same time, this is not just a how-to book that simply gives step-by-step directions on how to use a strategy. I wanted to include more than just the *how* but also some information on *what* and *why*.

As a word of caution, I have organized the strategies in this book in groupings that made the most sense to me. I also had a specific idea about how that strategy would be implemented. Like I said, this is a recipe book, not a book of guaranteed magical incantations. Thus, your implementation of any strategy is impacted by the conditions in which you attempt it, which I neither know nor can control. For these reasons, you should see my categorizations as a suggestions rather than an absolute. Therefore, you may find that your use of a strategy that I have listed as a tool to help students become compliant actually creates higher levels of engagement for your students. The opposite may be true too. I may have a strategy that is under the umbrella of helping to create interest but your students only achieve an engagement level of compliance with that strategy, at best. Again, the headings I used made the most sense to me as I included them and you should feel comfortable to reclassify them differently based on your knowledge, experiences, and conditions for use.

I also want to again spotlight the numerous and valuable contributions that others made to the creation of this book. This book would not be possible without collaboration. If I had not already known it before, I certainly know now that the collective intelligence of a group far surpasses the intelligence of any one person. Furthermore, through collaborating with others, any one person's load is lightened. For these reasons, I cannot emphasize enough that *everyone* has at least one strategy that they are an expert in that you might not have heard of before. All you have to do is ask, "Can you please share with me a strategy you use to…" build relationships, offer choice and voice, establish a learning-first culture, etc. I'm saying this because even though I want you to read this book and other strategy books, I also want you to connect with the people around you about what they're doing because you can learn so much from your neighbors—be it those in your physical Professional Learning Community or your digital Professional Learning Network.

Now What

In the book, *Building a Story Brand: Clarify Your Message So Customers Will Listen,* the author, Ronald Miller, explains that in stories there is always a hero and usually a guide. Despite being called a hero, the protagonist has challenges that must be overcome. For this reason,

> Heroes are often ill-equipped and filled with self-doubt. They don't know if they have what it takes. They are often reluctant, being thrown into the story rather than willingly engaging the plot. The guide, however, has already 'been there and done that' and has conquered the hero's challenge in their own backstory.
>
> The guide, not the hero, is the one with the most authority. Still, the story is rarely about the guide. The guide simply plays a role. The story must always be focused on the hero...[3]

In reading this book, you are the hero; this book is the guide. As you read, you will find tools you need on your quest to create classrooms where both the students and you are engaged in the learning.

In *Engagement is Not a Unicorn (It's a Narwhal)*, I included a call to action at the end of the introduction. I feel compelled to reiterate that message here. Specifically, as a former staff developer and a current administrator, I have seen and read a great deal about the challenges of measuring the impact of professional development (PD). If attending PD was enough, then all we would have to do was go to a session, and our work would magically change. That's unicorn nonsense. Clearly, that doesn't happen. In my experience, even when I go to a great PD session, I struggle to apply what I have learned right away. Then, as time passes, the daily routines overshadow the intention to change. Though the message of the PD was important and powerful, the impact was minor. I want to remind you that reading a book is also PD, and though your intent right now is to read this to make changes, it will likely be difficult to change your habits. To safeguard against this, I will repeatedly challenge you, the hero, throughout the book to do the following:

- **THREE**: Before you read, identify at least three people with whom you will share the ideas you're having as a result of your reading. It doesn't matter with whom or how you will share your ideas, it just matters that you will share.

- **TWO**: As you're reading, find at least two ideas that change you…it may be because you are surprised or unsure or intrigued. It doesn't matter why you change; you're just noting the change.
- **ONE**: When you're done reading, apply at least one idea. Don't limit yourself to a professional application; it could just as easily be a personal one. The point is that you do more than just read and think about engagement—it's that you take what you've read and thought and do something with it.

You have the choice about whether or not you want to attend to each of these questions for the book as a whole or if you prefer to think about answers for each chapter. This is because each person reads and digests their reading differently. So, if you haven't already done so, grab a pack of Post-Its, a highlighter, and/or a pen and get ready to make this book truly yours! The margins are big so you can write in them. After all, this book is yours. You own it. More importantly, in order to own the learning, you need to be in control of how to personalize the experience of reading this book.

Finally, this call to action is here at the end of the first chapter so you can mindfully read this book with the persistent, even nagging, question, *what am I learning and how will I use it?* While it is important for this book to impact your thinking, this book is the most meaningful if your actions change.

Chapter Summary

This chapter was about setting the stage for reading the rest of this book. To accomplish this, the Engagement Continuum and Matrix were shared and showed that there are really four levels of engagement: (1) Non-Compliance, (2) Compliance, (3) Interested, and (4) Absorbed. There were also ten highlights from the book *Engagement is Not a Unicorn (It's a Narwhal)*. Since this book is non-fiction, feel free to read it in any order you choose. Finally, reading this book will have the greatest impact when you try out what you're reading so don't be afraid to try—in fact, find someone to talk to about what you're trying to help hold you accountable and to be someone with whom you can share ideas.

Looking for even more information about ENGAGEMENT?

Please visit my website, www.LyonsLetters.com/learnmore, for print and digital recommendations including books, websites, videos, and more!

Reflection Prompts

1. Give an example of when you were at a specific level of engagement (non-compliant, compliant, interested, or absorbed). What was the task and what circumstances influenced your engagement?

   _____
   _____
   _____

2. Which highlight(s) made the most sense to you and why?

   _____
   _____
   _____

3. Were there any highlights that you have questions about? If so, which one(s) and why?

   _____
   _____
   _____

4. Name one thing you could do tomorrow based on what you learned from this chapter.

   _____
   _____
   _____

5. Tweet me @LyonsLetters to share an idea for a future reading or digital resource I should share on www.lyonsletters.com that would help someone who to understand engagement.

Persistent Questions

1. What have you done so far regarding the three challenge questions from Chapter 1?

    a. **Three:** Find at least three people with whom to share your learning.

    b. **Two:** Find at least two ideas that change you.

    c. **One:** Apply at least one idea from your reading.

    _____
    _____
    _____

2. What have you learned so far, and how will you use it?

    _____
    _____
    _____

Section I: Compliance Strategies

The next three chapters will address strategies to help prevent or move from non-compliance to compliance. This is a vertical move. Don't be fooled. Strategies to achieve compliance are both valuable and not the stopping point.

	Compliant	**Interested**
	Relationship to External Person and/or Consequence: High Relationship to Task: Low	Relationship to External Person and/or Consequence: High Relationship to Task: High
	Non-Compliant	**Absorbed**
	Relationship to External Person and/or Consequence: Low Relationship to Task: Low	Relationship to External Person and/or Consequence: Not Important Relationship to Task: High

Y-axis: Relationship to the External Person/Consequence
X-axis: Relationship to the Task

Chapter 2 addresses strategies to build or repair relationships. Chapter 3 focuses on communication strategies. Chapter 4 addresses strategies that focus on consequences (positive and negative). By the end of Section I, you will be able to identify actions that can avoid non-compliance altogether or shift someone from being non-compliant to being at least compliant.

Chapter 2

Relationship Building Strategies

"To improve our schools, we have to humanize them and make education personal to every student and teacher in the system. Education is always about relationships. Great teachers are not just instructors and test administrators. They are mentors, coaches, motivators, and lifelong sources of inspiration to their students."
~Ken Robinson

Recognizing Your Thinking Before You Read...

1. What is a strategy that you currently use that helps you build relationships with students, teachers, and/or families?

   _____

   _____

   _____

2. Think about a time when there was a difficult situation between two or more people. How did the relationship impact the situation?

   _____

   _____

   _____

3. What are signs of a strong relationship?

   _____

   _____

   _____

I Think I Can't, I Think I Can't, I Think I Won't

Imagine that you've encountered someone being non-compliant. The first question to ask yourself and/or that person is why. We need to be clear that the task the person is refusing to do is within their Zone of Proximal Development (ZPD) before determining that someone is being non-compliant for:

1. Reasons related to the relationship with the person assigning the task
2. Reasons related to the relationship with the consequences for doing (or not) the task

In other words, is the refusal to do the task because the task is either too easy or too hard (see Highlight 1 in Chapter 1)? If my homework was "Practice tying your shoes ten times on your own," I wouldn't do it. I don't need to spend time practicing tying my shoes because I already can do that so well that I could teach others to do it. I'd be bored. If my homework was "Respond to the following question: 'Given an arbitrary compact gauge group, does a non-trivial quantum Yang–Mills theory with a finite mass gap exist,'"[4] (which by the way is an unsolved problem in physics), I would not even bother because it was too hard. Though I can read every word of the question, I do not know what "an arbitrary compact gauge group" or "non-trivial quantum Yang-Mills Theory" or "a finite mass gap" are. Even if I took the time to look up what each of those terms means, there would be terms within those definitions that I wouldn't understand. I might as well be written in Sanskrit because I wouldn't understand that any better.

> **This is to say that the first question needed to ask regarding non-compliance is whether or not the assigned task is reasonable doable by the person who is supposed to do it.**

This is to say that the first question needed to ask regarding non-compliance is whether or not the assigned task is reasonably doable by the person who is supposed to do it. If not, then it doesn't matter how strong the relationship is between the person assigning the task and the person doing it. If not, then it doesn't matter how great or intimidating the rewards or punishments would be. The person assigned the work is highly inclined to opt-out and will appear to be non-compliant. Correctly diagnosing the cause of the non-compliance will assist the person assigning the task with the highest possible likelihood of shifting the non-compliant person to a higher level of engagement.

What's Your Type

In *Engagement is Not a Unicorn (It's a Narwhal)*, I describe three different manifestations of non-compliance:

1. **Rebels**: Those who will not do the task and don't care about the impact to the relationship or the consequences for (not) doing the task (think about the person at a meeting who always disagrees with the group no matter what the group says).
2. **Normalizers**: Those who will not do the task because it is more common to not do it than to do it (think about people who speed—that's everyone at least a little right).
3. **Activists**: Those who will not do the task because doing the task violates their morals or beliefs (think Martin Luther King, Jr. who was willing to go to jail or die rather than submit to man-made laws that violated his God-given rights as a human being).

Most people default to the notion of rebellion when thinking about non-compliance when, in fact, rebellion may actually be the least common manifestation. The most common is normalization of non-compliance since we are all non-compliant much of the time without even thinking about it. We don't think twice about going 60 mph even though the speed limit is 55 mph. Who only goes as fast as the posted speed limit? Speeding just a little is what everyone does, right? We justify that it's okay to whisper to our neighbor in a movie theater even though the screen told us "Silence is Golden." Hypocritically, we have normalized whispering but find actual talking or loud whispers to be rebellious. During the COVID-19 pandemic, even people who willingly wore masks in public would normalize a small gathering of friends or family who were not wearing masks because, for some reason, if you knew the people who you were gathering with, wearing a mask felt like overkill. These are all examples of normalized non-compliance. Normalizers generally do not even see their behaviors as non-compliant because no one else is following the written rules, therefore they're not doing anything wrong.

With activists, it can be not just difficult, but impossible for them to become compliant with the expectations because while you may call them non-compliant with the task, they actually see themselves as absorbed in their beliefs. If you were a vegan for moral reasons and I told you that you must eat this steak or else, don't be surprised if the vegan refuses even if you changed your relationship or the consequence. Remember, to go from non-compliance to compliance is a *vertical* shift. The reason for the refusal is not about the variables on the vertical axis of the Engagement Matrix—it's about the task itself.

A Fine Line

It is worth noting that reasoning behind behavior can change over time. In other words, the reasoning behind rebellion is frequently due to an inability to do what is expected. What manifests as a lack of skill is hidden behind the mask of a lack of will. Put differently, if I cannot do what you ask me to do, I may prefer to pretend to be unwilling rather than expose that I am actually unable. In this way, in its simplest form, rebellious behaviors may actually be a manifestation of a rebel's fears of being unable to do what is asked. If I can't do it, I won't do it.

> **What manifests as a lack of skill is hidden behind the mask of a lack of will.**

It does not take long for rebellious behaviors to become the status quo behaviors for a rebel. This means that the initial and intentional refusals can turn into habits and patterns of behaviors. This is how a rebel can transition into a normalizer.

On the opposite end, there are activists. Unlike rebels, activists have the skill to do what was asked. What they lack is the will. Those who disagree with an activist will interpret the behaviors as resistance. True activists are those who blaze the trail. Those who follow the path that is already there normalize the path for others to follow. Ultimately, depending on how well-traveled the path becomes, those who do not go down the path can become non-compliant.

Now What

Assuming the task is within someone's ability level, the strategies in this chapter are about establishing and improving the relationship between the person assigning the task and the person doing the task. Building relationships takes time and effort. Nevertheless, building relationships (versus changing consequences or a task) is the surest way to avoid non-compliance altogether. Here are five strategies to consider when seeking to create and/or improve relationships.

1. Being Seen
2. Check In/Check Out
3. Peer-to-Peer Mentoring
4. Targeted Assistance
5. Community Building Circles

Strategy 1: Being Seen

A common reason why teachers fail to build relationships with students is because they claim that it takes time away from their instruction. Yet, building relationships with students improves learning outcomes and does not have to require large amounts of time. In other words, small investments of time can yield high returns.

In their 2011 research, then Stanford Ph.D. student David S. Yeager and assistant professor Gregory M. Walton, researched the impact of "small" "social-psychological interventions in education—that is, brief exercises that target students' thoughts, feelings, and beliefs in and about school" and found that these

> can lead to large gains in student achievement and sharply reduce achievement gaps even months and years later. These interventions do not teach students academic content but instead target students' psychology, such as their beliefs that they have the potential to improve their intelligence or that they belong and are valued in school.[5]

In other words, when we target students' wellbeing, we help students build a sense of belonging and connection to the school academically, socially, and emotionally.

There are some students who have relationships with multiple adults within the school because the students are easy to connect with. At the same time, there are also students who can slip through the proverbial cracks. This strategy helps to identify students who may not have relationships with even one adult and takes steps to build those relationships.

The Being Seen strategy is designed to purposefully create relationships for all students. When speaking about why she has teachers build relationships with students, Principal of Cold Springs Middle School in Reno, Nevada, Roberta Duvall, declared, "Every child deserves to have at least one adult in this building who knows them by name."[6] It's one thing to say relationships matter; identifying whether or not it is happening is another. Hence the strategy.

See the "Being Seen" strategy in use here:
https://cutt.ly/BeingSeen

The teachers at Cold Springs Middle School use a faculty meeting early in the year to determine which students in the school have at least one adult who has a relationship with them. As Chris Ewald, a teacher in the school said, "It's probably harder for them to feel valued in the learning environment without that connection to the teacher."[7]

The strategy follows the steps outlined below:

1. Create a chart like the one in Figure 2.1 to determine who knows the students by:
    a. Name and face
    b. Academic status
    c. Something personal about the child
    d. A personal story
2. What do you notice and wonder after you have identified which students are known and unknown.
3. Develop an action plan to ensure that the students who are unknown have relationships with at least one adult in the school.
4. Share out the action plans so others can benefit from your ideas.
5. Implement your ideas.

Figure 2.1: Sample Chart to Find "Missing" Students

	Known by Name and Face	Known by Academic Status	Known by Something Personal About Them	Known by Personal Story
Nick	✓ X *	✓ X *	✓ *	✓
Riley	✓ X	✓ X	✓ X	✓
Nevaeh	✓ *	✓ *		

(In this chart, each separate symbol [i.e., the checkmark, X, and asterisk] represents a different adult who claims knowledge of the student in that row and column.)

I have also seen this done by putting each student's name on a separate piece of paper (I've used Post-Its, but it could be something with tape stuck to the back) and putting the pieces of paper around the room. The teachers then walk around and take the paper that represents each student only if they are able to say that they know something personal about the student. Then, the students who remain on the wall are the ones who are targeted for building relationships with.

No matter what process is used, the process must ensure that the relationships with the students are more than superficial. The goal is to guarantee that all students have an adult in the school with whom they have a relationship; it is not to inflate the number of students with whom relationships exist. Thus, it is better to err on the side of over-identifying the students who do not have a relationship than the other way around.

> *Alternate Use:* Adult-to-adult relationships are equally important. As Zacarian, Alvarez-Ortiz, and Haynes remind us in their book, *Teaching to Strengths*, "schools need to be not only the best places to learn but also the best places to teach and work."[8] A process like this could be used to target administrator-teacher relationships to ensure that each teacher has a relationship with at least one administrator in the building or district.

Strategy 2: Check In/Check Out

When talking about Check In/Check Out (CI/CO) Jim Wright, the author of numerous Response to Intervention (RTI) books and the website www.InterventionCentral.org, writes, "Students can be motivated to improve classroom behaviors if they have both a clear roadmap of the teacher's behavioral expectations and incentives to work toward those behavioral goals."[9] CI/CO creates this clarity for the adults identifying the discrete behaviors to focus on and by communicating this with the student, teacher, and the parent. This also gives students something to work towards by providing them with incentives for improved behavior. This strategy is designed for use with students for whom the general classroom behavioral plan alone is not effective.

The best use of CI/CO is when you have a team that includes the student, teachers, at least one support service provider (like a counselor, psychologist, and/or a social worker), and potentially an administrator. They will be the people who help develop the plan as well as those who review how it is going. The most important member of the team is the student because the student has to have voice and choice in the plan; the student needs to want the reward and understand that the plan is in service to the student.

In fewer than ten minutes, you can watch a video that shows how CI/CO works here:
https://cutt.ly/CICO

In their video, Tim McIvor and Brendon Ross, school psychologists from Nevada concisely describe how CI/CO works with visual examples and include a link to create the documents you would need.[10] Basically, a plan is created with a small number (approximately three) behaviors that you want to see more of. These are included in a tracking sheet (see Figure 2.2 for a sample) that the student is responsible for. The student meets with their CI/CO adult who is *not* their teacher for a couple of minutes at the start of the day.

Figure 2.2: Sample Check In/Check Out Form from McIvor and Ross

My Daily Progress

Name: _____

Date: _____

Goal: _____

Be Respectful
Act Kindly
Follow Directions
Be Responsible
Work Hard
Keep Focused
Be Safe
Hands and Feet to Self
Stay in Seat

Target Behaviors	AM Check In	Writing	Reading	Math	Science/ Social Studies	Specials
Be Respectful	2 1 0	2 1 0	2 1 0	2 1 0	2 1 0	2 1 0
Be Responsible	2 1 0	2 1 0	2 1 0	2 1 0	2 1 0	2 1 0
Be Safe	2 1 0	2 1 0	2 1 0	2 1 0	2 1 0	2 1 0

Total Points (___/36)   Parent Signature: _____

Additional Comments:

This person "checks in" with the student to see how the night was and how the day is going. The student, with any needed support from the adult, sets a target for the day of the number of points to earn by meeting the CI/CO plan's desired behaviors. The goal is to give the student a positive start to the day while also empowering the student. Thus, CI/CO explicitly links the student's behaviors and outcomes.

If the student is younger and only works with one teacher, the student checks in with the teacher at the end of each subject so that the teacher can indicate how the student did. This is meant to be another brief opportunity to give positive reinforcement to the student. In the event that the student needs to correct behavior, this can be done at that time too. If the student works with more than one teacher, the same end-of-lesson check in occurs with each separate teacher at the end of the class. The point here is to give timely reinforcement to eliminate the behaviors that are unwanted by acknowledging implementation of those that are.

At the end of the day, the student returns to the CI/CO adult to review the day's successes and possible struggles. This plan goes home with the student to ensure that the parent is also informed about the choices the student made and the impact of those choices. The hope is that CI/CO is a temporary scaffold that can be taken away when the student is consistently making appropriate behavioral choices.

Strategy 3: Peer-To-Peer Mentoring

Peer-to-peer mentoring is a strategy is based upon the work of Vorrath and Brendtro,[11] who promote the value of requiring "greatness rather than obedience" from youth. This approach draws youth into helping others. Rather than focus solely on the deficits or non-compliance of youth, this approach encourages youth to find what they have to give the world through an expression of their best self or greatness. As youth rise to a higher calling which requires giving one's best self to others, healing occurs from the inside out and social, emotional, and character development emerges.

Randolph Academy (RA), a public school in Western New York whose mission is to "support, empower, and educate students with emotional and mental health disabilities," strives to find approaches that offer students who have a history of non-compliance opportunities to feel empowered. For this reason, students at RA are encouraged to assume the role of a "positive peer," to offer support and help to other students in a way that upholds the school's norms of respect, responsibility, safety, goal direction, and "the classroom is sacred." When students act as a positive peer, they are commended for carrying out the helping role and affirmed for expressing their best self. This is referred to within the school's program as "finding their greatness."

On multiple occasions this strategy has improved the engagement of otherwise tough-to-reach teens who present as restless, unfocused, and non-responsive to the universal academic and behavioral interventions. These teens are in a futile and unproductive cycle of wandering the halls and defying redirection. They are caught off guard when they are assigned to serve as mentors to a "younger version of themselves," in the elementary wing of the school. Peer mentoring activities are supervised by a staff member, oftentimes including one-on-one reading time and playing simple board games.

Within RA, a common mantra is: "The best way to help yourself, is to help others." This is the wisdom behind the strategy of assigning peer-to-peer mentoring. An example of this occurred after a fight broke out between two tenth grade students. Immediately after, another student spontaneously went to comfort the student who was harmed most during the aggressive outburst. During a debrief with her counselor following the incident, the supportive student was commended for her empathetic and compassionate response. The counselor affirmed that her actions were an expression of personal greatness. In response, the positive peer reflected, "Yeah, I have courage when it comes to helping those who are weak, I am a protector."

When considering the idea of assigning an older student to mentor a younger student, do some background work first. Identify a couple of teachers who would welcome the help. Identify a scheduled time that is manageable. Determine parameters around the supervision of the peer-to-peer mentoring. Sometimes the school librarian or a school counselor are good resources. Gain parental permission, as appropriate. Decide on a time frame; usually three to four weeks is effective. Communicate expectations and suggested activities to the older mentor. Ask the adult who is supervising to provide a report of their observations and assessment each week. Connect the older student to a school counselor to debrief weekly regarding the mentoring experience.

Placing non-compliant youth in a helping role interrupts the pattern of non-compliance, and primes the pump for cooperation. Nothing melts defiance and non-compliance quicker than asking a student to assume a helping role. This strategy is so effective it is nearly magical, transforming non-compliance into higher levels of engagement.

Strategy 4: Targeted Assistance

On a smaller scale, another strategy employs the use of planned ignoring of non-compliant behavior, while inviting youth to help in some small way. One principal keeps boxes in the trunk of his car, at-the-ready for the occasion where he will ask the non-compliant, oppositional student to "help" him move the boxes. Truth be told, these boxes are heavy with obsolete files. But, they function well to provide an opportunity for a student to assume a helping role. Similarly, the school counselor needs "help" with a few things, *"Would you mind watering my plants?" Do you mind taking this envelope to the secretary in the main office?"*

The strategy of targeted assistance can be implemented within the classroom or the greater school community. Reflect on the student's individual strengths, talents and interests. Once you have identified these assets, create opportunities for the student to "help" others. Call on their expertise to "help" and honor them with appreciation and gratitude. It is hard to be non-compliant toward someone who appreciates your help.

Identify simple physical tasks that can be performed within various classrooms, offices and departments. Involve other staff to brainstorm a list of "helping" tasks. Clerical staff may need "help" with collating a mailing, delivering messages, collecting recyclable paper waste. Maintenance staff may welcome help moving chairs after an assembly, etc. Physical tasks, specifically, help get a person to get out of one part of their brain (the amygdala) and into another (their prefrontal cortex). Movement also helps create a dynamic of "me *and* you" instead of "me *against* you," so that we are not just in the same space, we are working together.

Strategy 5: Community Building Circles

Can you recall the last time you gathered around a campfire? Crackling fire. Friends and family. Young and old, engaged in unhurried dialogue, punctuated by silence and laughter. Relationships, connection, acceptance, respect. Harmony, balance. Deep listening. A sense of belonging. Community. Except for the fire, it is possible to create this same sense of community in classrooms through implementing community building circles. Community building circles are a restorative practice that is similar to classroom meetings, but with the added structure provided by use of explicit restorative principles and techniques. These circles are sometimes called talking circles, and have roots in ancient cultures throughout the world.

Community building circles have been implemented for many years throughout all classrooms, at all grade levels. In one classroom, the teacher may call the students to gather in a standing circle before instruction begins, to do a check-in circle, prompting, "Share a Fist to Five, telling us how you are feeling today." Students who display a closed fist are sharing that it is not a good day, while an open hand with all fingers raised indicates they feel their best. This quick check-in circle provides everyone with an understanding of how each person is coming into the class, and it gives the teacher knowledge of where extra support or understanding is needed.

On a weekly basis, a school-wide circle may require 15-20 minutes, and is guided by a script that is emailed to all teachers. The script serves as a "recipe" for facilitating the community building circle, including prompts to ask. Students and staff sit in an open circle, facing each other. A talking piece is passed to regulate who speaks. The prompts guide sharing on a theme. For example, the week before the Super Bowl, the theme for the community building circle could be teamwork. Another week, the circle theme could be the tree of life where in three rounds, participants share their roots (where they come from), their trunk (where they are now), their branches (the goals and dreams they are reaching for in the future).

Retired superintendent and restorative practices consultant, Lori DeCarlo explains, "Community building circles provide the foundation for our school culture, reinforcing a positive school climate. Through weekly circles, students learn the routines of the circle process, relationships are built and social and emotional skills are developed." Both community building and talking circles focus on building relationships among students and between staff and students. As such, implementing community building circles will support movement up The Engagement Matrix. To understand this point, let's look at the quadrants on the left hand side of The Engagement Matrix: non-compliant and compliant (see Figure 2.3). Increasing the strength of the relationship between the person assigning the task (the teacher) and the student is what moves engagement from non-compliance to compliance. Relationships between people are the "pixie dust" for building momentum for engagement because, as iconic educator Rita Pierson stated, "Kids won't work for people they don't like."

Figure 2.3: The Engagement Matrix

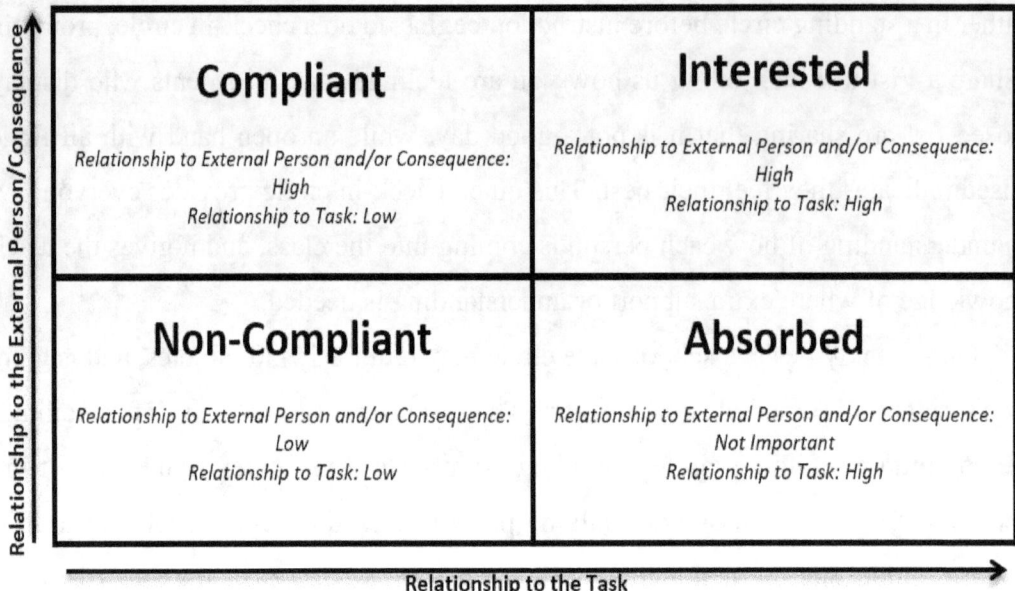

Community building circles are a simple strategy for building relationships. Not only relationships between teacher and student, but, also, peer relationships among students. Teachers at the elementary level are accustomed to dedicating time during the academic day for class meetings. To adopt the restorative principles and techniques needed to transform class meetings into community building circles is a small leap that is easily achieved. Teachers at the intermediate and high school level, however, often see things differently. *"We have content to cover! We cannot afford to waste time on kumbaya!"* Research provides a compelling answer to reassure these teachers that time given to community building circles is time well-spent. It is, in fact, an investment that results in increased academic achievement and fewer classroom management problems.

In a meta-analysis of over 200 studies, Durlak, et al. found that where social-emotional programming is implemented, learning benefits in multiple ways, significantly improving social and emotional skills, attitudes, behavior, and academic performance that reflected an 11-percentile-point gain in academic achievement.[12] Figure 2.4 details the benefits.

Figure 2.4: SEL Matters[13]

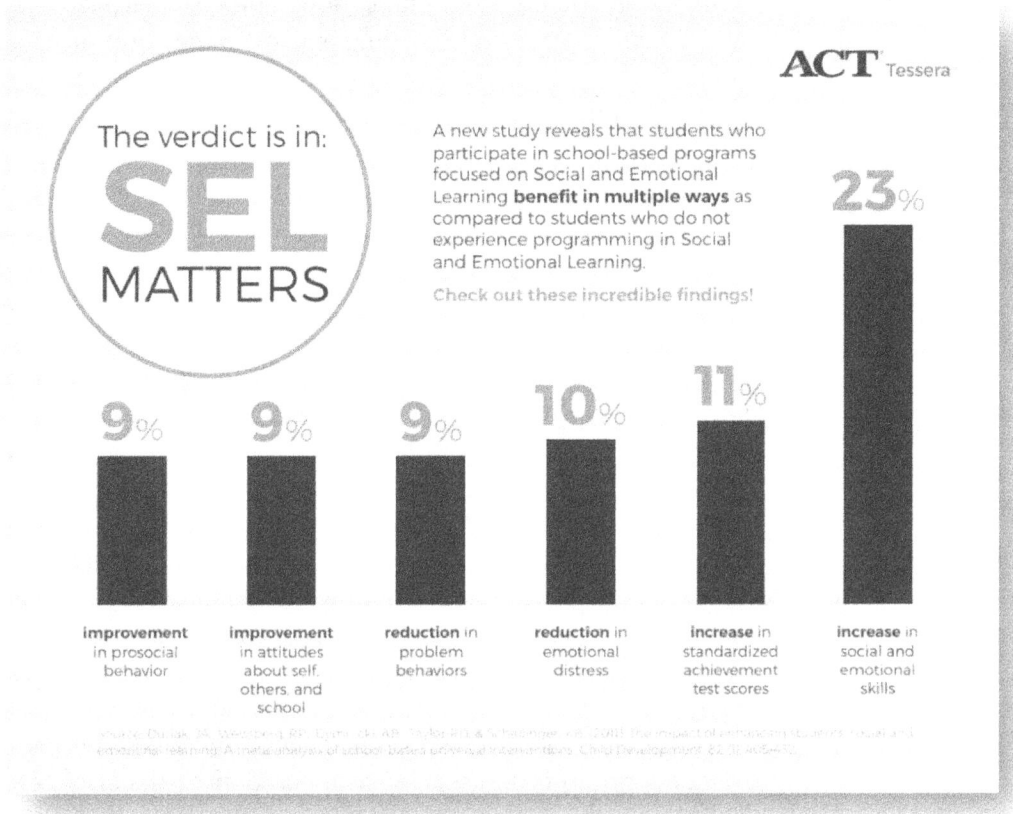

It may seem too good to be true, but this isn't the result of just one research study. It is a compilation of 213 research studies. Is there a teacher who would not want better academic performance, improved attitudes and behavior, fewer disruptions and incidence of non-compliance, and reduced student emotional distress? How can a teacher gain these benefits by incorporating community building circles into the classroom routine? Facilitating a community building circle is very simple, requiring only a basic understanding of restorative principles and circle process techniques.

Restorative Principles

Restorative principles are the values that provide the foundation for circles and the creation of a safe space for sharing. Figure 2.5 shows some of the important restorative principles for community building circles.

Figure 2.5: Important Restorative Principles for Community Building Circles

Respect Listen with respect and speak with respect	Too often, our societal communication habits have eroded the value placed on respectful listening and speaking. Community building circles are a place to explicitly teach and practice respect in communication.
Relationships Focus on relating and building relationships	The central purpose of community building circles is to make connections, getting to know one another on a human level. Over time, as relationships grow between members of the classroom community, the level of trust increases, also.
Emotions Self-awareness of feelings and emotions	Throughout the community building circle, opportunities are provided for identifying one's own emotions and expressing feelings.
Voice Equity of voice and it is okay to "pass"	Community circles provide equitable opportunities for sharing. Too often, the most confident voices dominate classroom communication. Community building circles, however, elevate the quieter voices, and equalize the more confident voices, achieving balance.
Role of Facilitator/Circle Keeper	The terms facilitator and circle keeper may be used interchangeably. The role is to create a safe space for sharing by introducing prompts and serving as a guardian of the circle's values and norms. When a violation of values and norms occurs, the facilitator will speak up and invite the group to discuss the values. The circle keeper is an equal participant in sharing. The facilitator may speak first in a round to model a response, or, they may speak last to avoid having too much influence. It is an adjustment for some teachers to learn the role of circle keeper. With experience, the circle keepers learn to "trust the circle," patiently allowing the group to respond and avoid being too directive. Student facilitators can be trained as circle keepers.

These restorative principles serve as an anchor for establishing effective community building circles. It is wise to refer back to these principles after each community building circle to reflect:

- Was communication respectful?
- Are relationships growing?
- Were emotions identified and feelings expressed?
- Was there an equal voice for all?

- Did the facilitator make sure the values and norms were honored?

Circle Process Techniques

The following simple techniques are important for creating a community building circle that is a safe space for sharing.

- **Circle Up!** It is very important to sit in a circle, preferably with no furniture in between people. This arrangement provides equality and balance, and allows everyone to see each other, enhancing openness. It also increases engagement, as there is "no place to hide."
- **Use a talking piece.** The talking piece is an essential element of the circle process and a distinguishing feature of community building circles. Simply, the person who is holding the talking pieces is the only person who speaks. When the speaker finishes, they will pass it to the person on their right or left. The pattern follows around the circle. The use of a talking piece slows dialogue, and reinforces listening skills for all, which improves the quality of communication. When selecting a talking piece, avoid objects like balls, which are made to be thrown. The best talking piece is one that has personal meaning that has been shared with the group. For example, one teacher brought a small paperweight from his desk to use as a talking piece. When he introduced the talking piece, he pointed out how it was made by his daughter in kindergarten and that it is her handprint on the paperweight. Explaining further, he shared that when he sees it on his desk each day, it makes him think of her and how much he enjoys being a father. This type of personal sharing enhances the value and respect for the talking piece.
- **Use scripts/prompts to guide conversation.** Most teachers understand the practical value of planning. This old adage applies to circles: "Failing to plan, is planning to fail!" Planning the community building circle script with written prompts ensures an organized and predictable time of sharing. Scripts are designed for a progression that begins with low trust prompts, and advances to prompts that go beyond the surface. Storytelling prompts are especially effective, as are prompts asking participants to share personal stories relative to the theme.

- **Review values and norms every time.** The first time a class circles up, it is important to elicit from the group some shared agreements regarding their values and what they need to feel comfortable sharing. A simple technique is to give each person a 3 x 5 card, asking them to write a value that is important to them in relationships. Then, pass the talking piece and give participants the opportunity to explain the value and why it is important. Norms can be established in the same manner. Norms serve as "guardrails" for how the group will operate and ensure emotional safety. Some common norms are confidentiality, listen with respect, speak with respect, and express acceptance. After values and norms are established, it is advisable to post these for the group as a reference, reviewing them at the beginning of every circle.

Various Community Circle Formats

Community building circles can be conducted in several formats, varying by the amount of time needed and complexity of the script. Figure 2.6 illustrates four different circles shown side-by-side in four columns. You can see, for example, that on the far left are "Check-In Circles," which take the least amount of time, whereas "Expanded Circles" on the far right take the longest; however, no matter which circle is chosen, there are commonalities.

The BIG Book of Engagement Strategies

Figure 2.6: Formats for Circles

Check-In Circle 3-5 minutes	Basic Circle 10-15 minutes	Intermediate Circle 15-20 minutes	Expanded Circle 20-30 minutes
			Opening Ceremony
		Mindfulness Activity	Mindfulness Activity
	Review Norms/Ground Rules	Review Norms/Ground Rules	Review Norms/Ground Rules
Check In	Check In	Check In	Check In
	Round 1	Round 1	Round 1
	Round 2	Round 2	Round 2
	Check out	Check out	Check out
			Closing Ceremony

Community Building Circle Scripts & Planning Template:

Figure 2.7 shows Randolph Academy's planning template used to develop community building circle scripts. Community building circles have a powerful, positive impact on the climate of a classroom. As the members of a classroom community see and know each other on a human level, connections are made that translate into a new level of compassion, empathy, and patience. As human beings, we are wired to be in relationship with each other. Community building circles meet this profound human need.

Click on this link to access a template you can use immediately
https://cutt.ly/CirclePlan

Figure 2.7: Randolph Academy's Level 1 Community Building Circle Planning Sheet

---

Randolph Academy's Level 1 Community Building Circle Planning Sheet

Opening Ceremony: *(Set the tone using an inspirational quote, story or song.)*

Mindfulness Activity: *(Relax the body and mind, reduce stress and prepare to participate in the community building circle.)*

Check In Round: *(Acknowledge how participants are feeling as they enter the circle)*

Review Values & Norms: *(The new group identifies the values and norms they will uphold to make circle time a safe place for sharing. These serve as shared agreements and should be reviewed before every circle—and referred to if a violation occurs.)*

Rounds: *(Written prompts to stimulate conversation on the theme. Participants speak their own truth, avoiding advice giving or persuasion.)*

1.

2.

3.

Check Out: *(Opportunity to provide a closing thought or take away.)*

Closing Ceremony: *(Facilitator acknowledges the efforts of the group and affirms the connections that have been made.)*

Chapter Summary

This chapter was about moving someone from the point of non-compliance to compliance by building relationships. Since humans are complex, unique, and unpredictable, not every strategy would be appropriate for every situation. First, you have to determine what the cause for the non-compliance is so you can determine if you need to focus on the relationship. After all, not everyone who is non-compliant is doing so because of the relationship. Also remember that if the task itself is outside of the Zone of Proximal development, the leverage is not with the relationship or the consequence.

**Looking for even more strategies to
BUILD RELATIONSHIPS?**
Please visit my website, www.LyonsLetters.com/learnmore, for print and digital recommendations including books, websites, videos, and more!

Thank you again to Lori DeCarlo for contributing Peer-To-Peer Mentoring, Targeted Assistance, and Community Building Circles—three strategies included in this chapter.

Reflection Prompts

1. Think of a time when you had to do a task that was outside of your Zone of Proximal Development. Was the task too easy or too hard? What did you do?

   _____
   _____
   _____

2. What is your go-to strategy to build relationships?

   _____
   _____
   _____

3. In your own words, why is building relationships important to engagement?

   _____
   _____
   _____

4. Name one thing you could do tomorrow based on what you learned from this chapter.

   _____
   _____
   _____

5. Tweet me @LyonsLetters to share an idea for a future reading or digital resource I should share on www.lyonsletters.com that would help someone who is non-compliant become compliant.

Persistent Questions

1. What have you done so far regarding the three challenge questions from Chapter 1?

    a. **Three:** Find at least three people with whom to share your learning.

    b. **Two:** Find at least two ideas that change you.

    c. **One:** Apply at least one idea from your reading.

    _____
    _____
    _____

2. What have you learned so far, and how will you use it?

    _____
    _____
    _____

Chapter 3

Communication Strategies

"The ability to listen is as important as the ability to speak."
~Sheryl Sandberg

Recognizing Your Thinking Before You Read...

1. How do you currently learn about your students and their families?

   _____
   _____
   _____

2. Think of a time when you were acknowledged for your work. Describe how that made you feel.

   _____
   _____
   _____

3. Have you ever been in a meeting where behaviors or communication did not go well? What happened and what proactive actions, if any, could have prevented this outcome?

   _____
   _____
   _____

The Bridge between Us

Though this line may sound like a Yogi Berra-ism (but isn't), improving relationships can be difficult if the relationship is one that needs to be improved. Put simply, if a relationship is already off on the wrong foot, then building a bridge towards improvement will take time, patience, and probably setbacks. Rather than administering consequences or changing the task, improving the relationship would be the ideal way to shift someone from non-compliance to compliance. This is why the preceding chapter of this book focused on building/improving relationships.

The space between relationships and consequences is often the space between intention and impact. This is because on the journey to build relationships we need to find common ground and that takes communication. When I know you, I hear you differently. Sometimes when I know you, I give you more grace and patience because I know your heart. Other times when I know you, I assume the worst because I have been hurt by you in the past.

Communication, when done well, is not just focused on what is said or written, but what is heard. In other words, communication should be two-way and inspire dialogue. Unfortunately, too often communication is less about asking good questions and instead becomes a contest of production—when we feel unheard, usually one of two outcomes is likely. First, unheard people may get louder. Another option is that people may get quiet. Either way, the result is disengagement.

Now What

The strategies in this chapter are proactive suggestions on how to foster strong two-way communication. That said, it is never too late try to make an improved second impression if the first impression fell short. Here are five strategies to create or improve communication.

6. Getting-to-Know-You Survey
7. Catch of the Week
8. Positive Communication
9. Creating Norms
10. Building Interdependence with Story-Based Learning

Strategy 6: Getting-to-Know-You Survey

We can all agree that gathering information about students improves the teacher's knowledge of the students. When children are in elementary school, teachers often ask families questions like:

- Does your child have a nickname?
- What does your child do for fun at home?
- Does your child have siblings?
- What are your concerns about your child?
- What do you see as your child's strengths?

As children get older, the parent is less and less the source of this information since teachers can ask the students directly.

What is less common, however, is seeking knowledge about the family and the family's experiences as students or what the family values about education. Yet, not only does the family impact the way a child will value the teacher, school, and learning in general, the family also impacts the school district at-large. For example, families are members of the school community who are able to elect the members of the board of education. Families will campaign for and against increases in school taxes which impact the resources—both physical and human—within a school district. Families can come to the board meeting to rally for whatever they value and that creates the culture within the school district you work. The reasons for connecting with families are numerous. This is why it is vital to see families as partners and to learn more about them.

Remember, the purpose of this strategy is to better understand others since the more someone feels understood, the stronger the relationship with that person will be. When we have strong relationships with others, we have a better understanding of what may or may not motivate them, and we are more likely to do something for that other person even if we may not be inclined to do it for someone else. In this way, taking the time to learn about someone else benefits both parties.

Asking questions about the child's reading behaviors at home, for example, helps the teacher and the school to understand the child because the family is the first ring of impact on the children. However, consider asking questions about the parents too. We need to know the family's after-school schedule, the family's philosophy on reading, and the family's beliefs about how the home and school come together. You can see in Figure 3.1 an example of a Home Reading Survey. This is just one example of a getting-to-know-you survey. No matter if the survey focuses on reading or any other behavior, skill, and/or content area, the intention should be to get a deeper understanding of students and their families. By tapping into parents' knowledge of their children, the teachers can improve their knowledge of the students and the families. Entire schools and/or districts could turn a survey like this into an electronic format so that they could collate the data to look for trends. Understanding the parents' behaviors and beliefs can inform school- and district-level initiatives because this understanding can influence the design, roll-out, and implementation of initiatives.

Alternate Use: Even if you are not a teacher of reading, and therefore are not interested in home reading behaviors of your students or their families, the intention remains: take the time to find out about your students and their families outside of school. This survey can easily be altered to ask about any content area.

Figure 3.1: Home Reading Survey with Questions about Parent Reading Experiences and Behaviors

Reading Survey

Families please complete this survey about your child's reading and the reading that takes place in your home. This survey is voluntary but will be extremely helpful as I continue to work with your child in reading. Thank you for your time and help in completing this. It is very much appreciated.

Child's Name:_____ Date: _____

1. How do you see your child's reading abilities? Is your child a proficient or struggling reader? Why?

   _____
   _____
   _____

2. To the best of your ability, please answer the following questions using the scale below.

	Always	Sometimes	Never
Does your child enjoy reading books to him/herself?	☐	☐	☐
Does your child enjoy reading books to others (younger siblings or parents)?	☐	☐	☐
Do you feel that your child is a motivated reader?	☐	☐	☐
If you read aloud, do you and your child have a running dialogue with questioning occurring about the story(ies)?	☐	☐	☐

3. How many minutes per night will your child read without having to be asked?
   _____ minutes

4. If your child does not read regularly at home please explain why. (For example, not motivated, other interests/activities, lack of books at home, etc.)

   _____
   _____

5. Would you like to change how much your child reads at home?

    ☐ Yes, I'd like my child to read a lot more

    ☐ Yes, I'd like my child to read a bit more

    ☐ No, I'm happy with how much my child reads

    ☐ Yes, I'd like my child to read a bit less

    ☐ Yes, I'd like my child to read a lot less

    ☐ Other_____
    _____

6. Does your child have books at home that are not from the school? Yes/No

7. Where does your child get books? _____

8. Does your child ever talk to you about books that they are reading? Yes/No

9. Are then any obstacles that get in the way of your child being a good reader? If so what?
    _____
    _____

What additional information, if anything, would you like us to know?
    _____
    _____
    _____
    _____

Thank you again for your help in completing this reading survey.

Optional Questions about Your Reading Experiences

1. When you were a child, did you like to read? Yes/No

2. What was your favorite book when you were in school? _____

3. What types of things do you read now?
    a. Books
    b. Magazines
    c. Newspaper
    d. Blogs
    e. Social Media
    f. Emails
    g. I don't really read much of anything now
    h. Other _____

Please check all of the following that apply:

- ☐ I would rather my child did other things instead of reading.
- ☐ We are not in the habit of reading at a regular time.
- ☐ My child would rather do other things than read.
- ☐ We don't have good books at home.
- ☐ I find reading difficult.
- ☐ I am too busy/have other things I need to do rather than read.
- ☐ Reading is not important to me.
- ☐ It's hard to read with my child because of my work.
- ☐ My child reads to me, but I don't read to my child.
- ☐ I don't understand the way the school teaches reading.
- ☐ No one likes to read in our house.
- ☐ It's hard to read with my child because there are other people I need to look after.
- ☐ I stress the importance of reading to my children.
- ☐ I read aloud to my children and encourage them to do so to me.
- ☐ I have a wide variety of reading materials around the house.
- ☐ My child has a library card.
- ☐ I have recently spent time with my child in a bookstore.
- ☐ Our family visits the public library.
- ☐ I encourage my child to set reading goals.
- ☐ I like to read.

Strategy 7: Catch of the Week

Confucius said, "Don't worry about being acknowledged by others; worry about failing to acknowledge them." I have found there is no better way to create and foster relationships with people than letting them know that you see the good work that they are doing. Be it for effort or for outcome, when you recognize people for their contributions they recognize that they matter to you. This recognition is the foundation upon which relationships are built.

The purpose for doing is this to create a culture of appreciation. This is reminiscent of the Zulus in Africa who greet each other with the word, "Sawubona" which means, "I see you." Our western greeting of "Hello" is just a formality to get the ball rolling. The Zulu greeting of "Sawubona" is deeper than that. According to Glen Pearson's Huffington Post blog, "It says, 'I see your personality. I see your humanity. I see your dignity and respect.' In the African village context, where everyone knows one another, it's an exceedingly powerful representation of understanding."[14] The response to Sawubona is "Sikhona" which translates to "I am here." The meaning of this exchange is meant to symbolize the power of recognition because the culture subscribes to the powerful idea that I do not exist until you acknowledge me or "when you see me you bring me into existence."[15]

Since 2008, I've been writing my staff a weekly email I call, "Lyon's Letters" (which is now the name of my website, blog, and social media handles). This weekly email is a way to share a little bit more about myself but also a medium in which I share what I am reading or seeing or hearing as it relates to the school/district. Lyon's Letters are optional reading. Pretty early in the writing of them I decided to end each of the Lyon's Letters with a "Catch of the Week." This Catch is a person who was caught doing something that week that was worthy of spotlighting.

Initially, I was the person who determined who that week's "Catch" was. In this role it was my weekly challenge to be on the lookout for people in my building who were standing out. This is fairly easy to do if you're okay with spotlighting the same people every week since from my experiences, about 20 percent of the people do about 80 percent of the work. The thing was, I was not comfortable only catching the same people over and over again—I wanted to share the wealth and I wanted to draw attention to people who are quietly doing great things. As a result of being thoughtful about who was doing what, I found myself walking around with a different lens—I was LOOKING for people who were doing good things. Not only that, I was looking to see people who I may not have otherwise seen so that I could catch people who weren't yet caught.

This was such a great experience for me because if left to my own devices, I fall into a rut. I see what I've always seen and I celebrate the people who are easy to celebrate. This is a universal pitfall. Who hasn't noticed this while teaching? A teacher in the span of a couple of minutes can ask a series of questions and called on the same student multiple times despite the fact that there were many students who were eagerly volunteering. These actions are not intentional—it is our default. This is why I was happy to be on the lookout for people who may have fallen off my radar.

Eventually, however, I realized something else...My Catches were people who *I* saw doing great things, but I can't see everything. Thus, I was missing a lot of great celebratory opportunities because I was the person who was doing the work. For this reason, I changed the rules for the Catch of the Week. I was responsible for being the Catcher for the first week of the school year. After that, the person who was last week's Catch was responsible for paying it forward and catching this week's Catch. There were two rules for the Catcher. The first is that they have to send me a short write-up (who was caught and why that person was caught) by 4:00 p.m. on Wednesday so I can include it in my postscript to my Lyon's Letter on Thursday. The second is that only someone with whom they do NOT work directly could be caught. In other words, this is meant to provide them with the opportunity to look beyond their usual circle.

Though I have no way of knowing for sure, it would not surprise me if 90 percent of people who open the weekly Lyon's Letters never read the letter itself but scrolled down to the bottom to see who was Caught. In some settings, each week, without fail, at least half a dozen or more people would Reply All to the email and give their congratulations or take the time to add additional sentiments to the hard work of the person who was Caught. In other words, it can be a love-fest that was not only staff/faculty endorsed, it was staff/faculty generated!

> *Alternate Use:* This same model could easily be modified for use in a classroom. The first week the teacher could acknowledge a student and that student could be asked to acknowledge someone else in the class and/or the school the following week.

Strategy 8: Positive Communication

Positive communication can serve at least two purposes. The first is to help build positive relationships. The second is that it serves as a positive consequence by providing feedback on good work.

People like interacting with someone who makes them feel supported. It is certainly easier to let one's guard down and take risks when working with someone who is benevolent. This is how positive communication builds relationships. Positive communication also provides feedback as a consequence for the work. This makes me think about one of my doctors. Obviously, she sees countless patients and when I have to get bloodwork or other tests, I am told upfront that, "no news is good news." My doctor is managing my expectations and wants me to know that the only reason she would call me is if the test results show that something is wrong. I certainly respect her time, but truth be told, I want a call either way. It's not that I want to add more work to her plate, but I worry that perhaps the test results show something troubling but maybe they forgot to call because they are so busy; not hearing anything can cause as much anxiety as hearing something. In the absence of information, I can draw my own conclusions. I'm not alone. Teachers want to hear good things about themselves. Students and families do too. There are also times when, in the absence of positive reinforcement or acknowledgement of good work, people can fail to recognize that their work was good and change course when they should have stayed the course. This lack of feedback can perpetuate less effective practices unwittingly.

I am sure that I do not need to tell you a medium to communicate. This strategy is all about positive personalization. That can take many forms. I have never met a teacher or student who is not motivated by positive communication. When my children were in elementary school, they received postcards from their teachers from time-to-time.

They were addressed to the children, but because it was a postcard and could be read by anyone who sees the backside, the parent was easily informed of the communication—which was always positive.

I would also encourage teachers to have their students take the lead in communicating what they are learning about via postcards or home/school journals. Positioning students as the lead communicators is brilliant because it is certainly easier for the teacher to find five to ten minutes for the students to write what they're doing than it is for the teacher to create time to write personalized communication to all families. Also when the student does the communication, the parent is more likely to read it. Finally, if there are home/school journals, it gives the parent a chance to respond—either directly to the child (in writing) or to the teacher. Having an authentic audience is key for writing and this is a prime way to achieve that. This is also a great way to integrate technology since students could be asked to communicate via a blog, a tweet, SeeSaw, Google Classroom, etc. The possibilities are endless and grow with the advent of new and better technology.

In thinking about how adults can use this strategy with adults, in one of my jobs, every Friday the faculty and staff would meet in the PD room and grab at least one "Caught Ticket" and catch someone else. "Tickets" like the ones in Figure 3.2 (each were printed four to a page and cut into individual "tickets") were strewn onto the tables.

There was no accountability with this. In other words, there was no sign-in sheet or attendance taken—it was on your honor. People could complete one, but often people did multiple tickets. Some were serious and others were funny. It didn't matter. I collected them and asked one of the secretaries to select one at random by pulling a ticket to be the winner of the best parking spot for the week. We would flip a coin. Heads would be the nominee, tails would be the nominator. Then, the secretary would distribute all the tickets into the mailboxes. The goal was to ensure that people felt positive connections to each other. In fact, most people, including me, saved and even hung up their tickets. Some people even took the time to write them during the week so they could do it while the idea was fresh. This could easily be done in a class with students too.

Figure 3.2: Sample Caught Tickets

Caught you BEING GOOD TICKET

Being GOOD means that you are extending and donating a part of yourself to others in a way that does not compromise or sacrifice values, standards, or what's important.

This week, I wanted you to know that I caught YOU being good when:
_____
_____
_____
_____
_____

Congratulations and keep it up!

Dear _____ (Date) _____

I wanted you to know that YOU really **stood out** to me...
_____
_____
_____
_____
_____

Strategy 9: Creating Norms

When talking about how students should behave, we usually use the term "rules." Many modern teachers recognize the when students are involved in the creation of the rules, the students are likely to be more invested in adhering to them. However, not everyone feels comfortable in facilitating the creation of rules.

First, I would encourage teachers to stop using the word "rules" altogether. Like with any group (students or adults) who will be working together on a recurring basis, before actually doing the assigned task, it is important to establish the behaviors and/or beliefs that will guide the interactions of the group. Rather than calling these actions "rules," I prefer calling them "norms" (though I have also heard them referred to as "commitments" or "agreements"). Taking the time to get on-the-same-page as a group helps that group become a functioning team.

My experience with creating norms is informed by the National Staff Development Council's "Tools for Schools"[16] newsletter from August/September 1999 which is dedicated to developing norms. Though the newsletter is intended for teams of adults, the information can and has been generalized to the concept of creating boundaries for behaviors with students too. With that in mind, the opening article, "Norms put the 'Golden Rule' into practice for groups," states, "Norms are the unwritten rules for how we act and what we do. They are the rules that govern how we interact with each other, how we conduct business, how we make decisions, how we communicate, even how we dress when we get together." In this way, norms make invisible expectations visible.

Read the National Staff Development Council's "Tools for Schools" newsletter here:
https://cutt.ly/Golden-Rule

Be it a classroom of students or with teams of adults, spending time creating norms that are consistently reviewed for "fit" is an important investment of time since norms are in place to proactively identify and address behaviors that people are likely to *struggle* with. Creating norms can take time—particularly for teams (children or adults) that are not accustomed to norms. Here are the steps I follow.

1. Provide categories of different behaviors (again, I use the National Staff Development Council's "Tools for Schools" newsletter from August/September 1999) to identify the categories of behaviors that this team may need to consider, like decision-making, use of confidentiality, and participation, as well as other categories like technology use or roles.
2. Ask the class/team members to brainstorm thoughts on individual Post-Its.
3. Break into small groups to draft the norms.
4. Report out brainstorms.
5. After the sharing, finalize the group's norms.

Depending on the group, this can take as little as fifteen minutes or as long as an hour.

When brainstorming norms, I ask people to think about classes or teams they have been members of in the past. What behaviors did that class or team engage in that were challenging? Examples for adults may include questions like:

- Did the meeting always start late?
- Was there a person who dominated the meeting?
- Were there people who were always on their computers but not because it related to the work of the meeting?

For students, examples may include questions like:

- Is shouting out something that we are comfortable with?
- Was there a time when someone took something from you without permission?
- Do you like it when a teacher calls a student out in front of others?

If you start with behaviors that are common pitfalls you will be able to create norms to address those things you are trying to avoid. For example, let's use the adult example of the annoying behavior of never starting on time. The norm could be "Start the meeting on time." The very fact that this behavior was named and a commitment to a positive behavior was identified means that everyone on the team will be inclined to hit the target that was set.

There is no need to create norms around things that the class or team already does well. Using the same example above, the norm "Start the meeting on time" was created at the first meeting and emerged because of experiences with teams where that was a problem. If the team always starts on time, then the norm of "Start on time" could be eliminated since it is not something that the team needs to be reminded to do.

It is important to revisit the norms frequently. As a class, you may revisit one norm a day or all norms once a week. With a team, depending on how frequently you meet, you may want to revisit all norms at the start of every meeting. Either way, the purpose of revisiting the norm is to use that as an opportunity to ask, "Are there any norms that we may need to change?" This might be a chance to say, "We always start on time, I'm not sure if we need to have that one anymore. However, I have noticed that we are having a problem ending on time." This review of the norms provides a reflection on the agreements that the class or team members have made to each other and gives everyone an equal opportunity and voice to raise a concern.

Since norms are in place to stave off unwanted behaviors, it should be expected that the unwanted behaviors may surface. Having norms makes it easier to address this when (not if) this happens. "Let's do a norm-check. I notice that we are not starting our meetings on time even though that is one of our norms. Do you think we need to change our norm to match our behavior" (because we are okay with our behavior), "or do you think we need to change our behavior to match our norm" (because we are okay with our norm). This is a non-judgmental question that revisits the initial commitment by the team and calls attention to the mismatch between the behavior and the norm. Again, this is an issue of non-compliance. The goal is to determine if the non-compliant behavior is worth changing or if the expectation should be changed. Either outcome is acceptable as long as the class or team is comfortable with the decision.

Classes meet with enough frequency and duration that creating norms makes sense. It is true, however, that there are teams where time does not allow for norm creation because that team may be very temporary. Nevertheless, it is important that there are common understandings between and among the team members. In this case, I use the team member rights and responsibilities in Figure 3.3, which shows parallel rights and responsibilities of all the members on the team. Though these are predetermined, I always offer team members the chance to comment on and, if needed, modify, and ultimately agree to these.

Figure 3.3: Team Member Rights and Responsibilities

Rights	Responsibilities
A. To be respected	A. To be respectful
B. To be heard	B. To listen
C. Share concerns	C. To seek solutions
D. To participate during meetings	D. To seek and share the input of those whom I represent between meetings
E. To disagree during the meetings	E. To publicly support decisions

Strategy 10: Building Interdependence with Story-Based Learning

In 2006, Distinguished Service Professor in the Department of Theater at the State University of New York Buffalo State College, Drew Kahn, directed a production of *The Diary of Anne Frank* in which the play was performed by two actors playing Anne: one who was the Anne in World War II hidden in the annex, and one who was a Rwandan genocide survivor. Both Annes used the same dialogue and demonstrated that not only is there is an "Anne Frank" in every genocide, but that through story, we

Watch Drew Kahn's TEDx video, "Telling a Story" here:
https://cutt.ly/Drew-Kahn

can give social justice a voice. From this production, the Anne Frank Project (AFP) was born. The mission of AFP is, "to use story as a vehicle for community building, conflict resolution, and identity exploration. Inspired by the wisdom of Anne Frank, AFP surfaces and shared stories stifled by oppression."[17] To achieve the mission, Drew works with communities and schools around the world and that is how I happened upon Story-Based Learning.

The work that Drew does starts more or less by merging the "Community Building Circles," strategy from the previous chapter and the previous strategy "Creating Norms" to establish an environment of safety and respect. Drew's circles are a part of a learning ritual whereby first interdependence is created to establish belonging and then he leverages that personal connection to foster learning connections. With his background in the performing arts, he has found a way through Story-Based Learning (SBL) to have students take learning (which is often acquired in a hidden manner because it is processed cognitively) and represent the learning through actions thereby giving students outlets for movement. These physical actions provide students with appropriate channels for being out of their seats and shifts learning from a passive experience at a desk to an active experience with others. In order to achieve an environment that supports this unique approach, you have to start by creating connection and safety.

First the Why

If you have spent any time on Facebook, you are more than likely familiar with the simple, beautiful story of Ubuntu (see Figure 3.4), which became the political philosophy of Nelson Mandela's leadership of South Africa. As the story goes, when Mandela was released from nearly three decades of wrongful imprisonment, he looked into the eyes of his captors and said, "Ubuntu," which translates to, "I am because we are." In that context it is more than forgiveness; it is the realization that his captors were in prison *with* him. By imprisoning Mandela they had, in fact, imprisoned themselves and all of humanity. Ubuntu is a very African idea that is difficult for our western minds to wrap around. When Drew brings students to Rwanda each year, he tells

Figure 3.4: The Story of Ubuntu[i]

them they will learn multiple important life lesson, but the most important one to bring home is, "We before Me," also known as Ubuntu. This belief is one that is foundational to a classroom of connections and interdependence.

This shared humanity is replicated in other cultural greetings beyond the Xhosa Ubuntu. From the Hindi and Sanskrit, the term Namaste is used to acknowledge the divine in another. The lengthier translation of Namaste' is, "I bow to the divinity in you. You bow to the divinity in me. When we are both in this place together we are One." That's a powerful hello, right? Rwandans greet each other in their native language Kinyarwanda saying, "Muraho." Muraho doesn't just mean hello; it means "I celebrate your presence!" What a beautiful way to greet each other—to celebrate another's existence in that moment.

It Takes a Village

This energy and ethos are what we must create as we use stories to build interdependence within our classrooms. Drew uses the term village instead of community in hopes of replicating the "We before Me" ideals of the villages he and his students visited in Africa. Western cultures typically look away from each other and throw a grunt in the general direction of our target without stopping—typical versions include: "Wassup?" "Hey," and "How you doin?" with the subtext being, "Please don't connect with me any deeper, I have things to do, whatever you do don't make eye contact." This is not a condemnation of western interactions, but an illustration of the work necessary to bring our students (and ourselves) to the village. Again, the purpose here to is to build relationships and foster communication to proactively safeguard against disengagement. After all, if you know someone cares about you, you are more likely to care both about that other person and what that person cares about.

Drew's vehicle to start connections is through the use of stories as communication. In order to build beautiful, engaging, meaningful stories we must connect by listening, trusting, respecting, sharing, collaborating, compromising, and contributing. These characteristics are inside of each of us. Too often, we are not asked to practice these ideas so they remain unfamiliar and dormant. Transitioning from operating as an individual to thinking about the village can be a difficult, abstract task. With this in mind, Drew simplified and clarified this process by creating the AFP Village Rules.

Circle Up

Before explain the Village Rules, it's important to note that Drew begins and ends the work with the students by forming a literal circle. This circle represents the physical formation of the village and represents the oldest story sharing shape there is. Mandated by the need for warmth and light, throughout history, tribes, clans, and nations gathered to conclude their days in circles surrounding the fire. There, amidst the dancing flames, magical stories were exchanged. These were not entertainment stories; these were *survival* stories. How did the hunt end? Why does the mountain spew fire? How can we grow more food? How can we protect ourselves from intruders? Thus, the circle is more than a shape for AFP classrooms—it is the sacred ritual that initiates and concludes the collective work each time the village meets. You will find that your students will crave this routine. AFP teachers regularly share how the circle provides important kinesthetic book ends to each day's work in class. We know that engaging the whole student (body, voice, spirit, and mind) is an important factor to their learning success. The physical warm-up work in the circle is fun, easy and flexible.

Village Rules

The Village Rules are a more interdependent variation of the previous strategy "Creating Norms" and are based on a similar idea from Brazilian drama theorist and activist Augusto Boal's book, *Theater of the Oppressed*—the acknowledgement that we create a unified work ethic totally committed to the task at hand before the work can begin. This is essential. Like children, we all need and appreciate rules. Without rules we are allowed to behave badly. Also like children, we might complain when given rules, but secretly we deeply appreciate the security resulting from the structure. Remember, there can be no freedom without discipline. Therefore the ultimate goal of the warm-up is to gain a complete freedom of our story building instruments—our minds, bodies, souls and voices all available to respond to the creative impulse of the moment. Drew wants students to have this freedom, but freedom is earned through practicing the Village Rules. Think of these rules as the ten commandments of story building.

The Village Rules are created each time a new process begins. They are created by the village and facilitated by the teacher. Drew suggests that while ten is a good number to aim for, the village should decide the eventual total number of rules. That said, Drew also always suggests the teacher provides the first few rules—these are mandated, unchangeable and non-negotiable. These first rules provide the teacher with the opportunity to model the language and format the rest of the rules will follow. These first rules will also send a strong message to your student village: first, there is a leader in this process and second, the leader (school) has clear priorities.

Here is an example of the Village Rules from a recent AFP story building process created by the village and its teacher:

- We agree that story is first.
- We agree to respect each other as collaborators and as people.
- We agree that our intention is to help each other tell the best possible story together as a community.
- We agree to send messages and requests through appropriate channels.
- We agree to evaluate each other by asking questions whenever possible, rather than making conclusions or delivering orders.
- We agree to consider anything for five minutes.
- We agree to discuss our differences with each other as they surface.
- We agree that we cannot do it alone and that we need each other.
- We agree that self-deprecation of any kind will provide obstacles in our work.
- We agree that a loving, caring, nurturing village is the foundation for our success.

You will note that the first three rules were created (mandated) by the teacher. These were essential and non-negotiable. As you build the Village Rules, there should be plenty of time to unpack the reasoning behind each rule. Encourage the students to ask questions and demand clarity. Be ready to explain why you believe the first few rules are important. We never number the rules as this would imply importance and priority. Each rule is as important as the rest. The village should determine the order of the rules, as one rule might flow better in one place than another—like a story. Encourage the village to be particular about language and word usage. Like each student, word choice matters deeply.

As you build the Village Rules it is an opportunity to model the process that lies ahead—you are rehearsing the story building as you build the Village Rules. For instance, if one student is especially quiet during this process, ask the student directly for input. After the student shares an idea publicly, celebrate that student's input, which will model inclusion for the village. Drew always makes a controversial suggestion to include in the Village Rules to entice student feedback. Something like, "We agree that secrets will help the process." The students will explode in disagreement and the teacher will agree to strike that idea from the rules. You have modeled compromise and the students have taken a step towards ownership of their village.

Spend time on the Village Rules. Encourage diverse opinions. Constantly and explicitly remind the village of how important these rules are. Edit, tinker, and change the wording until the village feels it is perfect. Allow for healthy debates between individual students—again, these are modeling opportunities for healthy collaboration. Practice the Village Rules as you create the Village Rules. Finally, develop a procedure for how the village will hold each other accountable practicing the rules during story building (class) time. These procedures should reflect the Village Rules and be very "Village-Rulesish" in their application.

While it would be wonderful for students to practice these collaborative ideals every moment of their lives, we only have contact with them during our scheduled meeting times; we can't follow each of them around all day, every day. So, tell them when they walk into the room; it is time for Village Rules, and it is a class requirement. You will find they will feel so proud of these rules that they will be attempting share them with their other communities and this transfer is great news. We want them to feel so strongly about their work that they must share it with others…this is kind of the whole point, right? There is nothing like the zeal of the convert.

Drew stresses that the final rule should be something along the lines of, *We agree that a loving, caring, nurturing village is the foundation for our success*, is crucial. This rule allows teachers to voice how serious they are about the village's treatment of each other. Loving each other is not optional; it is a class requirement; it is an *assignment*. This always opens the way to a healthy village discussion about loving, caring, and nurturing. Students typically have very little experience with useful definitions of these words that are applicable to their lives. They report surface definitions exported from popular culture, social media and Hollywood. They report a history of being told care and love are not to be discussed in school. They report unhealthy family obstacles to honestly understanding these words. Overall, they report a general dissatisfaction with their present definitions of these words and welcome the village opportunity to redefine them in healthy ways. Most importantly for the teacher, this conversation will surface personal feelings from the students about important issues that touch their hearts. These conversations will accelerate their relationships with each other, provide important scaffolding for their village, and set the bar for exploring high-staked content. Every effective story contains high-stakes content, so conversations like these model the work ahead of the village—they are, quite literally, rehearsing (simulating) content worthy of story.

Contemplative learning places an emphasis on the use of emotionally charged language in classrooms as an important piece of the whole education pie. You may find these high-stakes conversations awkward and uneasy to navigate initially. That's expected and understandable—it's not typical of most student experiences. However, as relationships are built over time, emotional content will eventually feel just as routine and expected as the academic content does. Emotions and feelings are not precious abnormalities to run from; they are natural parts of being human. How you, the teacher, facilitate these less familiar roads for your students will provide important vocabulary for their future bumpy life rides. You will undoubtedly be stretched and uncomfortable—that's important for your students to witness. You are human too, right?

A Moving Story

Once the Village Rules have been determined, it is time to move the creation of the village from the brains to the bodies of the students. This is a sequence you will repeat multiple times throughout the process: Think on your butt, act on your feet. There should never be a brain-focused discussion that simply stops at the end of the discussion. The brain introduces the idea, the body makes the idea into truth. Ideas that seem amazing in discussion often lose their shine when introduced to the body. This is a crucial lesson; thinking is an important first step to the nurturing of ideas, but never the entirety of the idea. Drew emphasizes that the body must be involved for the entire cycle of learning to be complete. Here's an extremely simple teaching recommendation: at any moment during the creative process when you are unsure of your student's certainty (i.e., thinking), provide the following direction: "Stand up and *show* me so we all understand." These impromptu rehearsals activate the thinking and will require the students to use each other to fully bring the thoughts out of their heads and onto the stage (e.g., you be the mountain, you be the giant). This is the magical bridge all ideas must walk across during the AFP story building process. Drew calls this transition from the head to the body "finding the truth." The villagers use their bodies as "truth vehicles." In this way, the Village Rules become truthfully and authentically owned in the circle during the AFP warm up.

When this process is new, the stories are about community-building rather than being content-related. As the group becomes a village, the shift to content starts. For example, in a science classroom, students could be asked to form a simple machine. In a math classroom, students might be asked in pairs or small groups to represent a fraction. The students collaborate and develop ideas on how to perform this abstract concept with their bodies and no words. Then the students take turns performing their story for the rest of the village and the villagers are able to guess what they are seeing and provide feedback to improve the performance and celebrate what went well. Students are often known to ask to get up or can be seen doing movements at their desks during a test because they are tapping into the physical memory of the actions used during the learning. This is the point! Drew wants students to not just memorize information, but to internalize learning in an environment where they connection to themselves, each other, and the content.

Chapter Summary

This chapter was about moving someone from the point of non-compliance to compliance by improving communication. How we speak and listen matters as much as what we say. This is why taking the time to get to know others, celebrate the positive, and proactively prepare for challenges is worth the effort. As the saying goes, no one cares what you know until they know that you care.

> **Looking for even more strategies for COMMUNICATION?**
> **Please visit my website, www.LyonsLetters.com/learnmore, for print and digital recommendations including books, websites, videos, and more!**

Thank you again to Drew Khan for contributing Story-Based Learning—
a strategy included in this chapter.

Reflection Prompts

1. In your own words, why is communication important to safeguarding against non-compliance?

   _____
   _____
   _____

2. What is something you would like to know about your students' families?

   _____
   _____
   _____

3. What successes have you had when students create rules? What were the struggles?

   _____
   _____
   _____

4. Name one thing you could do tomorrow based on what you learned from this chapter.

   _____
   _____
   _____

5. Tweet me @LyonsLetters to share an idea for a future reading or digital resource I should share on www.lyonsletters.com that would help someone who is non-compliant become compliant.

Persistent Questions

1. What have you done so far regarding the three challenge questions from Chapter 1?

    a. **Three:** Find at least three people with whom to share your learning.

    b. **Two:** Find at least two ideas that change you.

    c. **One:** Apply at least one idea from your reading.

    _____
    _____
    _____

2. What have you learned so far, and how will you use it?

    _____
    _____
    _____

Chapter 4

Consequence Strategies

"There is a role for carrots and sticks, but to rely on carrots and sticks alone is effective only when we employ donkeys and we are sure exactly what we want the donkeys to do."
~John Kay

Recognizing Your Thinking Before You Read...

1. In what circumstances are you okay with extrinsic motivation?

   _____
   _____
   _____

2. What extrinsically motivates you?

   _____
   _____
   _____

3. How do you currently identify and create meaningful motivators for others?

   _____
   _____
   _____

Caution Flags Ahead

While the last two chapters focused on relationships and communication, there are times when you can have a terrific relationship with someone and great communication, but there is still non-compliance. The best example of this can be seen between parents and their children when it comes to things like a keeping a room clean or doing the assigned household chores. I use these examples intentionally since most people are unlikely to achieve more than compliance when it comes to tasks that are literally or figuratively chores. The parents and children may have an amazing relationship, but there is still the chance of non-compliance. Using the Engagement Framework, you can see that there must be a change in the consequence for doing (or not) the task to shift from non-compliance to compliance (see Figure 4.1).

Figure 4.1: The Engagement Matrix

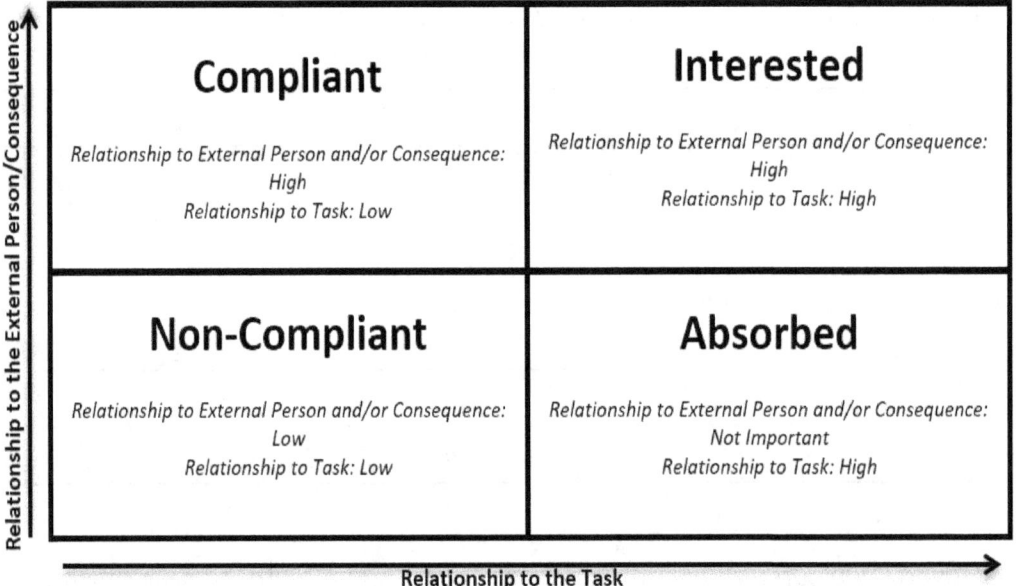

Remember, consequence is a neutral term and can refer to either a positive reward (carrots) or negative punishments (sticks). The most captivating and concise way to understand carrots and sticks, in my opinion, is through the work of Daniel Pink and the RSA video, "RSA: ANIMATE: Drive: The surprising truth about what motivates us." This video uses Pink's words as the narration while an animator uses dry erase markers to visually represent what Pink is saying. These videos are addictive, but that's not the point here. The point here is that maybe the reason the person is not doing what you want is that the person wants a better incentive to do it.

Pink will be the first and best to tell you that extrinsic consequences in the form of carrots or sticks should be used with caution. In the book *Drive*, Pink writes

Learn more about the ideas in *Drive* by watching this animated video: https://cutt.ly/RSADrive

> ...carrots and sticks can achieve precisely the *opposite* of their intended aims. Mechanisms designed to increase motivation can dampen it. Tactics aimed at boosting creativity can reduce it. Programs to promote good deeds can make them disappear. Meanwhile, instead of restraining negative behavior, rewards and punishments can often set it loose—and give rise to cheating, addiction, and dangerously myopic thinking.[18] (emphasis in original)

This is why we need to use consequences carefully and temporarily. In most cases, the point of the consequences should be just a momentary scaffold to help give someone the motivation to do the task. The long-term goal would be that the person doing the task sees the value in that work. I didn't like cleaning my room as a child so cleaning my room was linked with my allowance. As an adult, I do not need an extrinsic motivator to keep my spaces (room, house, office, etc.) clean because I see the value in doing it myself.

However, when we are not careful about using extrinsic motivators sparingly and temporarily, we can shift the focus from the task to the consequence. Here are two examples of when consequences can backfire. In the example of cleaning rooms, that would mean we would talk about the loss or achievement of getting the allowance rather than the loss or achievement of being tidy, clean, guest-ready, organized, etc. In schools that means we say if you do the homework, your grades will go up or don't do it and your grades will go down. This shifts the motivation from the task (learning) to the consequence (grades). If the purpose of school is to get good grades or avoid getting bad grades, then that would be okay. We know that this is not the purpose of school. School should be about learning about yourself, others, and the world through the content that it taught.

Thus, when using extrinsic motivators to shift from non-compliance to compliance, be sure to explain (a) the consequence is small and temporary and also (b) the difference between the consequence and the task. The clearer you can be with these two points, the more likely you and the person doing the task will be to achieve the task. For example, you can say, *since you're learning how to do this and may not be sure if you're on the right track, let's track your progress on this chart with a sticker every time you are successful. Doing this new task well is the goal, not getting a new sticker. The sticker is a marker of your progress.*

In addition to using extrinsic motivators sparingly, another precaution is linked to the fact that compliance is a deceptive state. Obviously, compliance is better than non-compliance in many cases. For that reason, compliance can feel like a victory when someone shifts from non-compliance to compliance. Nevertheless, compliance is just a lesser form of disengagement. We should also remember that when people are being compliant, they are doing a task they do not want to do and are doing it only for the consequences they receive or avoid for doing it. We should remember that given the choice to stop, compliant people will stop. We should remember that compliant people may do what they're told, but what you actually want are people who want to do the work/learning. This is why compliance lulls authority figures into believing that they are more than willing passengers on your train—you think they want to go along on this ride.

Finally, in classrooms, be on the lookout for students who are compliant with the behavioral expectations but non-compliant with the learning. This was Highlight 5 in Chapter 1 of this book. Students learn very early in school that as long as they are actively or deceptively compliant with not disrupting the learning of others, they are able to be passively non-compliant with their own learning. The teacher will not leave the small group to come tell the student who is being quiet but not reading to read. When there are so many students who raise their hands (behavioral compliance), as long as students don't shout out (behavioral non-compliance), the students who want to be non-compliant with the learning can often do so.

Now What

Now that you understand the necessary precautions when using extrinsic motivators, you are ready to consider your options. The next three strategies provide ideas on how to better incentivize others to do whatever the task at hand is that they may not want to do.

11. Wheel of Fortune
12. stickK Contracts
13. Everyone Gets an A

Strategy 11: Wheel of Fortune

In 1785, poet William Cowper wrote, "Variety is the spice of life." Nearly 250 years later, many people would still agree. The element of surprise can be motivating for some people who may get bored easily. The Wheel of Fortune strategy increases a students' engagement level because the positive consequence (which is earned) is determined by luck rather than skill and allows for the possibility of a range of consequences rather than just one.

The possibilities for how to create a wheel of fortune are limited only to your imagination. However, no matter what approach you use, there are some common criteria.

1. There must be multiple choices of positive consequences which could include, but are not limited to those listed below:

- Call home
- Note home
- Prize box
- PJ Day

- Additional free time
- Lunch with the teacher
- Electronic day
- No homework

- Extra time at recess
- Read to the class
- Hat day
- Note to principal

- Credit for school store
- Do the announcements
- Lunch with friends in the class
- Movie lunch

2. There must be a random chance of earning any one consequence; hence the name, "Wheel of Fortune."

If you happen to have or want to buy a vertically spinning wheel, they are certainly available for purchase. I would advocate that going to those lengths is unnecessary and would suggest the following options as possibilities to achieve the same result:

- **Dice:** Create a numbered list of ten possible consequences and number them 2-12. Have the students roll two dice and the number rolled equates to the positive consequence.
- **Board Game Spinner:** There are games, like Hasbro's Game of Life,® that have a spinner. Create a numbered list of ten possible consequences and have the students use the Life® spinner.
- **Student-Created Spinner:** Use a readily available spinner template online at sites like www.mathwire.com/templates/spinners.pdf, and create a list of possibilities equal to the number of spaces on the spinner.
- **BINGO:** Create a list of possible consequences and have them correspond to BINGO numbers. Using a spinning BINGO cage, select the consequence at random.
- **On-Line BINGO Generator:** Create a list of possible consequences and have them correspond to BINGO numbers. Using an online BINGO number generator like https://cutt.ly/BingoGenerator, the consequence is selected at random.
- **Out of a Hat:** Create a list of possible consequences and put them into a vessel from which the hidden consequences can be drawn at random.
- **On-Line Randomization:** Create a list of possible consequences and enter them into an on-line randomizer like www.randomresult.com.

I would strongly encourage you to be open to the possibility that students create the consequences. Certainly, this can be done as a class or group. Even better, particularly if using this strategy as an intervention for an individual student who is being non-compliant, have the student create a list of things that they would see as a positive consequence. For students like this, there may be a class generated Wheel of Fortune that applies to all students, but this student—who is demonstrating a lack of motivation from the general options—may be responsive to a more personalized approach.

> **A Word Of Caution...**Some may read this strategy and consider creating a "Wheel of Misfortune." Since the goal is to transition away from non-compliance to a higher level of engagement, fostering respect towards the other person is at a premium. Public punitive consequences will erode rather than create relationships and should be avoided at all costs with this or any other strategy.

Strategy 12: stickK Contracts

Have you ever really wanted to get healthier? You went out and got a gym membership, bought home fitness equipment, or invested in a diet plan but still failed to go, never used the equipment, and cheated on the diet so much that you actually gained weight? Perhaps, improved health or fitness are not enough to get you off the couch. As the saying goes, the road to hell is paved with good intentions.

Maybe, instead of good intentions, you need some type of negative consequence. If you visit www.stickk.com, you can sign-up to pay money to a charity that you hate if you do not follow the commitment you established for yourself. For example, let's say that you wanted to exercise for at least thirty minutes four days per week. If you made a stickK contract, you would indicate your exercise goals and if you did not hit those targets each week, you would pre-select an amount of money that would be paid to a person or organization that you did not want to support.

Like the idea of stick but are interested in an alternative? Here are some alternatives: https://cutt.ly/stickk

If you are a staunch member of a political party, you might select that $100 would be paid to a cause that supports the opposite views every week you did not hit your target. In other words, the large negative consequence of having your money go towards a cause that you fundamentally disagree with incentivizes you to do what you already wanted to do but were not motivated enough to do. You can even identify an independent verifier of your actions to whom you would report your success or failure. This would be an added layer of insurance to make sure that you stuck to your goal. After all, it might be easy for "Normalizers" to lie to the website and say that the goal was met each week so as not to pay the literal and figurative price of the anti-incentive. It might be harder to lie to your friend who you asked to hold you accountable.

> *Alternative Use:* Though this strategy specifically uses a website, you would not have to go to those lengths. Also, the website is not one I recommend using with students. Instead, I would recommend asking students to think about stick consequences as a means of self-discipline. In other words, help students to motivate themselves by creating healthy boundaries. This would likely take one-on-one coaching to encourage (a) self-reflection on the desired outcome and why it matters and (b) thinking through healthy but meaningful non-incentives like doing a set of 10 push-ups or having to do a chore for their sibling. When using this with students, be careful that you are doing so in a way that allows the students to have accountability—something they are doing for themselves and with choice and voice. After all, *you* do not want to be the stick for a child.

Strategy 13: Everyone Gets an A

In his book *Skin in the Game: Hidden Asymmetries in Daily Life*, Nassim Nicholas Taleb sums up the theory of loss aversion in this straightforward way, "What matters isn't what a person has or doesn't have; it is what he or she is afraid of losing."[19] The point here is that future benefits feel more abstract than a present benefit. For this reason, people work harder to prevent the loss of a current benefit than they do to achieve the same outcome in the future.

Teacher, conductor, and musician Benjamin Zander describes what this means in schools beautifully in the YouTube video, "Work (How to give and A)." In this video

Zander explains that he tells his students that they all have an A for the course at the start of the course. By doing this, rather than working to *get* the A, the students work to *keep* the A (loss aversion).

Zander takes this one-step further by building in a Ulysses Contract, or a decision made in the present that binds you to actions that will benefit you in the future. See Chapter 3 in *Engagement is Not a Unicorn* for a thorough explanation about Ulysses Contracts. Zander achieves this by having the students write a letter to him at the beginning of the term that is dated for the end of the term. The letters all begin with the same opening, "Dear Mr. Zander, I got my A because…" In the letter the students write what they did to justify this "extraordinary grade…and fall passionately in love with the person they're describing." Even better, Zander says "the person I teach is the person they described in their letter."[20] Thus, as their teacher, Zander is holding them to the highest level that they hold themselves and expecting the students to meet their own expectations.

Watch Benjamin Zander's video "Work (How to give an A):" https://cutt.ly/Zander

Positioning the students as the people who determine what their A looks like is genius because it shifts the motivation from extrinsic—*this is what the teacher says I have to do to earn this A*—to intrinsic—*I am doing this because I said that I would.* Indeed, doing this could cause the rare shift from non-compliant to absorbed. That is to say, the student is not actually striving to get the A (extrinsic), but striving to fulfill their word (intrinsic).

> *Alternate Use:* This same process could be used with adults related to their year-end evaluation scores. Here the outcome would be to earn an evaluation rating of Highly Effective and the letter would be to the evaluator: "I got my Highly Effective score because…"

Chapter Summary

This chapter was about moving someone from the point of non-compliance to compliance through the use of consequences. In truth, determining the best consequences for any one person is couched in the knowledge you have of that person—meaning, the better the relationship, the more likely you are to find a consequence that will be of consequence to someone else. As well, the more choice and voice you can offer with determining the consequences, the better. After all, the person receiving the consequence is often the best person to identify the most meaningful reward or punishment. It bears repeating that not everyone who is non-compliant is doing so because of the consequence; there could be a leverage point with the relationship (see the previous chapter). Also remember that if the task itself is outside of the Zone of Proximal Development, the leverage needed is not with the relationship or the consequence.

**Looking for even more strategies to
CREATE CONSEQUENCES?
Please visit my website, www.LyonsLetters.com/learnmore, for print and digital recommendations including books, websites, videos, and more!**

Reflection Prompts

1. How do you create an environment that uses extrinsic motivators but ensures that obtaining or avoiding the motivator is not the task?

   _____
   _____
   _____

2. In your own words, why is it important to keep carrots and sticks as temporary and minimal?

   _____
   _____
   _____

3. What is your go-to strategy for creating carrots (rewards or incentives)?

   _____
   _____
   _____

4. What is your go-to strategy for creating sticks (disincentives)?

   _____
   _____
   _____

5. Name one thing you could do tomorrow based on what you learned from this chapter.

   _____
   _____
   _____

6. Tweet me @LyonsLetters to share an idea for a future reading or digital resource I should share on www.lyonsletters.com that would help someone who is non-compliant become compliant.

Persistent Questions

1. What have you done so far regarding the three challenge questions from Chapter 1?

    a. **Three:** Find at least three people with whom to share your learning.

    b. **Two:** Find at least two ideas that change you.

    c. **One:** Apply at least one idea from your reading.

    _____

    _____

    _____

2. What have you learned so far, and how will you use it?

    _____

    _____

    _____

Section II: Interest Strategies

The next three chapters will address strategies to help prevent or move from compliance to interested. Assuming that people are already compliant, this is a horizontal shift to the right and is therefore a change in the relationship to the task. Interested is the entry point to engagement and should be the minimal target we aim to achieve in schools for both the students and the adults.

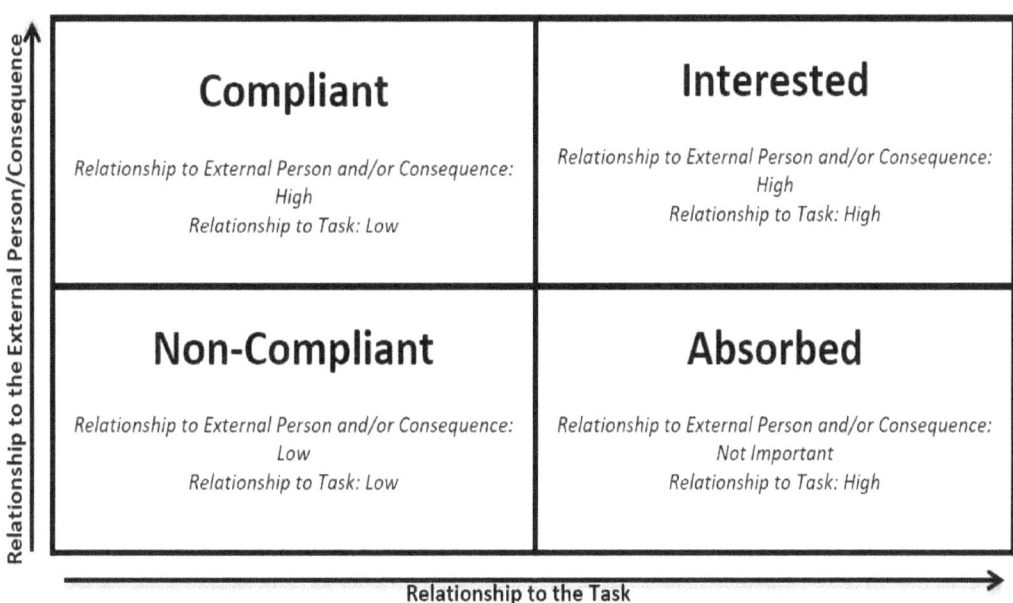

Chapter 5 in Section II addresses strategies to create choice and voice in tasks. Chapter 6 addresses strategies to change the task. Chapter 7 addresses ways to approach scheduling differently. By the end of Section II, you will be able to identify actions that can avoid compliance altogether or shift someone from being compliant to being at least interested.

Chapter 5

Choice and Voice Strategies

"Freedom is not the absence of commitments, but the ability to choose yours."
~Paula Coelho

"The voice is the muscle of the soul."
~Alfred Wolfsohn

Recognizing Your Thinking Before You Read...

1. What are common barriers preventing choice with tasks?

   _____
   _____
   _____

2. What are common barriers preventing voice with tasks?

   _____
   _____
   _____

3. In what ways do you create opportunities for others to take the lead regarding the design of tasks now?

   _____
   _____
   _____

You Have Crossed Over

The strategies in the previous three chapters of this book focused on lessening disengagement. As I say, compliance is worthy of celebration if someone was previously non-compliant. However, compliance is not true engagement; it's just a lesser form of disengagement.

Interest, on the other hand, is true engagement. Some would like to minimize interest because it is not the highest level of engagement—absorption. However, it is not possible for anyone to be absorbed in everything all the time. Interest, however, should be the goal for all classrooms in all schools every day. When people are interested, they have crossed the threshold from *disengaged* to *engaged* because *interested* is the most basic level of engagement. The question is, how do we get there? The direction to go from non-compliance to compliance was vertical and related to extrinsic motivators (consequences and relationships). Making the shift from compliance to interested is a horizontal move regarding the relationship to the task.

It's important to remember that interest gets students to a point whereby they are more than just willing to do the work—they want to do the work—at least for that moment. However, when the bell rings or the unit is over, the student is no longer willing to continue. This is because when people are only at the interested level, the enjoyment is both temporary and also extrinsically motivated—the student enjoys the task but would quit if the extrinsic consequence(s) was taken away. For students, the consequence is in the form of grades, for adults, it's in the form of their paycheck.

Thus, to increase engagement, we must strengthen the relationship with the task. Doing so happens through focusing on who is doing the task as much as what needs to be done. The more the authority controls the creation of the task for those who are doing the task, the more likely the feelings towards that task will be compliant (at most). The more voice and choice those doing the task have in the creation and/or selection of the task, the more likely the feelings towards that task will be interested (at least). Remember, it is not a bad thing to aim for getting to the interested level. This is where engagement starts.

What's Your Type

In *Engagement is Not a Unicorn (It's a Narwhal)*, I shared that there are at least three main types of interested people: (1) willing participants, (2) professionals, and (3) strategists. Before we go into the strategies on how to shift from compliance to interest, let me explain these manifestations of interested people.

Compliant people do the work, but interested people do more than the minimum because they willingly participate in the task. In classes, willing participants raise their hands before being called on. When working in groups, students' "heads are down and butts are up" (in the air) because they're leaning in to see what's going on. When it is time to share their learning, willing participants volunteer to go first because they want others to hear what they did. While having discussions, willing participants offer their ideas. In fact, willing participants may even be on the cusp of absorption because they may be absorbed in the *process* of learning even if the topic, content, or other variables are only interesting (or vice versa). However, you know someone is at the interest level (and not absorbed) based on what happens when the bell rings or you take away the grade. Willing participants will stop doing the work whereas absorbed people continue.

A second manifestation of interest is a professional. The term professional actually has two meanings. The first refers to how people behave. You might say, "Wow, you were such a professional in how you approached that angry person. You acted like it didn't bother you even though it must have been difficult when she raised her voice at you." The second refers to people who are paid for their work. Here you're talking about the difference between an amateur (someone who does the task recreationally) and a professional (someone who is paid for doing the work). Both of these meanings of professional apply to this type of interest since hallmarks of being interested are that you like the work (therefore, you behave professionally), and you like the compensation (meaning you are a professional who is paid).

The area(s) in which we became a professional was probably influenced by areas in which we were once absorbed. This is because many of us tried to find a way to get paid to do the thing(s) we loved to do. In a sad twist of fate, when we make money doing the thing we love, we often decrease our engagement in the task. Why? Simply put, when we did the thing we loved for the joy of doing it, we never had to worry about extrinsic compensation. When we do it professionally, we have pressures that we didn't have before—can I make my car payment doing this? Can I pay my rent this month if I do this? How will I eat? These pressures can have a depleting impact on our level of engagement, meaning our desire to do the task is replaced by our need to make money by doing the task. Consequently, the thing we were once absorbed in becomes the thing we're now only interested in.

Interested people can also be "strategists." Strategists are those who do the task because they are very attracted to the consequences. In comparison to professionals who liked what they were doing and found a way to get paid to do it, strategists liked the payment and found a way to like the task.

Strategists are students who take an AP course in a subject that they minimally like (at best). They're smart enough to do the work but, more than that, they recognize that there is a certain prestige in taking APs. Strategists may start doing the work not because they really like the work, but because they think others will like them more because they did the work. If they find they actually like the work, they shift from being compliant (I'll take this course because it looks good) to interested (the course looks good and I like it). Another example is when students commit to volunteering so that they can have something to include on their National Honor Society applications. Though they started for the outcome, if they are interested (and not compliant), they end up enjoying the experience. With both of these examples, though, because the students are only interested in the AP course and volunteering, they would not continue doing it unless they got the reward for their time and effort.

We do not outgrow this. As adults, we are just as likely to say "yes" to additional work or even a promotion because we want others to view us as capable, we want a raise, and/or we want the status that comes with the title that we acquire. This doesn't mean we're selling out; it means we're getting ahead. Again, what we're interested in is our job, and if we're going to do it, why not get the highest pay we can? If I like this and you're willing to pay me to do it, that's a win-win.

In summary, here are the three manifestations of what interested people look like:

- **Willing Participants**: People who temporarily enjoy what they are doing and the consequence they get for doing the task.

- **Professionals**: People who find a way to get compensated for things that they like (not love) to do.
- **Strategists**: People who like the prestige or power that comes from doing the task.

Who Says

In order to shift from compliance to interest, the task must be changed. The question is, who is able to change the task? Chances are, it's the authority. For students, that means it is the teacher, for teachers, that means it is administration. However, it doesn't have to be. In fact, it is easier and more interesting for the authority when choice and voice are provided to those who are doing the task. Why? Differentiation is harder to create if the only person responsible for developing those options is the authority. However, if the authority is able to tap into those who are doing the work to have a say in what and how the task gets done, then the authority can focus on providing guidance rather than providing options or motivation.

> **Differentiation is harder to create if the only person responsible for developing those options is the authority. However, if the authority is able to tap into those who are doing the work to have a say in what and how the task gets done, then the authority can focus on providing guidance rather than providing options or motivation.**

Now What

The strategies in this chapter are about making a horizontal move on The Engagement Matrix from left to right. To do this requires a change in the task. Keep in mind that the task, itself, is likely something done *in service to* the desired learning outcome. If that's the case, then the task is not the learning; the task is a method to achieve the learning. Put another way, the learning is the destination and the task is the vehicle used to get to the destination. For this reason, it is actually not difficult to create options (choice and voice) to achieve arriving at the destination in a way that allows for creativity, options, and/or input. Choice refers to options. Voice is the ability to give input regarding decisions (see Highlight 7 in Chapter 1). For example, in order to demonstrate an understanding of how to conjugate verbs in Spanish, you could have all students complete a worksheet; however, the worksheet is not the destination—it's the vehicle. In truth, the students could complete the worksheet or write a paragraph or have a conversation or make a video, etc. Certainly it is easier for the teacher to have the students all do the same task, but that doesn't mean the task is engaging for those doing it. Since people can find interest in unnecessary tasks, being interested doesn't mean that the task you are doing is relevant, challenging, or appropriate. We need to guard against making tasks that sacrifice the learning for enjoyment. As I wrote in *Engagement is Not a Unicorn*, "Learning without fun is too common, but so is fun without learning."[21]

The next six strategies are designed to make the task more engaging through offering choice and/or voice.

14. Directed Volunteers
15. Coalition of the Willing
16. All, Most, Some Learning Targets
17. Earn a Badge
18. Playlist
19. Audiobooks

Strategy 14: Directed Volunteers

In the field of education, we are often in need of assistance from parents and community members to come in and help us. Unfortunately, just because we are in need and someone is available doesn't mean that the person who can help is the person who is best able to help. In fact, sometimes the person who is available is *not* helpful. This gap between the need and the skill is common. What's more, because so often the same people volunteer, there can be both burnout and resentment.

As someone who doesn't have family in the area I live, I do not have family to tap into when it's time to fundraise so this is a commitment that I try to avoid. As a mom who works outside of the home during the school day, I know that I am never going to be able to be a "Room Mom." Yet, given my role as an educator, if the school needs someone to sit on an after-hours committee to weigh in on decisions regarding new report cards, curriculum, etc., I'm your girl! I have a specific niche of both skill and availability, and I am not alone.

I am someone who is a sucker for a good leadership book even if the book is technically for a non-educator audience. Case in point, Dr. Samuel Chand's book, *Who's Holding Your Ladder: Selecting Your Leaders*. As a former pastor and college president, Samuel Chand has had to rely on many volunteers to ensure that the work he is doing can be accomplished. After all, places of worship and schools are often in need of assistance (free labor). This is why I was excited to read his chapter "How Do We Recruit Volunteers?" in which he writes, "Stop asking for volunteers."[22] His point is that if you want to ensure that you get the best person for the job, you need to recruit for the job as though you were paying someone to do it.

People in need of volunteers should first proactively ask potential volunteers what they can and would be willing to do. Then when there is a need, it is easy to review the inventory of skills and reach out to those who indicated they could help in that way. Chand's inventories are aligned to the needs he has in his church; educators would align their needs for the school. One way to think about it is in three general categories—who has gifts of time (can be there), talent (can do the work), or treasure (can provide money or other resources). If those are the large categories, you could break them down into more discrete skills. For example, you may be interested in those who are good at:

- Event planning (to help with upcoming events)
- Fundraising (to help raise money)
- Organization (to help with sending letters, filing, grading papers, etc.)
- Supporting students directly (to help with activities in the classroom)
- Understanding education (to help with committee work on academics)
- Advocacy (to help with policy or law)

Once you establish the skills that would be valuable, you then send out a questionnaire to build your inventory. At this point you are not asking for anyone to do anything other than to share what they can and would be willing to do. When a need arises, you look at your inventory and you recruit. "Hello Mr. Chamberlin. Earlier in the year I sent out a questionnaire to see what skills you have and would be willing to provide to the school if needed. I'm reaching out because you said that you would be willing to help plan events. As it turns out, we are looking to do just that. Let me give you some details so you can decide if this is something you're still interested in..."

The good news is that you know Mr. Chamberlin's able to do event planning but Mrs. Greene, who you know would say yes if asked, has indicated that she is better suited for supporting students directly in the classroom. Mrs. Greene may have been compliant if asked to event plan, but she's very interested in being in the class with kids. Mr. Chamberlin may have appeared to be disengaged because he would not have volunteered before to do the event planning (either because he didn't know about it or he thought that someone else might step-up) but now he's interested because he was asked.

> *Alternate Use:* There is no reason why you couldn't think of skills that you need from your students in your classroom and build an inventory around that. This could be for those students who like to clean-up, those who like to assist the teacher, those who like to assist other students, etc. The same is true for teacher voluntary activities like committees, advisories, etc.

Strategy 15: Coalition of the Willing

In a meeting a couple of years ago, I heard someone describe responses to change as one of three types of people on an island as shown in Figure 5.1.

- **Swimmers**—those who are willing to try something new and dive right in. They will leave the safety of their current island in order to swim towards the new, potentially better island. They are seen by others as fearless and maybe even reckless. (In Figure 5.1, this is the figure in the water on the far right.)
- **Shark Spotters**—those who are afraid to leave the safety of their current island even if the other island is rumored to possibly be better. This is the majority of the island inhabitants. They are willing to try something new only after the Swimmers try it first and come back unharmed. (In Figure 5.1, this is the middle figure with the thought bubble of the shark.)

- **Flagpole Holders**—those who cling tightly to the flagpole on the current island and refuse to let go even when most people have already left the island. These are people who resist change even if their island is sinking. (In Figure 5.1, this is the figure on the far left clinging to the flagpole.)

Figure 5.1: Swimmers, Shark Spotters, and Flagpole Holders[23]

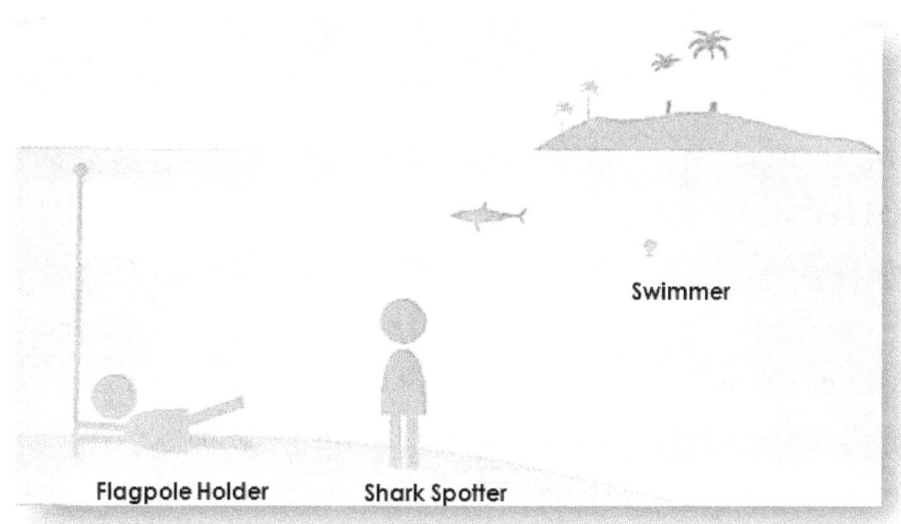

It's important to understand that if you plot these three types of people on a graph, you would end up with a bell curve. The majority of people are shark spotters and you have about 25 percent of people who are going to be Swimmers and 25 percent who will be Flagpole Holders. The question you have to ask is how will you get the majority of people from their current location to the new location?

In reality, most people are not going to follow the Swimmers; they will follow the Shark Spotters. If you are not a Swimmer, you look at Swimmers as people who are willing to try anything and that is not a good thing. The only way that Shark Spotters try something is if another Shark Spotter says it's okay. Shark Spotters are like the boys in the old Life Cereal commercial who are skeptical to eat Life.

Watch the Life commercial here:
https://cutt.ly/Mikey

Kid 1: What's this stuff?

Kid 2: Some cereal. Supposed to be good for you.

Kid 1: Did you try it?

Kid 2: I'm not gonna try it. You try it. *Kid 2 slides the bowl towards Kid 1.*

Kid 1: I'm not gonna try it. *Kid 1 slides the bowl back to Kid 2.*

Kid 2: Let's get Mikey!

Kid 1: Yeah!

Another kid, Mikey, is at the end of the table and Kid 2 slides the bowl towards Mikey who now has the bowl in front of him.

Kid 2: He won't eat it. He hates everything. *Noise of crunching cereal.* He likes it! Hey Mikey! *Mikey is revealed eating the cereal. Then Kid 1 and 2 are seen eating the cereal.*

It's only when Mikey (the person who is seen as the skeptic) gives the cereal his approval, do the others decide they're willing to try it too. In schools, that means that people are likely to feel better about trying something new when the skeptic becomes the convert or at least the person who is willing to try. Put differently, being told to try something new by the administrator or by the person who is always open to change is not nearly as compelling as it is when it comes from the person who is seen as the resistor.

Watch Derek Sivers' TED Talk on First Followers here:
https://cutt.ly/FirstFollower

In his 2014 TED Talk, Derek Sivers, professional musician and entrepreneur, explains why people follow other followers. Though the leader needs to be brave and willing to be ridiculed, the leader cannot "create a movement" alone. The leader needs a "first follower" who can be embraced as an equal. When that happens, the first follower demonstrates that it's okay to join. The *followers* (not the leader) attract other followers to join the movement and then the followers "emulate the followers, not the leader." Eventually the participants develop momentum because now you have a critical mass of people and it is finally a movement. "As more people join in, it's less risky" and eventually, it's not a risk to be a part of the movement—it's a risk to oppose it. "If you really care about starting a movement, have the courage to follow and show others how to follow."[24] Here are some tips I use to help encourage first followers.

1. **What problem are you trying to solve?** Why is this important and what change do you want to make?

2. **Who else is impacted by this problem?** If you can explain why this is important, you can help determine who else might be willing to try something different.

3. **What other options exist?** You are probably not the only people who have this problem. Find out what other people are doing and talk to them about what they tried. What similarities and differences exist between their problem, context, and solution and yours? There is no need to reinvent the wheel, but there is also no need to think that their solution will be exactly what you need either.

4. **To pilot or not to pilot?** It's often very important to do a test-run of a change before diving head-first into a massive overhaul, but doing so can require a large investment of time and money. Moreover, the training required may ultimately be for naught if you decide to go in a different direction. As well, the pilot may not be a true representation of what it will be like when people become familiar because there may be an implementation dip. It may be advisable to visit those who have committed already to the change and ask them about their implementation. This can save the time, money, and training.

5. **Do you have the right people?** So often those who want change avoid those who do not. I would strongly encourage those who are considering change to enlist someone who is less willing. First of all, during the planning phases this person can inform the group of pitfalls that they should avoid; it's better to know those when planning rather than during or after the rollout. Secondly, this person then becomes a symbol of inclusion and validity. They are your Mikey. If you can get this person on board, other Shark Watchers are more likely to become followers.

6. **Communicate, communicate, communicate!** No one should be surprised by what is happening. Not only should there be meeting summaries following every meeting, but these summaries should have all participants' names on them. The summaries should be first shared with the team members for approval and then sent

to the masses. I usually end the written summaries with something like, "If you have any questions about this work, you are encouraged to reach out to any member of the committee" and then have their names listed alphabetically. After all, if you're not doing anything wrong, there is no need to appear that you are working in secret.

Strategy 16: All, Most, Some Learning Targets

The word differentiation has left such a bad taste in people's mouths that I have worked in places where we actively avoided using this term. While we can make differentiated instruction very complicated, we can also make it very easy. This was my challenge several years ago when the school I was working at started to dive deeply into learning targets. While doing some research in how to write strong learning targets,

Read Doug Belshaw's blog post about learning targets here
https://cutt.ly/Doug Belshaw

we discovered a way to make them differentiated. Based off a blog post by Doug Belshaw, "Learning Objectives: The Basics,"[25] we realized that this approach was unbelievably easy and made a world of difference to both the teachers and students. We began to call this the "All, Most, Some" (AMS) learning target. Not only were the teachers able to create learning targets, the learning targets they created were differentiated and empowered the students to know the expectations for both process and product.

The idea behind the AMS learning target is that the teacher identifies a target that all students should be able to do. Using that same target, the teacher identifies an outcome that is aligned to the task that all students should be able to do, but slightly more challenging so that most (but not all students) can achieve that portion. The final piece of the learning target is an objective that only some students will be able to achieve because it is the most challenging. You can see what this would look like in the example in Figure 5.2.

5.2: All, Most, Some Learning Target Example

All	All students will list all the simple machines and gave an example of each.
Most	Most students will identify how two simple machines work together and how this synergy improves what either could do independently.
Some	Some students will draw their own invented machine which solves a problem and includes at least two simple machines.

What makes this easy is that the teacher is able to identify a learning target and bump it up or down in complexity to achieve differentiation. As well, based on the students' achievement of the learning targets, assessing the level of learning the child is capable of is clear to both the teacher and the student. This is because this lesson target always follows the same rules:

- **Struggling:** Students who cannot accurately complete the "All" portion of the learning target. These students demonstrate a lack of the basic skills and/or knowledge needed to complete the most basic objectives even if provided support from the teacher.

- **Developing:** Students can accurately complete the "All" portion of the learning target independently. These students only demonstrate the below-level skills and/or knowledge needed to complete the most basic objectives independently but cannot accurately complete the "Most" portion of the learning target even if provided support from the teacher.

- **Proficient:** Students can accurately complete both the "All" and "Most" portions of the learning target independently. These students demonstrate both basic and on-level skills and/or knowledge needed to complete the learning target independently, but cannot accurately complete the "Some" portion of the learning target even with or unless provided support from the teacher.

- **Highly Proficient:** Students can accurately complete the "All," "Most," and "Some" portions of the learning target independently. These students demonstrate below-level, on-level, and above-level skills and/or knowledge needed to complete all pieces of the learning target independently.

For ease and/or to think about how to communicate this with students and families, see Figure 5.3, which shows a very straightforward rubric to use with the AMS learning targets.

Figure 5.3: All, Most, Some Learning Target Rubric

	A Student at this Level will...			
	Struggling	**Developing**	**Proficient**	**Highly Proficient**
Accurately Completed Learning Target	No	Yes, but only the All	Yes, but only the All & Most	Yes, the All, Most, & Some
Teacher Support Needed	For the All Portion	For the Most Portion	For the Some Portion	No Teacher Support Needed
Student Proficiency Level	1	2	3	4

Using this rubric, students would eventually never need to ask the teacher during a lesson "What's my score?" or "What should I do when I'm done?" If a student says, "What's my score?" the teacher can reply with, "What have you done? Were you able to do it independently or did you need my help?" The only piece a student may not be able to answer with certainty is whether or not the work is accurate. When sharing the learning target with the class, the teacher can say, "Today, I expect all of you to do...Most of you will be able to...Some of you who are ready for a challenge can try..."

> **A Word Of Caution...** There are students who may want to attempt the "some" portion who will not accurately complete the "most" portion. There are several reasons why this could happen including the competitive nature of students. Therefore, you may want to initially have students submit or show you their work (if the assignment is in class) before permitting them to attempt the "some" portion. The point of the AMS target is not to have students compete with others or to have

> students blast through more work. AMS targets assist you, as the teacher, in creating easy differentiation to challenge your students wherever they may be and to allow you learn more about what your students are capable of so you can better address their needs. As well, AMS targets allow students to improve their understanding of what they're capable of and make informed decisions about what they need to do to learn.

Strategy 17: Earn a Badge

If you were ever a Boy or Girl Scout or are a parent or troop leader, you know that in order to earn a badge, there are specific tasks that are required. Figure 5.4 is an example from Boy Scouts using the Animation Badge requirements and Figure 5.5 shows an excerpt from the Girl Scouts Animal Helpers Badge requirements. You can see in both that there is choice in what is needed to accomplish the intended learning. It is important to note that in both there are high levels of interaction and reflection regarding the learning. In other words, though the badge is earned through the completion of tasks, the purpose of the tasks is to tap into the intrinsic interests of the person completing it and to be able to take the learning beyond the procurement of the badge. Imagine now that this same structure was created in a classroom.

5.5: Boy Scouts Animation Badge Requirements[26]

Requirements

1. General knowledge. Do the following:
   a. In your own words, describe to your counselor what animation is.
   b. Discuss with your counselor a brief history of animation.

2. Principles of animation. Choose five of the following 12 principles of animation, and discuss how each one makes an animation appear more believable: squash and stretch, anticipation, staging, straight-ahead action and pose to pose, follow through and overlapping action, slow in and slow out, arcs, secondary action, timing, exaggeration, solid drawing, appeal.

3. Projects. With your counselor's approval, choose two animation techniques and do the following for each:
   a. Plan your animation using thumbnail sketches and/or layout drawings.
   b. Create the animations.
   c. Share your animations with your counselor. Explain how you created each one, and discuss any improvements that could be made.

4. Animation in our world. Do the following:
   a. Tour an animation studio or a business where animation is used, either in person, via video, or via the Internet. Share what you have learned with your counselor.
   b. Discuss with your counselor how animation might be used in the future to make your life more enjoyable and productive.

5. Careers. Learn about three career opportunities in animation. Pick one and find out about the education, training, and experience required for this profession. Discuss your findings with your counselor. Explain why this profession might interest you.

Figure 5.4: Excerpt from the Girl Scouts Animal Helpers Badge Requirements[27]

> **STEP 1: Explore the connection between humans and animals**
>
> The lives of humans and other animals have been linked for thousands of years—and the connection keeps getting stronger!
>
> **CHOICES – DO ONE:**
>
> ☐ **Find out how views of animals have changed over the centuries.** People used to think animals had no feelings, and they didn't always let cats and dogs sleep on their beds! Find 10 examples of how and why the human-animal connection has changed over time, then share what you've learned with friends, classmates, or a group of younger girls.
>
> OR
>
> ☐ **Watch a documentary series on the human-animal connection.** Then host a screening party about it. Come up with five topics or questions to discuss. For instance: How are certain animals, such as dogs and cows, viewed and treated in different parts of the world? Why?
>
> OR
>
> ☐ **Show how animals helped at key points in history.** Where would humans be if we hadn't began to use oxen to plow fields? What would have happened in 1776 if Paul Revere hadn't been able to ride his horse? Pinpoint five moments when animals took a role in human history, then share one—or all—in a skit or video show for friends and family.

There are two suggestions to consider before starting this process. The first is to start small. I would not recommend creating a whole book of badges to start; rather think about one unit that might lend itself to this structure. The second piece of advice is to find a friend so you can pool your creativity, thereby multiplying the ideas while dividing the pressure to invent tasks (two heads are better than one).

The key to doing this successfully is to be willing to (a) generate multiple pathways for the students to demonstrate success, including but not limited to students having the chance to work collaboratively and/or independently and (b) be open to the possibility that your first attempt at this will ultimately need revision. The goal is to get started so you can revise later—not to delay starting until it is perfect. So, if you're willing to take the risk, you'll do the following:

1. Clearly identify the intended learning.
2. Determine what the students would need to show someone (you, their classmates, etc.) in order to demonstrate they have achieved the intended learning.

3. Create tiers of tasks—some that are required and some that have choice—that students would do to demonstrate their learning.

Since this will be just as new for the students as it is for you, it will be important to frontload the learning with clear directions and expectations. Then, because the learning was planned in advance behind the scenes, you will be available to the students during the learning work time to assist them when and if they need it. You will also be able to monitor the learning in case there is instruction that you didn't plan for but might be needed.

Eventually, and this would take quite a bit of time to create, you could have a classroom where students in the same classroom are working on different badges because their learning would be determined by their interest in different topics. As well, you would invite the students at the end of the experience to offer suggestions for changes to the process that you could incorporate into my modifications. Imagine, for example, that you created a unit on biomes and by the end of the unit, students might all need to earn at least three of six possible badges. Each badge would be related to the unit, but since the work is self-paced, you might have a couple students working together on one badge, while you're doing a conference with students who may be working on different badges but all need support with a skill like citations, while the rest of the class is working independently on their learning. The iterations of how this could look in your classroom truly are endless.

Strategy 18: Playlist

Melissa Laun, a former teacher and staff developer who is the Director of Special Education and Grant Writing in Lewiston-Porter Central School District, where I work shared this strategy with me. I saw her use this strategy with teachers and asked her to share the Playlist strategy here for you.

When you think of the term "playlist," classroom instruction is probably not the first idea that comes to mind; you probably think of a playlist in iTunes or, for a real throwback, a mixtape you gave a crush with a list of their favorite songs on the cassette you recorded for them (yes, I said cassette). When I saw Melissa using this strategy, it was actually very close to a musical playlist—which is a list of songs that you choose to listen to—except with this instructional strategy, participants are given options of tasks to complete to show their learning.

Melissa was introduced to an instructional playlist in 2016 when collaborating with Education Elements (EE)—an educational consulting organization—to learn more about the personalized learning. When the consultants from Educational Elements (EE) provided her team with overviews of the work they would engage with that day, EE used the playlist. Melissa shared,

> We were given a Google document that had multiple links on the topic that we were able to self-navigate. They gave us a set amount of time and sent us on our way. It was a refreshing experience. I had some knowledge of personalized learning, but I was by no means an expert. The playlist gave me the opportunity to skip the novice stages and start at a more advanced level.

In essence, playlists give the learner choice over *when, how, and what they do* during the learning process. Since we all enter learning at different entry points, the playlist allows learners to start where they need and go as in-depth as they would like. For example, Melissa presented to a group of teachers on developing instructional strategies for collaborative teaching. The teachers ranged in experience from first year teachers to tenured and all differed in support roles. Melissa created several playlists on effective strategies they could use in their classrooms to support collaborative teaching. Figure 5.6 is an example of the playlists Melissa developed on Specially Designed Instruction (SDI).

Figure 5.6: Sample Playlist

Specially Designed Instruction Playlist

This playlist is specifically designed for educators to learn more about Specially Designed Instruction (SDI). Below you'll find a series of activities focused on specific content that allows you to control your path, pace, or modality.

How it works: Click on any of the links. Read/play/listen to the link. If you like what you are reading/listening to, you can continue. If you are not digging it, close that link and try a new one. You are required to be thoughtful and you are responsible for your own learning.

Learning Target: Provide teachers with several effective and research-based strategies to implement in their inclusive classrooms

TITLE & LINK	DIRECTIONS	TO DO
Guidance Document: Lesson Plan Template Accessing the Common Core for Students with Disabilities NYSED Regional Special Education Technical Assistance Support Center (RSE-TASC)	1) Read the guidance document from NYSED. 2) Complete the reflection sheet. 3) Be prepared to share your thinking.	Reflection Sheet *This link will force you to make a copy. If for some reason it does not, please make a copy of the document before filling it in.*

Specially Designed Instruction
United Federation of Teacher
	1) Read the description of SDI.
	2) Choose from A or B.
	   a) Complete the chart on SDI features.
	   b) Browse the section **What are some examples of specially designed instruction in various domains?** and complete the takeaway reflection sheet on the specific strategies.
		a) SDI Features Chart
		This link will force you to make a copy. If for some reason it does not, please make a copy of the document before filling it in.
		
		b) SDI Instructional Strategies
		This link will force you to make a copy. If for some reason it does not, please make a copy of the document before filling it in.

Considerations for Specially Designed Instruction Kansas SED	1) Read through the chart from Kansas SED 2) Complete the get **Connect - Extend - Challenge** protocol	Connect - Extend - Challenge *This link will force you to make a copy. If for some reason it does not, please make a copy of the document before filling it in.*
Specially Designed Instruction Learning Modules Maryland Online IEP Electronic Learning Community	1) Complete the module by clicking on the different buttons below the title. You do not have to do the Wrap -up. Example: 03: Specially Designed Instruction	While you are viewing this module, go through the process and complete the various pieces to learn about SDI.

By giving teachers/learners a playlist, she didn't have to waste time trying to get everyone at the same place in their understanding in order to move on in the lesson. She could honor where people were in their understanding of the topic and build from there more easily.

There are a few important components to an instructional playlist.

1. **Learning Objects:** First, there should be an attached learning target or objective on the playlist. This learning target will provide clarity as to what participants should be able to do by the end of the lesson/ time.
2. **Student Ownership:** The playlist should be structured in such a way that participants are offered control over their pace and path for learning.
3. **Options:** As noted in the example, another component to a playlist are the resources and activities provided for participants to browse and complete. Depending on the learners, you can differentiate activities and levels according to "must dos" and "may dos." Again, this provides a certain level of control to the learner. The resources can be anything! It can be a video, article, website, memes, blog, etc. The list is endless. The activity then can be broken down by levels on Bloom's Taxonomy, by must dos/may dos, level of ease, or even product.

As with any strategy, there are some challenges. When it comes to playlists, you should expect that there might be a learning curve with technology—be it if you're working with children or adults. Therefore, creating hyperlinks is a must. As well, this strategy is one that requires adequate time for both introduction of the work and then time to complete the tasks. Finally, as already mentioned, playlists often have videos so learners will need to have headphones and/or a separate space for listening.

Despite these challenges, there are many reasons why playlists increase engagement.

- **Learner Choice:** Learners decide what they want to engage with and how they want to show their knowledge/comprehension of the topic.
- **Built-In Assessment:** Learners determine where they start in the learning process (i.e. Novice, Competent, Expert).
- **Built-in Accountability:** There is a deliverable that must be completed by the predetermined end time.

- **Learner Pacing:** Learners determine how fast they move through the playlist to get to where they need to be.
- **More 1:1 Time**: Because learners work independently, the teacher/facilitator has the ability to meet with learners one-on-one and provide feedback.
- **Highly Customizable:** Playlists can be anything you want it to be and can be customized for your group of learners. Adjustments can easily be made because playlists are digital.

Strategy 19: Audiobooks

When I was the Director of Elementary Education, I used to create sign-up sheets where I would make myself available to visit classes for about twenty minutes and volunteer my time. I would tell the teachers I would come in as a sub for that time if the teacher wanted to visit or work with a colleague (if they signed-up for back-to-back sessions, that would forty minutes). I would offer to run a center. I could work one-on-one with a student. I could read to the class...the time was theirs and I was happy to be there. Most of the time, teachers would invite me in to read to their students. I always had the teacher pick the book because I wasn't sure what the students had already read or not. I loved every minute of those visits! During the read aloud, I was the only one with the book. The students did not have a copy in which they followed along; students simply sat in their seats or on the rug intently listening as I read the book and showed them the illustrations at the end of every page.

Read alouds are commonplace in primary classrooms. I cannot even imagine a primary teacher who isn't reading to the class regularly, if not daily. In part this is because the students may be too young to read to themselves. Also, most of the books that are read to children have reading levels that far exceed what the children are capable of reading independently. "Children can listen on a higher language level than they can read, so reading aloud makes complex ideas more accessible and exposes children to vocabulary and language patterns that are not part of everyday speech."[28] This is just one small reason why read alouds are so important in primary classrooms.

Nevertheless, even when the children are capable of reading to themselves, they are still excited to listen to the adult read to them.

So if this is all true, why is it that listening to a book rather than reading it yourself becomes taboo at a certain age? Even among adults why is the idea of listening to an audiobook considered by some to be cheating? Interestingly, audiobook popularity is on the rise. According to the blog post, "Audiobook Trends and Statistics for 2020," by Michael Kozlowski, the Editor in Chief of *Good e-Reader*,

> Digital audiobooks continue to be the fastest growing segment in publishing. Not only is the entire publishing industry making more money, but there is more choice available for customers. Last year audiobook sales increased by 16% in the United States and generated over $1.2 billion dollars in revenue, whereas in 2018 it only made $940 million, an increase of 25% from 2017. You know what is surprising about that $1.2 billion digital audiobooks made? Ebooks only made $983 million, so for the first time ever, US audiobook sales have eclipsed ebook sales.[29]

Certainly not everything can be read to a child nor an adult. However, we need to ask what is the goal?

If the goal of the reading is to become a better decoder of words, then there is no substitute for actually reading the text. Trust me. I have a master's degree in reading. I get it. However, there are other important goals that go beyond decoding. Vocabulary development and comprehension are critical and do not require a student to actually read a text. This is why we do read alouds in the first place.

So, on one hand, read alouds are good for children who are not yet able to read independently to develop their vocabulary and comprehension skills without the task of developing their phonemic awareness, phonics, or fluency skills. On the other hand, audiobooks are good for anyone who can already read independently but wants access to more challenging text than what can be read independently. Audiobooks are also great for people who are looking to enjoy a text without the burden of actually having it in hand, i.e., while doing something else. In fact, "the average audiobook users are affluent men, aged between 18 and 34 years old, who listen to at least four audiobooks every 12 months. Their main reasons for doing so include entertainment and brain stimulation. Overall, men, far more than women, listen to audiobooks while working, commuting and running outdoors."[30] I am a competent reader of text, but I *always* have an audiobook (or two) on my phone and listen to them while I drive, make dinner, fold laundry, etc.

Check out this link for audiobook apps for kids:
https://cutt.ly/Audio-Apps

The purpose of allowing students to listen to audiobooks rather than to force them to actually read the text is to provide students with choices in how to accomplish the thinking and learning from the book. This is the difference between reading to learn and learning to read. If you are working with a student on learning *how* to read, audiobooks are not going to be the best bet. If, however, you are working with that student in reading to learn, audiobooks might be a welcomed option for you and your students to consider. In other words, if the goal of the task is related in some way to vocabulary development and/or comprehension of the text and not to learning how to decode, then offering the choice in how the student acquires the knowledge of the text is worth a shot to increase engagement. After all, the critical thinking about the text remains intact through reading or through listening to an audiobook.

Chapter Summary

This chapter was about moving someone from the point of compliance to interest through the use of choice and voice strategies. Choice refers to options. Voice is the ability to give input regarding decisions. These strategies were about a change in the task in order to make a move from the left to the right on The Engagement Framework. Interest manifests in at least three ways: (1) Willing Participants, (2) Professionals, and (3) Strategists. No matter how interest manifests, interested people enjoy the tasks temporarily *and* they need an extrinsic motivator to do the task; if they were intrinsically motivated and/or they had more than a temporary enjoyment of the task, they would be absorbed.

> **Looking for even more strategies to**
> **CREATE CHOICE AND VOICE?**
> Please visit my website, www.LyonsLetters.com/learnmore, for print and digital recommendations including books, websites, videos, and more!

Thank you again to Melissa Laun for contributing Playlist—

a strategy included in this chapter.

Reflection Prompts

1. Think about a time when you had choice or voice. How did that impact your engagement in the task?

   _____
   _____
   _____

2. Think of a time when you did not have choice or voice? How did that impact your engagement in the task?

   _____
   _____
   _____

3. What is your go-to strategy for incorporating choice?

   _____
   _____
   _____

4. What is your go-to strategy for incorporating voice?

   _____
   _____
   _____

5. Name one thing you could do tomorrow based on what you learned from this chapter.

   _____
   _____
   _____

6. Tweet me @LyonsLetters to share an idea for a future reading or digital resource I should share on www.lyonsletters.com that would help someone who is compliant become interested.

Persistent Questions

1. What have you done so far regarding the three challenge questions from Chapter 1?

    a. **Three:** Find at least three people with whom to share your learning.

    b. **Two:** Find at least two ideas that change you.

    c. **One:** Apply at least one idea from your reading.

    _____
    _____
    _____

2. What have you learned so far, and how will you use it?

    _____
    _____
    _____

Chapter 6

Change the Task Strategies

"The most dangerous phrase in language is 'we've always done it this way.'"
~Rear Admiral Grace Hopper

Recognizing Your Thinking Before You Read...

1. What is the difference between a task and a learning outcome?

   _____
   _____
   _____

2. How can changing a task increase or decrease engagement?

   _____
   _____
   _____

3. Think of a time your engagement increased because the task was changed. What was the task and how did it change?

   _____
   _____
   _____

Yeah Right

I know. It seems almost laughable to say that if you change the task, you can increase engagement. Thank you Captain Obvious. However, before you roll your eyes or close the book, I want to remind you that many of the **tasks** that we ask others to do in education are not required; the requirements are the standards, and the options are the tasks used to achieve the learning of the standards. Put another way, the learning outcomes are required, but the inputs used to achieve those outcomes are determined at the classroom level.

The feelings of being trapped by the tasks are created when the adults feel like they are disempowered and do not have the ability or autonomy to have choice themselves. Accordingly, the challenge is that it is not easy to design tasks that students to want do around information that students *have to learn.* Indeed, there seems to be a paradox that suggests that if students have to learn X, they won't want to learn it AND what they want to learn about is Y. In other words, the things students want to learn about are not a part of the curriculum and so what is a teacher to do? This is an inverse relationship.

As a result, with the ever-growing focus on common and rigorous standards, teachers have reduced the "frills" from their lessons, like projects and choice, in favor of teacher-directed, whole-group instruction. Why bother getting to know your students' interests, learning styles, or preferences if you are handcuffed to curriculum? It's not like you can be responsive or inclusive to this knowledge of your students' differences or needs anyway, right? Ironically, this establishes a mindset that is the exact opposite of what research says are best practices in terms of having students learn because the students want to know more. Thus, both the teacher and the student feel like they just need to suffer through the boring mandates, lessons, and tasks to check the box that this information was covered. The reality is that the most common reason for mind-numbing, uninspiring tasks is because the *teacher* feels bored or helpless. Let's not act surprised when there are teachers who feel disengaged, discouraged, trapped, and

> **Let's not act surprised when there are teachers who feel disengaged, discouraged, trapped, and like they're just going through the motions who have students who feel that same way in that classroom.**

like they're just going through the motions who have students who feel the same way in that classroom.

The Journey and the Destination

This reminds me of the difference between standards, curriculum, instruction, and assessment. Though I shared the differences among each of these terms in *Engagement is Not a Unicorn*,[31] it bears repeating here. When you understand the differences among these terms, you can see that there is a great deal that can be done to change the tasks that students are assigned.

> *It can be confusing to understand the differences between standards, curriculum, instruction, and assessment. Each of these are described below using a metaphor of travel. That is, if the standards are the destination (let's say Chicago), the curriculum is the vehicle (car, boat, bus, plane, etc. used to arrive at the destination). The instruction is the approach or route used to get to Chicago—I chose the scenic route, you chose a shortcut. Finally, in this metaphor, the assessment is the GPS that tells us if we actually arrived in Chicago, if we broke down along the way, or we made even better time, got past our destination, and are in Kansas City.*
>
> - ***Standards:*** Standards are the *expectations* for what students should know and be able to do at each grade level. The standards answer the question, "What is the destination for the intended learning?"
> - ***Curriculum***: Curriculum is the *content* that gives students access to the standards. According to Robert Marzano,[32] it should be both:
>   - *Guaranteed* (i.e., all students, regardless of their teacher or school will have access to the same content, knowledge, and skills across the district).

- ○ *Viable*[ii] (i.e., the curriculum is realistic in scope and has made careful decisions to narrow the universe of knowledge into developmentally appropriate and challenging learning targets for the students in the district).

    Ultimately, the curriculum is the common and reasonable plan used to teach students the learning goals embodied in the standards and prepares students for success for the next grade level. The curriculum answers the question, "What is/are the best vehicle(s) for all students to arrive at the destination?"

- **Instruction**: Instruction is the *approach* (route) a teacher uses to ensure that all students learn the content. Instruction is fluid and changes depending on the teacher's abilities and the students' needs. Instruction is a variable in the learning "equation" since how a teacher chooses to teach the content is highly dependent on the students, the resources, and the teacher's own knowledge of the content and pedagogy. This explains why two teachers can tackle the same curriculum differently. The instruction answers the question, "What are the best approaches I can use to ensure all students arrive at the destination?"

- **Assessment**: Assessment is the *measure* of what students have learned. This is fundamentally different from what teachers have taught because students may not demonstrate learning of taught material and this explains why not all students answer all questions correctly all of the time. Assessment is able to identify what students know as well as identifying if the curriculum and/or instruction are meeting the needs of our students or require revision. The assessment answers the question, "Where are the students in relation to where they are supposed to be?"

[ii] I strongly agree with Marzano's research on a guaranteed and viable curriculum and I would also add that curriculum needs to be contextual. In other words, though a curriculum could be both guaranteed and viable, if the contextual constraints (time, human or other resources) cannot support the curriculum, it doesn't matter if it's the best curriculum ever because its implementation in that context is not the best ever.

Managing Expectations

Remember Highlight 9 from Chapter 1 of this book, "No one is capable of being absorbed in everything all the time"? While the absorption strategies are later in this book, I want to remind you that although it is not possible for any one person to be absorbed in 100 percent of all things at all times, it should be the aim of schools that all students are at least interested in all classes 100 percent of the time. That does not mean that there are some tasks that must be done that are not that enjoyable and are unavoidable (like state-mandated assessments). However, these tasks should be the exception, not the rule.

Now What

The next fourteen strategies provide ideas on how to change tasks in order to increase engagement.

20. Peer Feedback
21. But Why Does This Matter
22. Don't Kill the Wonder
23. Talk Moves
24. Notice and Wonder
25. Math Accountable Talk
26. Esti-Mysteries
27. Which One Doesn't Belong
28. You Can Make It
29. Modeling
30. Strategy Share
31. Intermittent Practice
32. 4DX
33. Read for Speed

Strategy 20: Peer Feedback

Feedback comes in many forms, but it is commonly provided by the superior to the subordinate. This can be teacher-to-student or administrator-to-teacher. Either way, the feedback is often boiled down to a number, e.g., a percentage of accuracy for students or a rating for a teacher. You are an A. You are Effective. As soon as a label is assigned, the opportunity for true feedback to elicit reflection or change disappears. It's not that the superior is not able or qualified to provide feedback, but, out of compliance, the evaluation necessitates a score.

Unfortunately, for all the time we spend training superiors in evaluation of subordinates, we spend very little time explaining to subordinates how they are being evaluated. Then, when there are times that we ask them to do peer-to-peer feedback, they struggle. Perhaps if we spent as much time empowering those who are being evaluated to understand what they are being evaluated on, they would not only improve in their own abilities, but also improve in their ability to provide feedback to their peers.

The reasons to have students provide feedback to each other abound. Not only do students benefit from the process, but indirectly, "teachers will receive feedback on their pedagogical practice."[33] In this way, peer feedback sounds like a win-win. Nevertheless, I know that peer feedback can be very challenging. Educator and author of the book *Peer Feedback in the Classroom: Empowering Students to be the Experts*, Star Sackstein writes,

> Giving students this responsibility is not without its pitfalls. Students don't always step up to the challenge and may falter in their ability to help their peers. There can be many reasons for this, but it often comes down to one of two things: a lack of individual student agency or interest or unclear expectations and follow-through from the teacher. Understanding where the breakdown happened and then finding a solution for the particular problem is important. The feedback process isn't designed to happen in a vacuum; the challenges that arise can actually strengthen students' learning, collaboration, and leadership skills. [34]

When I taught high school, I used peer feedback. In the beginning, it was more challenging than I thought because I did not provide the necessary scaffolding to support the students' success. As I better understood the need for scaffolding and adapted, peer feedback became easier and something that truly improved the students' work. Here are some of the tips to keep in mind.

1. **Model.** It is best to use a sample and share it with everyone. Do a true "I Do" and use a think-aloud to show that you're looking for. Transition to "We Do" after you allow the students some think time to process independently. Then have students do "You Do" with just one part.

2. **Start small version 1.** Focus on one component at a time for feedback. For example, you may have students complete a full word problem in math. Instead of asking students to look at the problem to ensure that the problem was set up correctly, the computation was correct, *and* the answer was correct, just focus on if the problem was set up correctly. When the students master the ability to determine that one aspect in their peers' work, then add the next step.

3. **Start small version 2.** Focus on one question at a time. For example, there may be ten problems the students had to do for homework. Do not have students look at all ten problems; have them look at just one. The goal is to have the students be able to provide quality feedback in small doses before scaling up.

4. **Understanding warm feedback.** Because feedback should be specific, we do not want students giving un-actionable praise like "good job" or "I like this." Teach them how to give specific feedback on work that is well done. Give them sentence starters or examples like, "You did this well because you…" or "When you did _____, I could easily see _____."

5. **Understanding cool feedback.** Because feedback should be specific but it is hard to tell a peer there's something to improve, teach them how to give specific feedback on work that needs improvement. Help them frame their cool feedback in the form of a question and give them sentence starters or examples like, "I wonder if you instead tried _____ if your point would be strengthened" or "Have you considered…?"

6. **Create accountability.** Make sure that the people who provide the feedback are accountable because they sign their name or initials to the feedback they give. This allows the receiver to follow-up with questions later, if clarification is needed. This

also ensures that the teacher can intervene if someone is not meeting expectations for the feedback they're providing.

7. **Reflection.** The feedback certainly helps the person receiving it, but it also gives insight to the person providing the feedback. Since they are peers, the students giving the feedback are able to reflect on what they saw from their peers to use within their own work. This makes the process reciprocal.

I used a Peer Editing Form (see Figure 6.1) that students would staple to their papers. We would sit in a circle and students would pass their paper with the form to the right. The students would have the paper for a set amount of time (about five to seven minutes). When the timer rang, the students would pass the paper to the right again. With the new paper, they would read it and answer the second prompt on the paper. When the timer went off, they would pass again. This happened for as many times as there were prompts. This gave the students multiple examples of student work to look at; however, it is certainly not necessary to pass the paper—one student could review another's for all of the prompts. Again, depending on your students, you may want to focus on one prompt at a time before adding on all prompts.

Figure 6.1: Peer Editing Form

Name_____   Date_____

Peer Editing Form

Sometimes it is easier to identify the strengths and weaknesses of someone else's work than it is to do that for ourselves. Furthermore, reading others' work can often inspire one to improve. For these reasons, it is now time to read the writing of your peers.

First Reader: Silently read the piece. In the box below, tell the author whether or not the introduction drew you in. If it did, explain why. If it did not, make a suggestion on what/how to improve.
Reviewer's Initials _____
Second Reader: Silently read the piece. As you read, focus on the conventions of the writing. Make the needed suggestions using our proofreaders marks. In the box below, give the author tips to improve conventions in this piece.
Reviewer's Initials _____
Third Reader: Silently read the piece. As you read, highlight all the words, phrases, and/or sentences that are the most effective or have an impact on you as the reader. In the box below, recommend places to improve and suggest ways to do so.
Reviewer's Initials _____
Fourth Reader: Silently read the piece. Consider the writing in terms of the author's voice. In the box below, explain how the author drew you in and/or make recommendations on how the author could improve the writing to engage the reader.
Reviewer's Initials _____
Fifth Reader: Silently read the piece. Consider the writing in terms of the assigned task. How well did the piece meet those requirements? In the box below, make recommendations on what could be done to better meet the requirements of the task.
Reviewer's Initials _____

*A Word Of Caution...*Angela Stockman (@angela_makewritng) is a talented author, teacher, and consultant. Check out Angela Stockman's great tips she posted on Instagram for explicitly sharing "when peer review works" and "when it doesn't."

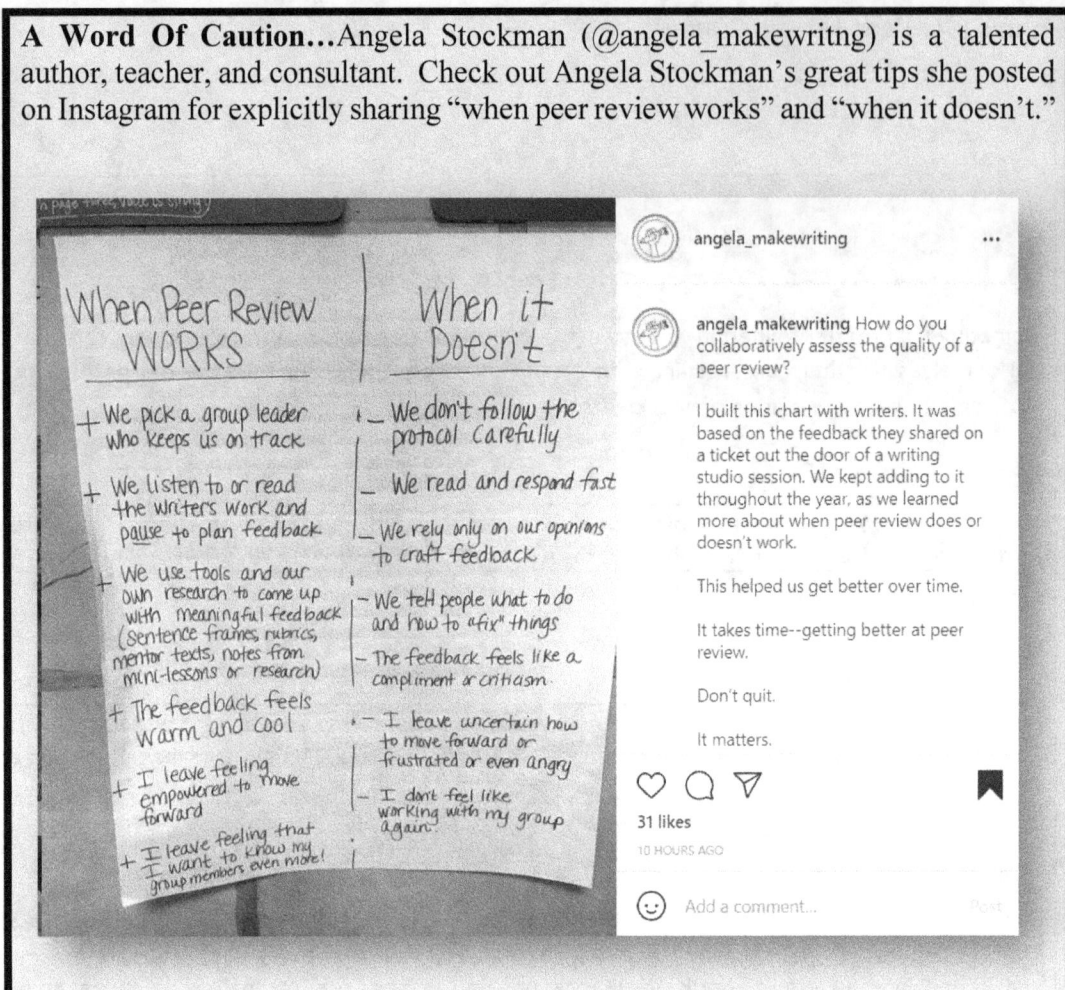

Alternative Use: Let's not forget that peer feedback is also powerful for adults. *Education World* called peer feedback a "form of professional development that improves teaching practices and student performance."[35] Peer feedback between adults can take several forms including lesson studies, peer coaching, and peer observations, to name the most common. The article, "The Power of Peer Feedback" shares these "Critical Elements of Teacher Observation as Professional Development."

- Ensuring school leaders advocate and support teacher observation as a valid form of professional development
- Building a community of trust among faculty
- Establishing a school-wide commitment to the approach

- Separating observation from the teacher evaluation process
- Declaring the purpose for teacher observation and a commitment to its outcomes
- Inviting teachers to first participate in the process as volunteers
- Allowing *time* for teachers to observe other teachers
- Organizing scheduled meetings, coaching sessions, and follow-up conversations
- Creating teams that share students
- Selecting specific strategies and skills on which to focus during an observation session
- Instituting a way to measure the impact of observation

As with all strategies in this chapter, the purpose of peer feedback with adults is to encourage the power of feedback. This power shifts us from the compliance-based exchanges that tend to occur when the feedback is from an administrator to the teacher as a result of the required evaluation.

Strategy 21: But Why Does This Matter

Simon Sinek's book *Start with Why* explains the importance of communicating the purpose of tasks. He uses what he refers to as the "Golden Circle" to illustrate why you should start with why (see Figure 6.2).

Figure 6.2: Simon Sinek's "Golden Circle"[36]

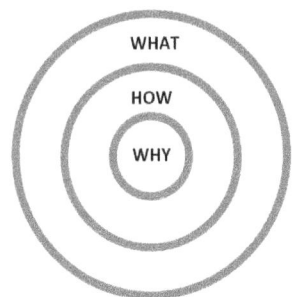

WHAT: *Every organization on the planet knows WHAT they do. These are the products they sell of the services they provide.*

HOW: *Some organizations know HOW they do it. These are the things that make them special or set them apart from their competition.*

WHY: *Very few organizations know WHY they do what they do. WHY is not about making money. That's the result. WHY is a purpose, cause, or belief. It's the very reason your organization exists.*

Though you are likely not reading this book because you have a business, you do have a classroom or a school that you lead. If you are a teacher, do you explain what the students are learning and how to do whatever they need to do? If so, that's what most teachers do. "Here's the learning target. I'll model for you how to do this. Now it's your turn. Go." Sinek argues that this misses the point since "People don't buy what you do, they buy why you do it."[37] Again, you may not literally sell anything, but figuratively you sell learning.

Sinek says that by starting with why "we can communicate from the inside out, [so] we're talking directly to the part of the brain that controls behavior, and then we allow people to rationalize it with the tangible things we say and do. This is where gut decisions come from."[38] Unless you explain to me why I should care about different types of government or Shakespeare or solving for X, you leave it to chance that I will be able to intuitively recognize the purpose of the task. If I do not, then the purpose of doing this work is for the grade or because you told me to, and fails to spark interest in me. If you want to get me, tell me why it will/should/does matter to me. Or better still, ask me what my WHY is and allow me to do work that links to me. This simple question could actually elicit absorption.

The same thing is true if you are an administrator working with adults. For example, when interviewing several potential interns, the first question I asked was "Why are you pursuing your administrative certification?" The answer to this question elicits the purpose of the work and that should never be "to make more money" or "to ensure the buses leave on time." The answer should be about the purpose and beliefs like "to create positive learning experiences for even more students than I am able to reach in the classroom" or "to ensure that all members of the school community from students to parents to teachers know that they are valued in the learning process." Yet, how often do we hear administrators share the reason why they became administrators outside of an interview? When we understand why they do what they do, we are more likely to be interested in the things that we do with them.

Imagine the last new initiative that your administration presented to you. Was that initiative rolled out with the why first? Was there a concerted effort to explain the purpose of the initiative and how that connected to the purpose of the district, the purpose of the administration, and/or your purpose? Probably not. If not, then the initiative likely felt like another thing that needed to be done. And you did it compliantly. If the why was shared, then the initiative likely felt like an opportunity to improve and grow. When we start with why, we are excited about doing it because the thing we are doing makes sense. This is what brothers and authors Dan and Chip Heath write about in their book *Switch: How to Change Things When Change Is Hard*. In their book they use an analogy of The Rider (reason), The Elephant (emotions), and the Path (the steps needed) and argue that you need alignment among all three in order to most easily facilitate change. In the classroom, I would argue that all three are needed to facilitate learning. Hence, you need to appeal to the reason and emotion behind the learning with clarity in how the learning will happen.

Watch a brief video narrated by Dan Heath that explains the Rider, Elephant, Path metaphor here:
https://cutt.ly/Heath

It is hard enough to learn even when things are concrete and tangible. It is even harder when things are abstract and vague, yet it is the teacher's job to provide clarity. When starting with WHY, the learning is not just about answering the sometimes difficult question of *when will I use this*, but the question of *why do I need to learn this?* The right answer to this question should never be *because it's on the test*.

I may be going to educator purgatory by saying this out loud, but most of what is taught really depends on the preferences of the teacher; the standards are determined externally, but the curriculum and especially the instruction are highly connected to the teacher, not the government, the district, the building, and especially not the students. Mrs. Jones doesn't need to use this specific experiment to teach mitosis and Miss Pritchard doesn't need to use this problem set to teach Pythagorean Theorem. Mr. Smith doesn't need to use this writing prompt to teach opinion writing and Ms. Salvatore doesn't need to use that text to teach the battles of World War II. What's more, the reason why games like "Are you Smarter than a Fifth Grader" exist is because much of what we learn in school we do not need to know in order to function as adults. So if most of what is taught in schools is traditionally linked to the teacher, then what is school all about? It should be about learning and the classes should be designed to support that end.

This doesn't mean that students do not need to be tested on the content or skills they're learning, but that these are the WHAT. Understanding the difference can be difficult. To help explain it, I point to the blog, "Three Teachers Talk," where Amy Rasmussen, a high school English teacher, writes about the impact *Start with Why* had on her work as a teacher. Figure 6.3 shows how Rasmussen shares her why, how, and what. Notice that she goes from the inside out.[39]

You can do this too. Reflect on and share your WHY, HOW, and WHAT. Just as important, have your students take time to identify their WHY, HOW, and WHAT. This will provide you leverage when teaching more abstract or less interesting content because you can redirect yourself and your students to the WHY of learning. It's not just the test, it's about the learning process.

Figure 6.3: Amy Rasmussen's Why, How, and What

> **WHY**: Everything I do as a teacher, I believe in helping my students identify as citizens, scholars, and individuals whose voices matter. I believe our world is better when individuals understand their value, believe in their capacity to cause change, and take action to better the world around them.
>
> **HOW**: The way I challenge my students is by making my classroom safe and inquisitive for my individual learners, with instruction that centers on trust, esteem, equity, and autonomy. Through the rituals and routines in my workshop classroom, students gain a sense of belonging, identify themselves as readers and writers, develop their voices, advance in literacy skills, and take risks that have the potential to change their worlds and the world around them.
>
> **WHAT**: And I happen to teach English by modeling my reading life and writing life.

Alternate Use: If you are an administrator, what is your Why, How, and What? Reflect on this question share this with those whom you work including your colleagues, the families, and students.

Strategy 22: Don't Kill the Wonder

If you are not a science teacher, you have probably never heard of Paul Andersen, a science teacher who has become an educational consultant and YouTuber. Andersen is credited for the now ubiquitous phrase among those familiar with the Next Generation Science Standards (NGSS), "Don't kill the wonder." This phrase is a critique of the traditional approach to science instruction, but can be generalized to all instruction. Traditional instruction is designed to tell students what they will do/see and then have them do it themselves. In a science classroom, that means the teacher would frontload the terms and then model the lab. It would be the job of the students to watch, take notes, and replicate. Andersen advocates that classrooms are places to teach students how to tap into their curiosity, not to kill it, saying, "'Show them something amazing, something cool and let them figure out how it works.'"[40] In the science classroom, this is referred to phenomenon-based teaching, but this constructivist approach can be modified to any discipline.

Since this strategy is couched in science, that's what I'll highlight and then I'll share some possibilities with other disciplines. However, the possibilities are limited only by the teacher's willingness to allow students to explore.

To best understand what phenonema-based learning (PhenoBL) is, here are some brief guidelines for PhenoBL in the science classroom.[41] The guidelines are taken directly from www.twigeducation.com. As you read these guidelines, consider how they can be generalized to other disciplines.

1. **Getting real**: The real world is the bedrock of PhenoBL – providing a much-needed starting point that is repeated at every stage. Students and teachers choose to focus on a real-world phenomena: rain, space travel or perhaps something problematic, like soil erosion. Students study a phenomenon that interests them, and use scientific enquiry and problem-solving skills with the aim of understanding it and demystifying it.

2. **Question and more questions**: PhenoBL thrives on curiosity, and so students are encouraged to question what is around them. It's not a revolutionary concept. Centuries ago, Socrates used a similar method of questioning to guide his students: in order to find the right answers, they had to know how to ask the right questions. PhenoBL echoes this approach, prioritising *how* over *why* in order to inspire students to make observations.

3. **Contextualise**: Phenomenon-based learning builds tangible connections between curriculum theory and the real world, but it also serves to link the various, separate subjects that students learn in schools: the Egyptian pyramids display an acute knowledge of physics engineering, both of which require precise, complex calculations, and the study of fossils and sedimented craters – a perfect mix of

geography and science–have helped scientists come to understand the Earth's biodiversity millions of years ago.

4. **Change in a teacher's role**: PhenoBL recasts the teacher's role, changing them from a provider of knowledge to a guide that helps students find knowledge on their own. This might initially be a slightly uncomfortable proposition for both teachers and students – watching students struggle prompts many teachers to want to jump in with the answer. But stick with the altered lesson structure: the aim is still to achieve learning goals.

5. **Other skills**: The beauty of PhenoBL is that it also integrates the learning of important social skills, such as clear communication and the ability to function in a team. PhenoBL also encourages the use of other pedagogy models: project-based learning, integrated-learning and inquiry-based learning, to name just a couple.

If that's what the teaching looks like, what makes a good phenomenon? According to Laura Henriques, Faculty Member in Science Education C.S.U. Longbeach, "It has to be something that makes the students ask questions" as well as something that they are able to "refer back to that multiple times throughout the unit."[42] Molly Ewing, Achieve Senior Program Associate, adds that it would be something that students are able to "connect to their lives and their interests," to further students "learning in a purposeful way," and students need to use the discipline to explain it.[43] In other words, it can't just be cute or odd; it has to be something that can be explained through disciplined-based study.

Teachers achieve this by showing the students something that piques curiosity—a short video (e.g., a spider capturing an insect), a photo (e.g., the Northern Lights), or a live demonstration (e.g., a can of regular soda and diet soda in water—one sinks and the other floats). These are all shown *without* frontloaded explanations or vocabulary instruction, etc. Clearly, the students will be interested in what they are seeing and because the wonder is still alive, they will be driven to figure out what is going on. Taken directly from www.NextGenScience.org, the side-by-side comparison of "Prior Thinking about Phenomena" to "Thinking about Phenomena Through the NGSS" is helpful in understanding what makes good phenomena (see Figure 6.4).

Figure 6.4: A Comparison of Old and Current Thinking about Phenomena[44]

PRIOR THINKING ABOUT PHENOMENA	THINKING ABOUT PHENOMENA THROUGH THE NGSS
If it's something fun, flashy, or involves hands-on activities, it must be engaging	Authentic engagement does not have to be fun or flashy; instead, engagement is determined more by how the students generate compelling lines of inquiry that create real opportunities for learning
Anything students are interested in would make a good "engaging phenomenon"	Students need to be able to engage deeply with the material in order to generate an explanation of the phenomenon using target DCIs, CCCs, and SEPs
Explanations (e.g., "electromagnetic radiation can damage cells") are examples of phenomena	Phenomena (e.g., a sunburn, vision loss) are specific examples of something in the world that is happening—an event or a specific example of a general process. Phenomena are NOT the explanations or scientific terminology behind what is happening. They are what can be experienced or documented
Phenomena are just for the initial hook	Phenomena can drive the lesson, learning, and reflection/monitoring throughout. Using phenomena in these ways leads to deeper learning
Phenomena are good to bring in after students develop the science ideas so they can apply what they learned	Teaching science ideas in general (e.g., teaching about the process of photosynthesis) may work for some students, but often leads to decontextualized knowledge that students are unable to apply when relevant. Anchoring the development of general science ideas in investigations of phenomena helps students build more usable and generative knowledge
Engaging phenomena need to be questions	Phenomena are observable occurrences. Students need to use the occurrence to help generate the science questions or design problems that drive learning
Student engagement is a nice optional feature of instruction, but is not required	Engagement is a crucial access and equity issue. Students who do not have access to the material in a way that makes sense and is relevant to them are disadvantaged. Selecting phenomena that students find interesting, relevant, and consequential helps support their engagement. A good phenomenon builds on everyday or family experiences: who students are, what they do, where they came from

So if all of this explains what it looks like in a science classroom, what could it look like in a different discipline? Figure 6.5 shows some possible examples.

Figure 6.5: Non-Science Examples of Phenomenon Based Learning

Discipline	Phenomenon Examples
Art	Show students different pieces of clay (before the first fire, after the first fire, and after the last fire). Ask them to explain the differences and why they are different. Allow them to make modifications to their theories throughout the unit.
English	Play the Telephone Game with students and note how the message changed from the first messenger to the last. Why? Have students create their theory and allow them to make modifications to their theories throughout the unit.
Math	When teaching odd and even numbers, show students that whenever two odd numbers are added together, they form an even number. Why? Have students create their theory and allow them to make modifications to their theories throughout the unit.
Physical Education	Show students how to properly throw a ball *without telling them how it's done* and ask them to explain what's happening and how it works then let them test out their theories allowing them to make modifications to their initial explanation throughout the unit.
Social Studies	Show students an image of the Berlin Wall coming down. Without telling them what's going on, ask them to explain it. Why was the wall there and why would people celebrate its destruction? Allow them to make modifications to their theories throughout the unit.

Strategy 23: Talk Moves

If you have ever watched or participated in base- or softball practice, you know that there are times when one child is up to bat and everyone else on the team is in a holding pattern watching the batter. The pitcher throws the ball and the batter swings as everyone else watches. Waiting. Swing. Miss. Pitch. Here's another option. The child can hit the ball and then it's up to one or two children in the field to try to catch the ball. Even so, everyone else is watching. Waiting. Wondering what will happen. Even in a game, after every pitch, the adult (umpire) comments and then the game can proceed.

Questions and discussions in a classroom can feel the same way. The teacher is the pitcher and lobs a ball out there. Sometimes it's to one student (the batter). Sometimes it's to the class (the field). In this scenario, one student answers and then throws the ball (the answer) to the teacher and the teacher catches it and throws out another ball (question) to one student or generally to the class. The teacher can be just as bored by this dynamic and wistfully hopes that some kid will "catch the ball."

Now think of a soccer game where the children are all on the field passing the ball to each other, sometimes having the ball taken away by someone on the other team. The action is constant and the adult monitors the play only commenting when needed, e.g., when the ball has gone out of bounds or when a player violates a rule (like being offsides). Questions and discussions in a classroom that is more like a soccer game would feel very different. The teacher might provide the class with the specs of the field (i.e., the topic for discussion), but the game would be played by the students. Students would question each other and not go back and forth between the adult and one student.

Certainly there are many ways to achieve questioning and discussions in classrooms to be more like soccer than like baseball. Specifically here, I want to focus on the strategy called "Talk Moves." With this strategy, the teacher provides students with a list of sentence starters to act as scaffolds on how to ask and answer each other's questions without the need for the teacher to be directly involved in the discussion. See Figure 6.6 for an example of sentence starters developed by teachers at King Middle School in Portland, Maine.

Watch students from King Middle School use the Talk Moves Print Out here:
https://cutt.ly/TalkMoves

What's important about this strategy is that is not just a strategy that can or should be used in a humanities course (e.g., an English, social studies, and/or world languages), but is just as powerful within a science, math, or other classroom where students may not be accustomed to engaging in real discussions. For example, in a science classroom where students may be observing a phenomenon (see Strategy 22), a teacher might have prompts embedded with science-specific vocabulary, like, "Tell me more about your observations of the phenomenon" or "What model do you have in your head about what you're seeing?" In a math classroom, some prompts might be, "Can you explain how you got your answer?" or "Another strategy you can use is…" Even in courses like physical education, talk moves can be used. For example, "When I saw you demonstrating this skill, you did _____ well" or "A suggestion that might have changed the outcome of the game would be…"

No matter what content Talk Moves is used with, Dr. Pamela Cantor, Founder and Senior Science Advisor for Turnaround for Children notes, "Children are going to struggle a bit, depending on how confident they feel, in speaking up in class. And yet…teacher[s want] everybody in the class to feel valued. So the kids are all learning phrases that can inspire other kids to contribute more easily."[45] The point here is that when students are given prompts to use as a means to assist their discussions, the discussion among all students improves because now all students have points of entry.

Figure 6.6: Talk Moves Print Out[46]

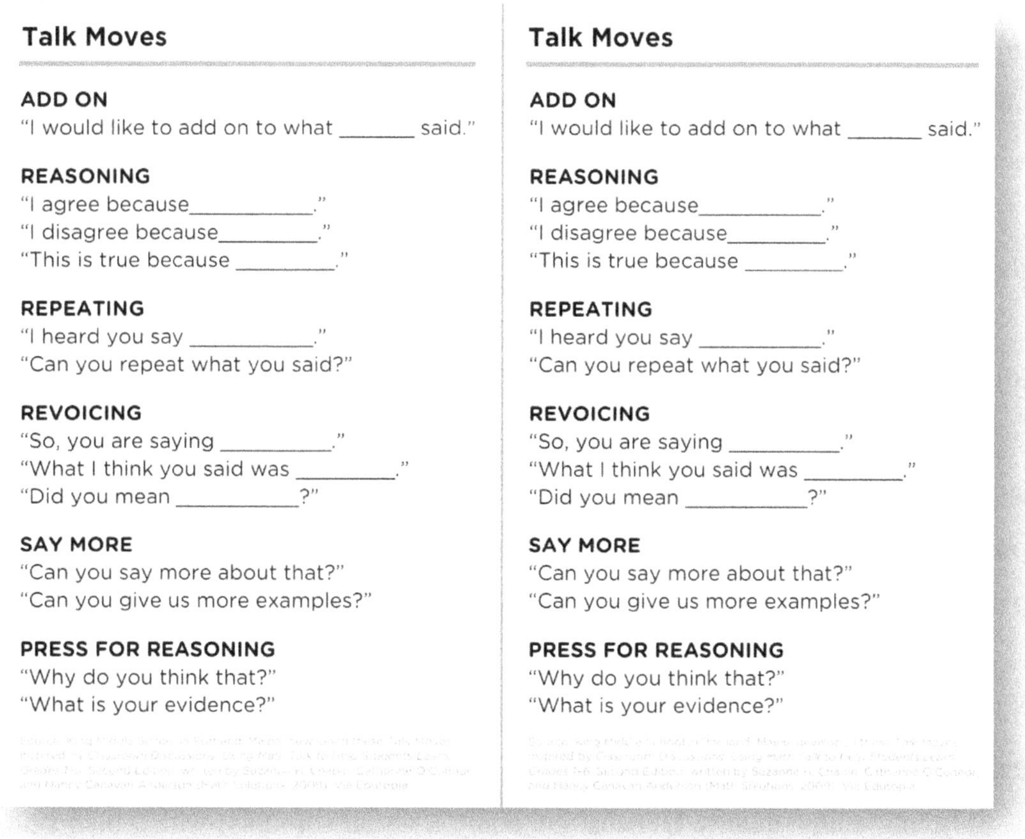

Talk Moves

ADD ON
"I would like to add on to what _______ said."

REASONING
"I agree because___________."
"I disagree because_________."
"This is true because _________."

REPEATING
"I heard you say ___________."
"Can you repeat what you said?"

REVOICING
"So, you are saying __________."
"What I think you said was _________."
"Did you mean ___________?"

SAY MORE
"Can you say more about that?"
"Can you give us more examples?"

PRESS FOR REASONING
"Why do you think that?"
"What is your evidence?"

Talk Moves

ADD ON
"I would like to add on to what _______ said."

REASONING
"I agree because___________."
"I disagree because_________."
"This is true because _________."

REPEATING
"I heard you say ___________."
"Can you repeat what you said?"

REVOICING
"So, you are saying __________."
"What I think you said was _________."
"Did you mean ___________?"

SAY MORE
"Can you say more about that?"
"Can you give us more examples?"

PRESS FOR REASONING
"Why do you think that?"
"What is your evidence?"

> ***Alternate Use:*** Integrating better question and discussion techniques with adults during faculty meetings and professional development not only improves the likelihood that they will be interested, but also models how they can use them with students.

Strategy 24: Notice and Wonder

Most educators have heard the old adage "You do not need to reinvent the wheel," but seasoned teachers know that even when we "borrow" something that we find, we nearly always make it our own. This is how teachers Elizabeth (Liz) Buck and Nina Calarco approached the strategy for the classroom routine "Notice and Wonder." Liz and Nina adapted Sara Van Der Werf's "Stand And Talks," which Van Der Werf credits as a spin-off of "Think, Pair, Share." In Liz and Nina's version of Notice and Wonder, they begin with a selected QFocus (explained below) where students are given something tangible to observe such as an image, video, graph, data-table, demonstration etc. with a partner. The student-pair will engage in dialogue using only the prompts, "I notice…" or "I wonder…" to activate their thinking and curiosity about the given stimulus. Students are encouraged to come up with as many notices and wonders as possible and are discouraged from any further discussion during the allotted time. The process continues as students choose both a notice and a wonder that they find most noteworthy to share out.

This strategy is typically used to introduce a new concept or topic because this gives the teacher an opportunity to listen for the students' prior knowledge, misconceptions, and areas of curiosity about the subject matter. Sara Van Der Werf suggests using this strategy five to eight times within a two-week period but, in their practice, Liz and Nina found success using the Notice and Wonder strategy on average one to two times per week in their math and science classrooms.

The procedures found to be the most successful when implementing Notice and Wonder are shown below. However, the two components that Liz and Nina feel are essential when using this strategy are:

1. Selecting a high quality QFocus (generally a visual stimulus) with which students can interact.
2. Creating and maintaining Notice and Wonder norms.

Step 1: Selecting a QFocus

When choosing the stimulus that will be the focus of the students' Notice and Wonders, Liz and Nina take a very similar approach to the Right Question Institute's concept of a QFocus.[47] A QFocus is a "stimulus for jumpstarting questions and is usually a statement, phrase, image, video, or alaural aid, math problem, equation, or anything else that gets the questions flowing."[48] The same is true when students generate Notice and Wonders, which in turn leads to great questions, student curiosity, and more in-depth student-centered learning.

Here are some things to keep in mind when selecting and using your QFocus:

- **Each pair of students should have access to a tangible QFocus whenever possible.** This may be a visual on a half-sheet of cardstock, access to a video, a physical model, or demonstration.
- **Whenever possible, each pair of students should have access to their own copy of the QFocus.** (sometimes this is not possible). Keep in mind that all students must be investigating the same QFocus so that the whole group debrief is focused on the same concept.
- **There should not be a question associated with the QFocus.** Students should simply make observations in the form of Notice and Wonders, not looking to find the answer to a question.
- **When adapting visuals, tables, graphs etc., consider removing names, titles, values, and details.** This will encourage students to generate more of their own ideas.
- **Choose strange and thought-provoking images and videos whenever possible.** Figure 6.7 has two math examples that Nina used and Figure 6.8 has two science examples from and Liz.

Figure 6.7: Math Examples

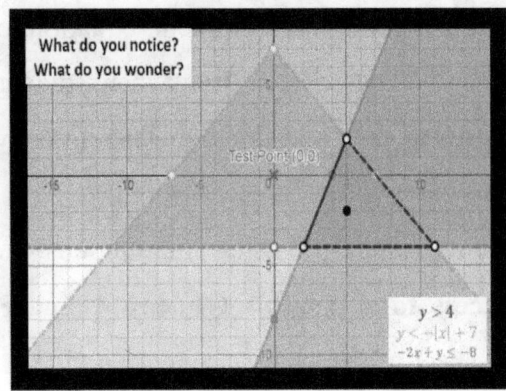

https://www.saravanderwerf.com/

Figure 6.8: Science Examples

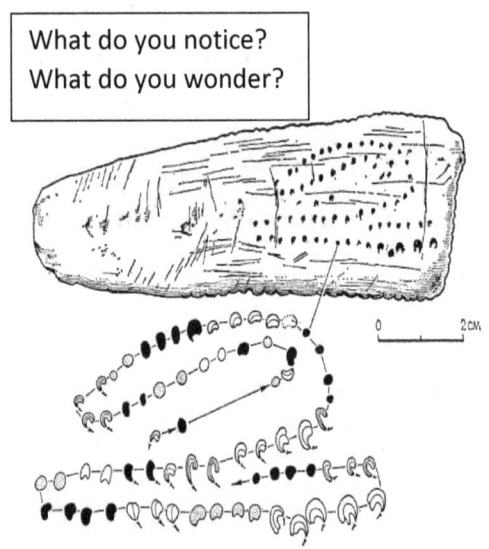

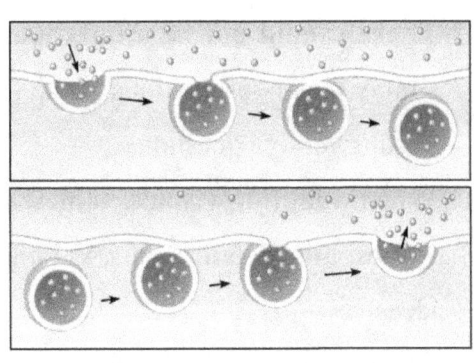

Step 2: Creating and Maintaining Notice and Wonder Norms

When creating and sharing your Notice and Wonder norms, be very deliberate with your students. Share the graphic with them, discuss and model what these expectations look like, and then reinforce the norms through student recall several times until the routine has been firmly established. Some of the tenets you will see below seem to be common sense, but they are in fact, very purposefully designed to support classroom culture and a sense of community.

To strengthen relationships and the overall emotional safety in the classroom community, encourage students to work with peers that they do not usually pair up with. You will probably be surprised to find out that one of the key components to success is having the students actively moving and remain standing. Peter Liledahl's work on Building Thinking Classrooms[49] shows research on how having students work vertically (standing), versus at a desk, changed the engagement in classrooms. Liz and Nina experimented with both options and their informal research showed vastly better results when students were standing.

Figure 6.9 has the Notice and Wonder Norms that Liz and Nina shared with their students. They have these norms on the smartboard as a prompt so that students are cued into the fact that they will be participating in a Notice and Wonder activity.

Figure 6.9: Sample Notice and Wonder Norms

Notice and Wonder Norms
~ Nothing in your hands
~ Stand tall...no leaning or sitting
~ Stand up from your desk and find a partner across the room from you
~ Choose a partner you do not usually work with
~ You will be working in Groups of 2
~ If you do not have a partner come see me
~ For the next ___ minutes you will be talking...*the entire time*
~ You will need to find at least ___ things...
if you run out of ideas just repeat some that you have already said.
*You should be talking the **ENTIRE TIME!***
~Really simple things are ok...

Step 3: Executing the Notice and Wonder in Class

Below you will find the sequence Liz and Nina use when executing a Notice and Wonder activity in their classes. You are encouraged to take these guidelines and make them your own. Adapting and fine tuning this process occurs over time. In fact, if you speak with Liz and Nina, they would tell you that they modified the Notice and Wonder routine when they had to instruct remotely due to COVID-19.

1. Ask students to pair up with a student they do not usually work with.
2. The pair will work together for the allotted time (usually 1-2 minutes, dependent on level of complexity), trying to come up with as many notices and wonders as possible.
3. Teacher is walking around the room, monitoring the level of engagement, listening for misconceptions, key words, insightful notices and wonders, etc.
4. Once the time is up, while still standing, each pair of students are required to give what they perceive is their best notice or wonder, which the teacher will record on the whiteboard, smartboard, etc. to be displayed.
5. When recording the information, be sure to avoid praising, restating, clarifying, or asking questions. Do not judge "correctness" of responses. Later discussion will amend thinking as needed.
6. Once all groups have contributed, they are to return the QFocus artifact (if it was a concrete object) and return to their seats.
7. Once the activity and recordings are complete, the teacher facilitates a whole group discussion where you may want to make some observations/comments..." lots of students noticed..." or "I can see that many of you are wondering..."
8. This discussion can then be used to inform your instruction, address misconceptions and further spark student inquiry.

Liz and Nina experienced many unintended positive outcomes when implementing the Notice and Wonder strategy in their classrooms. Through their informal observations and student feedback, they compiled a list of noteworthy outcomes that occurred in their classrooms:

- Student discourse not only improved during the designated "Notice and Wonder" time, but was also observed in day-to-day activities and routines.
- Students were observed working with a wider variety of classmates without encouragement from the teacher.

- Students showed an improvement in their ability to formulate questions. The quality of the questions grew over time, and the students' ability to self-assess their work improved dramatically.
- Students displayed a greater awareness of details. This was especially noticeable when students would interpret complex directions and when reading complex data tables.
- Students took more ownership in their learning. They began to display more confidence in their ability to determine relevant information. The amount of times students would ask the teachers "Is this right?" decreased over time.

Strategy 25: Math Accountable Talk

Student engagement during mathematics is usually at the compliant level as students work through workbook pages that have been assigned to them. I have watched Molly DiPirro, a math coach and staff developer with Access Mathematics, shift students and teachers to the next levels of engagement through various activities (Math Routines) that can be done in conjunction with any math program. Molly uses a variety of activities along with the strategic moves of student accountable talk in order to make these shifts. Depending on the schedule, math routines are usually done for about fifteen minutes outside of the Math Block. They are seen by the students as fun activities because often there is more than one answer or there are multiple strategies to find the answer. The math routines are written to be low floor/high ceiling activities; every student has an "in" to the problem (the low floor) and the activity can also be challenging for students with greater readiness (the high ceiling). The other key that Molly believes must be in place for a higher level of engagement in mathematics is the culture of the classroom. The culture needs to be one in which all students are comfortable speaking, they know that all solutions are accepted, that mistakes are looked upon as a learning experience, and that all strategies are welcomed and examined.

Molly described student accountable talk as the key to engaging students in all work. Accountable talk ensures that all students feel their voices are heard, helps to clarify their ideas and allows for time to adjust their thinking. Accountable talk is important for all subjects, but it is essential in mathematics as students are exploring their way around many ways to solve a problem. Accountable talk starts with practice. Students need to practice turning to each other. Upper elementary and secondary students might turn their desks to face each other while primary students might be on the carpet knee-to-knee, eye-to-eye. Students need to practice speaking to each other. Both partners need time to speak and hear/discuss each other's strategies. The three moves that Molly uses during a math routine are shown in Figure 6.11.

Figure 6.11: Accountable Talk Moves

Move 1: Turn and Talk	Move 2: Paraphrasing	Move 3: Adding to Someone Else's Thinking
• 30-40 seconds long • Teacher listens (does not engage) in on conversations in order to find strategies to be shared • Ensures students can share their strategy or answer with someone, even if they are not called upon to share with their class.	• "Can you repeat what that student just said?", "Can you explain how they arrived at that answer?"	• "Do you have something to add to their strategy?" "How is your strategy like _____'s strategy?"

Accountable Talk is guided by the teacher, but led by the students. The teacher's role is to ask questions and facilitate or clarify the conversation, with the students doing the explaining.

Strategy 26: Esti-Mysteries

Another accountable talk strategy that Molly shared is called Esti-Mysteries by Steve Wyborney. The Esti-Mystery starts with showing the students a glass filled with objects. Students make an estimate of how many objects they think are in the glass (see Figure 6.12).

The students in the class I watched Molly teach were anywhere on the continuum from interested to absorbed. They were excited to share their estimates, but Molly really focused on asking the students to explain why or how they came up with the estimate. They discussed as a class which estimates would be too low and estimates that would be too high and why. The next step of Esti-mysteries are the clues. One clue at a time helps students hone in their estimate.

They can be found at:
https://cutt.ly/Steve Wyborney

Figure 6.12: An Example of an Esti-Mystery

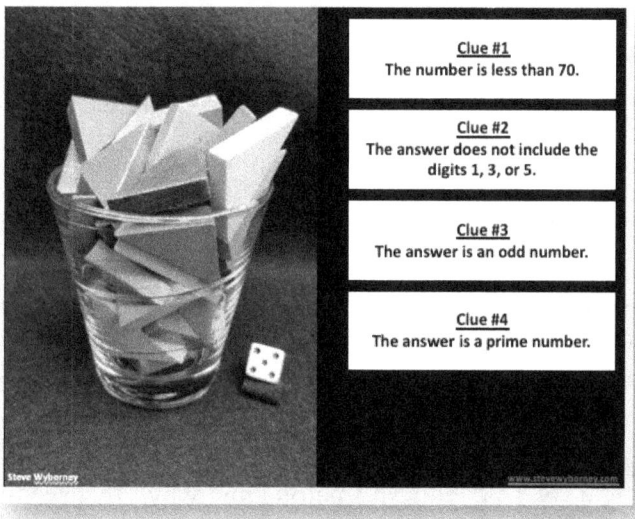

Students were excited to be able to change their estimate or keep their original one based on the clues given. Molly allowed those students who wanted to use a 100s grid to help keep track of the clues and their guesses (see Figure 6.13). Molly explained that many students will make and write their own Esti-Mystery at home to share with the class. This supports the high engagement of this activity.

Figure 6.13: Students Using a 100s Grid in an Esti-Mystery

Strategy 27: Which One Doesn't Belong

The accountable talk called Which One Doesn't Belong is another highly engaging math routine. Which One Doesn't Belong shows students four quadrants that have something in common. Students take a few minutes to quietly find one box that doesn't belong before they share. The students are to explain what the three quadrants have in common that theirs does not.

Many examples to be used in classes can be found on: http://wodb.ca/

The engagement is high because there is no wrong answer; students justify in their own words which one doesn't belong and why. In a secondary math classroom, the examples could be four different graphs of parabolas, whereas in an upper elementary classroom, you might show four different mixed numbers with improper fractions. In the following first grade example (see Figure 6.14), one student could state that the top right does not belong because the other three are pictures and that one has numbers (low floor). Another student might explain that the top left does not belong because the other three all show ways to make twelve and the top left shows seven. This strategy, in particular, helps students to understand that correctness lies in their reasoning since there are multiple acceptable answers. This relates to the Standards for Mathematical Practices, which are as important as content standards, though often underexplored or discussed.

Figure 6.14: A Which One Doesn't Belong Example

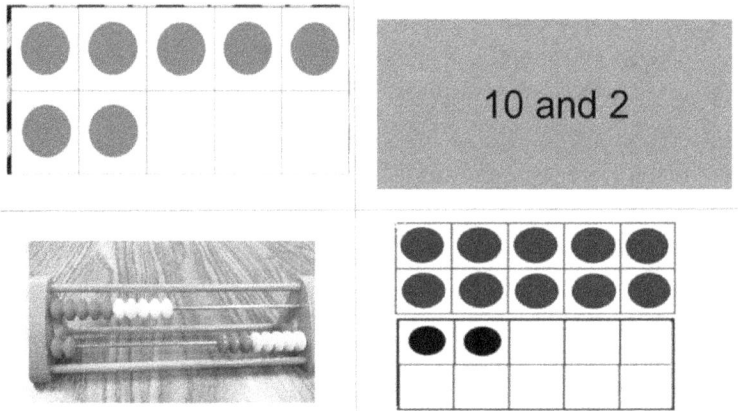

Alternate Use: This strategy could easily be modified for other content areas. For example, show four different balls for physical education, four different paintings for art, four different presidents for history, etc.

Strategy 28: Can You Make It

In this strategy, students are asked to make a target number using eight to ten other numbers. These numbers are not chosen randomly. They are chosen for the various ways students can use them to make the target number. Again, this activity is a low floor, high ceiling activity. The students have many options in this activity and the teacher guides the students to compare their number combinations to other students. This is a great math routine that not only supports students' use of mathematical language, but allows for differentiation and engagement from all students. Students are asked to find as many different ways as they can to find the target number. Again, in a secondary classroom, the target could be a fraction or polynomial and students are told they must use multiplication, fractions, or other more advanced mathematical skills. Figure 6.15 shows an elementary example.

Figure 6.15: A Can You Make It Example

<pre>
                    13

          7   6   3   8   2
          5   10   20   15   1
</pre>

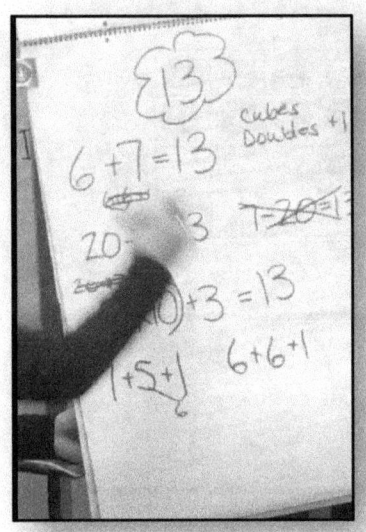

Strategy 29: Strategy Share

Though there are many times in school when there are right and wrong answers, usually, there are several possible pathways to arrive at the answer. For example, if you are writing an introduction to an essay, one student might choose to start with a question and another student may choose to start with a bold statement. If you are working on a math problem, one student may use skip counting to arrive at the answer and another student might use an array. In social studies, one student might use evidence to support their claim that comes from the Constitution and another might use evidence from the Bill of Rights. You get the point, not every student will use the same method to achieve the outcome.

Knowing how students come to their solution is often just as, if not more, important as the answer at which they arrive. This is why it is common to ask students who have math problems to "show their work." How common is it, however, to ask students to verbally explain their thinking to the class so that the students metacognitively think through what they did? Not only does this position the student as the teacher for the other students, but it gives the teacher insight into what the student was doing as the student worked through the task.

In math, we call this strategy a "Number Talk." Number Talks originated as a book of the same title by Sherry Parrish. The students are highly motivated and engaged during this routine. Number Talks focus and support students in number sense, fluency and mathematical vocabulary. Number Talks is a math routine that supports flexible thinking, while allowing students to share and hear different strategies and therefore support many ways to solve a problem. This is the basis for the high student engagement during this routine. Number Talks give students a series of smaller problems that build on each other to teach or reinforce a particular strategy.

> **The book *Number Talks* provides many of the equations that can be used for grades K-5 and the steps and videos to Number Talks can be found in this link: by Alycia Zimmerman:**
> **https://cutt.ly/NumberTalks**

This routine is done mentally. It is meant to support quick strategies to solve an operation. Outlined below are Zimmerman's Steps for a Typical Number Talk.[50]

1. Teacher presents an expression or problem for students to solve mentally.
2. Allow adequate "wait time" for most students to come up with an answer. Students can signal with a thumbs up when they have solved the expression.
3. Initially, invite students to share their answers only, not their solutions.
4. Then ask for student volunteers to share how they solved the problem.
5. For each student who shares their solution strategy, chart their thinking on the board. Make sure to accurately record their thinking; do not shape or correct their response.

6. Have several students who used different strategies share their thinking with the class.
7. Invite students to question each other about their strategies, compare and contrast the strategies, and ask for clarification about strategies that are confusing.
8. Three more problems related to the first equation are then given to be worked through the same way as the first.
9. The facilitator accepts wrong answers in order to lead to powerful conversations and often clear up common misconceptions.

I have seen Molly DiPirro use Number Talks with students to boost student engagement. The students were eager to participate thanks to some easy routines that Molly put in place. Figure 6.16 shows a poster of useful Number Talk hand signals and below are some of the prompts she uses.

- Can you explain your strategy?
- How is your strategy like _____'s? (the previous strategy shared)
- Can you name your strategy? (e.g., Adding in parts, counting back on a number line by 10s and 1s, used the doubling/halving strategy)
- Does anyone have a different strategy to solve the problem?
- Can you share the strategy your turn and talk partner explained to you?
- Is the model I made on the board what you did in your head?

Figure 6.16: Number Talks Hand Signals

A beautiful example of a Strategy Share can be seen in Drew Crandall's third grade math class at Lakeridge Elementary School in Seattle, Washington. I certainly would encourage you to watch the entire video because Drew's teaching is impressive throughout the entirety of the lesson, but the point at which he does the Strategy Share comes at 21 minutes into the lesson. Just prior to this point in the lesson, Drew asked the students to indicate if they had "a strategy to solve this equation." Drew wrote

"24÷4=_" on the chart paper. After giving the students some independent think time, he asked the students what their answers were and wrote them on the chart. Students were then told to talk with their partner to share *how* the students solved the problem. When the students were called back to his attention, Drew asked students to share their strategies for solving the equation while he wrote them on the chart. This is the Strategy Share.

Watch Drew Crandall use Strategy Share with his students here:
https://cutt.ly/StrategyShare

Through seeing their peers' strategies, the students are able to expand their various options of how they can work through a problem. The students who are less confident can feel validated. The students who are incorrect can learn through listening. The teacher can identify patterns of confusions and misconceptions, applications of taught strategies, and inventive student strategies that show insights.

As is true for all strategies, the effectiveness is a direct result of the learning environment established by the classroom teacher. For this reason, teachers need to be deliberate about creating an environment of risk-takers where participation is expected, not optional, and mistakes are perceived as opportunities to learn. As well, students should be told explicitly that agreement and disagreement is with ideas, not people. This means that your best friend might say something that you disagree with because the purpose is not to create agreement, but to solve problems accurately, demonstrate flexibility, and to do so respectfully.

Strategy 30: Modeling

Imagine that you're sitting at a workshop to learn more about the Next Generation Science Standards (NGSS), when the facilitator asks you to take a look at a phenomenon he has brought with him. It is an apparatus called a "Wonder Tube" made of PVC pipe that has four total strings coming out of it, two on each end. Each string has a pom pom attached. He asks the participants to view the device as he pulls on each of the four strings separately and then asks them to show their thinking about

If you're curious, here is the link to the device he used (minute 1:24):
https://cutt.ly/TheWonderTube

what was happening. Since the device in action seems to defy the laws of nature, you would probably see people with looks on their faces like, "Show my thinking? What does that mean? I don't know how that thing works!" Nevertheless, participants would turn to each other and begin to discuss. There would be many ideas shared about what they saw.

Now imagine the facilitator joining the table and reminding the participants to show their thinking by drawing what they were thinking on some paper he provided—think, "a picture is worth a thousand words." Each person would attempt to draw images from their own mind on paper. The number of ideas about the functioning of the device, the construction of the device, and even the materials from which the device was made would be numerous and reveal the thinking of each of the different participants.

The purpose of the example above is to highlight the process of making a model of thinking. I learned about this new form of modeling when working with Susan Cyrulik, a staff developer and former middle school teacher. Traditional modeling is what you probably experienced when you were in school. Susan, for example, told me about making a model of an editable cell when she was in middle school. In the traditional form, models were items that were three dimensional, placed on the table for manipulation, or held in the teacher's hand for demonstration. In anatomy, that was the upper torso of the human with the organs exposed. In chemistry, it was using pipe cleaners and beads to construct an atom. In all of these cases, there was only one correct answer for constructing and using the model.

Modern modeling is different. Now, modeling is a science and engineering practice to teach students to "use and construct models as helpful tools for representing ideas and explanations. These tools include diagrams, drawings, physical replicas, mathematical representations, analogies, and computer simulations."[51] In this way, a model is a tool for gauging the understanding of what a student is thinking in relationship to the phenomenon (stimulus) provided and can be used to develop questions, make predictions and explanations, analyze and identify flaws in systems, and communicate ideas. Models then, are revised over time when influenced by measurements, observations, and other learning happening in the classroom.

Developing and using models is incorporated into all of the science standards from kindergarten to twelfth grade, with scaffolded integration and measurement throughout the grade bands. The Next Generation Science Standards and the K-12 Science Frameworks have worked diligently to produce literature and descriptions around scientific modeling, inclusive of a rubric found in Appendix F on the NextGenScience.org website.[52]

Here is the link to Appendix F from the NextGenScience.org website:
https://cutt.ly/NextGenRubric

Integrating modeling into the science classroom offers an opportunity to increase modalities of learning. Again examples of models include diagrams, drawings, physical replicas, mathematical representations, analogies, and computer simulations. Additionally, Susan would also add dramatization and storyboarding to the list. The tools for modeling mentioned here tap into kinesthetic, tactile, and visual modes for learning that could have been overlooked in the more traditional approach of having a discussion.

Students who resonate with these tools of expression, then, are more likely to increase their participation in the science classroom. Modeling should honor the thinking and support the growth of thinking over time. When a student's thinking becomes visual in nature, the teacher is able to evaluate where the student is in the process of learning the content. Modeling, therefore, is a practice that will grow over time as students learn the process and the purpose for modeling.

How will you know if you are having the students model or having them complete an art project? It isn't a model if it doesn't have the following.

1. **Models need to be revisited and revised.** Students should be asked to model their thinking when introduced to a phenomenon and multiple times throughout their learning. Initial modeling can be done individually. Over time, the class should

work toward having a singular model to represent the science content accurately and they work to figure out the phenomenon. Revision of the model into its final form with accurate science is the outcome that is desired.

2. **The model construction and use should build over time**. The content of the model will not be accurate at the onset since the phenomenon may be unfamiliar to the student. Ultimately, with collaboration and science investigation, the model will grow in its accuracy. As the accuracy grows, the model can be used as evidence in scientific discussions.

3. **Models show a process or have functionality**. Models on paper can show processes by using arrows and labels. If the model is three dimensional in nature, then movement can provide functionality to show a process in place.

Susan Cyrulik fell in love with modeling and wanted to use it with every teacher and student that she came in touch with. It was in a session that she ran that I saw her demonstrate what modeling in science looks like. When I asked her about it she said:

I asked colleagues to show me their thinking (draw it out) while having a conversation. I took the process of modeling into many classrooms, from grades K-12 to see if the process worked to show thinking. I experienced great success and realized some patterns that led to me to develop some tips and tricks to get started and create rules for what is and is not a model.

Here are some tips Susan shared with me.

- **In starting to have students create models of their thinking, start slowly**. Younger students need assistance with the basics of drawing. All drawing starts with shapes, then shapes become more elaborate to form images. Accurately drawing what you see is another skill. Young students love to use color in their drawings. Color is appropriate in science, but students may need reminders that they are using a scientific eye to observe and that grass is green not rainbow colored. The art teacher in your building is an excellent resource for teaching the students to draw with all of the skills noted above. If you don't have an art teacher to work with, there are some incredible instructional YouTube videos out there for learning to draw.

- **If modeling is new for your students, you may want to take the first pass at modeling as a group.** Have students sketch their own ideas individually so that they can contribute to the class model much earlier in the process. The use of arrows and labeling can then be modeled as a whole class so students come to understand their importance in showing a process. You can then have students participate in a carousel protocol or collaborative learning structure so they can share, compare, and alter their models. Students can then create a consensus table model and then eventually land on a whole class model that is grounded in scientific fact.

- **Assist students in understanding that arrows have different meanings in different situations.** Specifically in science, arrows are used to show direction, transformation, and even phase changes. That is a lot of meanings for one symbol. Teaching students to label their arrows with their thinking is important to the modeling process.

Strategy 31: Spaced Repetition

If you've ever read *Classroom Instruction that Works: Research-Based Strategies for Increasing Student Achievement* by Robert J. Marzano, Debra Pickering, and Jane E. Pollock, you will recall that this book uses meta-analysis, or a process that "combines the results from a number of studies to determine the average effect of a given technique."[53] In layman's terms, that simply means the authors looked at a large amount of other people's research and determined from the average results what works and doesn't work. In fact, the authors identified nine strategies that demonstrated the highest "probability of enhancing student achievement for all students in all subject areas at all grade levels."[54] Throughout the book, the word "pattern" is used over eighty times. Why? Because our brains are wired to look for patterns—be it similarities or differences (the first strategy) or when summarizing and notetaking (the second strategy), or when creating non-linguistic representations (the sixth strategy).

For a moment, go back to your days as a student in school studying math. My guess is that your lesson for the day had to do with a very specific and discrete concept—for the purpose of this example, we'll say it's adding two-digit numbers. The teacher showed you how to do this and during the class, you probably had some practice problems where you added two-digit numbers. To ensure that you learned addition of two-digit numbers, your homework had more problems that included what? You guessed it! Addition of two-digit numbers. Sound familiar? By the way, this example is true for almost every student in every class in every grade. When kids study history, we teach them about this specific time period and ask them questions (be it homework or tests) about that specific time period. In world language classes, we have them conjugate the same verbs they studied in the same unit. In class after class, day after day, we informally and formally assess students exclusively on what they're learning in that moment. Certainly, there is nothing wrong with this approach that emphasizes patterns; however, if we want long-term learning, there is a better way.

Patterns are important to learning. However, patterns can sometimes hinder, not help learning. Several years ago, I read a book whose title escapes me now (which is ironic given the purpose of this strategy is about long-term learning). This book was about the science of learning and memory. While there were many fascinating accounts from the book, the one that stood out the most spoke about an experiment where test subjects were asked to identify different artists' art after studying the artists' different styles. Pamela Hogle explains the experiment on LearningSolutionsMag.com:

> Participants looked at multiple examples of the work of each of several artists. In the massed learning condition, many works by the same artist were presented in succession; each viewing session presented a different artist. In the spaced learning condition, participants viewed a mix of works of different artists within each viewing session. All participants were later asked to view images of **different** works from the same artists and to figure out which artist had created them.
>
> Participants in the spaced learning condition reported less mind wandering than those in the massed condition. Their recall of the information was better than that of learners in the massed learning condition, and spaced learning led to a better ability to apply the information to a new problem—correctly identifying the artist who created works that they had not seen previously.[55] (emphasis in original)

The reason the participants in the spaced learning condition out-performed those in the mass learning condition had to do with patterns. Our brains are wired to look for patterns. Once the pattern is identified, our brains relax (wander) and our cognitive load is eased.

Undoubtedly there are times when easing cognitive load makes sense. I would much rather be in a car with a driver who has a decreased cognitive load since that driver is one who is more experienced and does not have to be overly aware of their actions since driving has become appropriately automatic.

When it comes to true learning (as opposed to temporary memorization), we have to keep our brain on its toes. According to The Center for Transformative Teaching and Learning, this is the difference between short- and long-term memory.

Unfortunately, teachers (who are often under constant pressure to push more learning on their students in shorter periods of time) often fail to help students shepherd new knowledge into their long-term memory. That means that students can often hold onto it just long enough to grasp it in the immediate term, but fail to store it successfully for later recall. In short, their active working memory doesn't have the capacity to write or revise the knowledge schema in their long-term memory."[56] (emphasis in original)

We've all been there, of course, as both teachers and students. Further, as I sit here writing this as an adult, I marvel at how many tests I took in school where I received the highest marks only to not know that information anymore. This is why adults with college degrees may still struggle to help their children with elementary school homework—everyone knows that much of what is taught in schools is not really learned.

In her post, "Why Straight-A Students Haven't Learned As Much As You Think," Managing Editor of InformEd, Saga Briggs, writes:

A cognitive phenomenon called "fading" is particularly responsible for failed memory retention. According to the fading theory, the trace or mark a memory etches into your brain is like a path you make in the woods when you continually walk along the same route. If you don't take that same path, it eventually becomes overgrown until it disappears. In the same way, facts that you learn are forgotten when you don't review them.[57]

Just like we can train our muscles to run and lift and jump but they will atrophy if not used, our learning can be trained by continuous repetitions or not. When students learn information briefly and in ways that are contained to certain units or lessons (i.e., mass learning conditions), they will know that information only well enough to be successful for those units or lessons unless the students continue to be exposed to that knowledge.

One easy and underutilized antidote for fading is spaced practice. Going back to the earlier example of the math class where the lesson, in-class practice, and homework exclusively focused on two-digit addition, we should not be surprised that the students doing those tasks became familiar with the expectation, and the cognitive load decreased. How much? Well, since the task became routine, the students likely stopped *thinking* about the task and shifted to automation.

Let's imagine, however, that there were some problems that focused on the day's learning and there were problems that focused on past learning as well. Would that not only increase the students' attention to the task, but also through the continued intervals of practice, increase the students' maintenance of the learning that was intended? In other words, the easiest strategy to decrease fading and increase the odds that the learning will shift towards long-term memory is to continue to include questions on the

Visit Thomas Frank's post to watch a video on spaced practice and find links to software designed to support spaced pratice:
https://cutt.ly/Spaced-Practice

current homework and assessment that address previously studied information (in addition to what is currently being taught). This revisiting will create greater levels of need to truly learn and master the information that students may have previously only learned for the single assignment or assessment.

I am a big fan of Thomas Frank's strategy for spaced practice as well. In short, you have flashcards that have information on it that you are learning. However, these are not just regular "flashcards" with a term on one side and a definition on the other. There is an interactive nature to them that makes them effective. This is not about drill; it's about practice. This practice makes a difference in how that information is processed, stored, and retrieved when flashcards are constructed in this way. These cards will ultimately end up in five different stacks or boxes:

1. Box 1—Review Daily
2. Box 2—Review every other day
3. Box 3—Review once per week
4. Box 4—Review once every other week
5. Box 5—Retired (study before the test)

All cards begin in the first box. As you get them correct, they move into Box 2. If you get them correct in Box 2, they move to Box 3, and so forth. If you get them wrong, they move back to Box 1 even if they were all the way into Box 5 (see Figure 6.17).

Figure 6.17: Thomas Frank's "Analog Spaced Repetition System"[58]

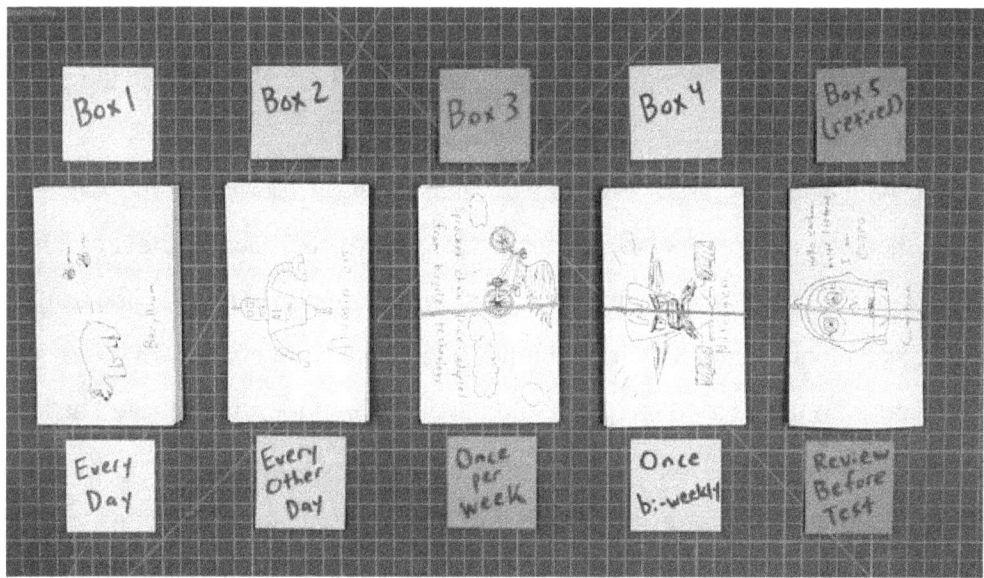

Strategy 32: 4DX

When I started my position as the Assistant Superintendent of Curriculum, Instruction, and Technology, I wanted to get the lay of the land in my new district. In order to do that, I set up one-on-one interviews with all of the administrators and created a survey to administer to all of the teachers, staff, and board members. The survey questions and interview questions were identical—it just wasn't feasible for me to meet one-on-one with more than just the administrators. The first question I asked was, "In your own words, what is the district's most important goal? Please do not say something like 'educating all students' or 'keeping students safe.' These are assumed. The goal would be the thing that we're trying to accomplish in order to educate all students or keep them safe." Here's my question to you as you're reading this: *how consistent do you think the response was to this question?*

Before I share the answer, I want you to consider the implications of what could happen when the goal is unclear. After all, how would anyone (teacher, student, coach, athlete, etc.) or any organization achieve their most important goal if there is no agreement on what they're working towards? Before I share the answer, I want you to consider whether or not you think that you could identify what the most important goal is in your organization with consistency.

Now I want you to think about the fact that if you're a teacher, do your students have goals for the year or the unit? What do you want them to walk away knowing and being able to do? I'm not talking about the lesson objectives, but what is the single most important learning outcome that they should be aiming for?

Not knowing what the goal is would be like having a football game where in addition to the football players on the field, there are also baseball players, chess aficionados, a quilting bee, and people who were lying around trying to work on their tans. All are very appropriate in their own time and place, but together it's a mess. The football players who understood the game and the purpose of their roles would be very frustrated by the people who didn't know what they were doing and who got in their way. Perhaps the football players could organize everyone in such a way as to clear the field and/or teach the others how to play, but more than likely, the football players would just give up in frustration.

Goals give clarity to the work and are really at the heart of the cliché, "We need to work smarter, not harder." It's the idea that energy is finite and should be focused on getting the right job done in the right way. I think everyone would agree that it's hard to achieve a goal if you don't know what it is.

Spoiler alert. The interviews and surveys showed that people were working really hard, just not on the same things. The most common response from the survey to the question about what was the most important goal was a response about preparing students for the real world/future/life skills/jobs and, as you can see, this was me just lumping this theme together. Even then, this response was given fewer than twenty percent of the time and that was only from the faculty, staff, and board survey; no administrator said anything about this in their responses. In part, the reason for the inconsistency had to do with the fact that as a district every administrator and team or department created their own list of goals. Though we are a relatively small district, this meant there were hundreds of goals that people were working on. No wonder no one knew what the most important goal was.

I learned the value of goal clarity when, in a previous job, I was introduced to the Four Disciplines of Execution (4DX). In the book by the same name, authors Chris McChesney, Sean Covey, and Jim Huling, break down four steps (disciplines) to use to achieve what is most important. Though I am going to share what these four simple steps are, do not mistake their simplicity for being easy to enact. Simple to understand and simple to do are not the same—if they were, we would all be at our perfect weight with perfect credit scores; though we all understand how to do these things, it takes discipline to put them into practice. For this reason, the first step before trying this may be to read the book *The Four Disciplines of Execution* or at the very least, check out some of the links I'll share at the end of the strategy.

I also want to point out that this strategy is equally useful no matter if you're looking to create a personal goal as an adult, or you're working with students to create academic, social, or behavioral goals. The Four Disciplines are ones that make creating—and more importantly—achieving goals possible. Figure 6.18 provides a visual for how 4DX works. Again, the disciplines are relatively straightforward, but executing them takes focus and determination. Yet, as they say, with great risk, comes great rewards.

Figure 6:18: The 4 Disciplines of Execution[59]

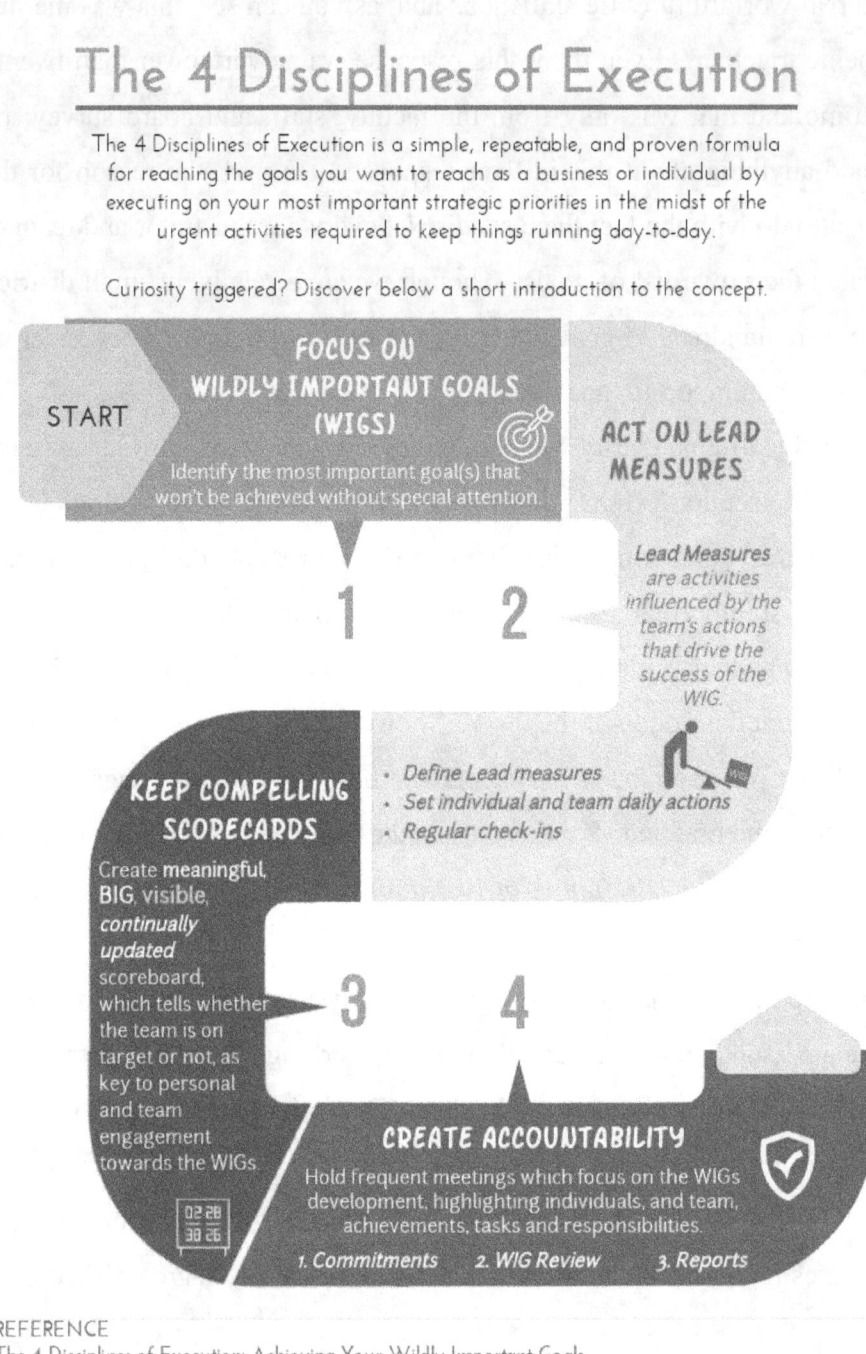

- **Discipline 1: Focus on the Wildly Important**

    This is the point at which you identify the most important goal, in the book referred to as the Wildly Important Goal (W.I.G.). The "whirlwind" of our work comprises of about eighty percent of what we do, yet that swirl is most likely not the work that matters the most, even though we spend the most time with it. That's okay. Accomplishing goals is not necessarily a function of reducing the whirlwind (you probably can't) nor spending more time on the W.I.G. Accomplishing goals is about getting clarity on what is wildly important and creating a system to pay attention to it. W.I.G.s, by the way, are those things that matter so much that even if we were able to accomplish every other goal, if we didn't accomplish this one goal, we would be unsuccessful. W.I.G.s are also specific and have a "start line, finish line, and a deadline." In other words, they can be measured. It's the difference between saying, "I want to lose weight" (not a W.I.G.) and saying, "By March 31st of this year, I will lose twenty pounds."

- **Discipline 2: Act on the Lead Measures**

    If we continue with the idea of weight loss as the W.I.G., you won't know you achieved the goal until March 31st. 4DX refers to that ultimate goal as the "lag measure." If we only focus on the lag measure, we won't be doing much. As the saying goes, "weighing a pig won't make it fatter." The inverse is also true. If you're trying to lose weight—stepping on the scale won't make you slimmer. Losing weight requires specific actions. Lead measures are the *actions* that you do no less than once a week in pursuit of achieving the goal. Lead measures should be seen as powerful levers that take this big rock and move it in the direction of the finish line. With weight loss, certainly taking the action of making and reviewing a vision board once a week could be lead measures (actions), but they do not have high leverage. Better lead measures would be exercising for at least thirty minutes at least five days each week and eating no more than 1,200 calories each day. Those lead measures

    o Can be done daily (therefore meeting the criterion of occurring at least once per week)

- Are high leverage because you can predict by doing these actions that the goal will be achieved
- Are within your control
- Can be monitored

- **Discipline 3: Keep a Compelling Scoreboard**

    Even if you have never played a sport in your life, you could watch just about any game/match and tell within seconds by looking at the scoreboard who is winning and how much time has passed and/or remains. The ability to monitor at a glance your progress on the lead measures is at the heart of Discipline 3. The scoreboard should be public because it shows you whether or not you're winning or losing. This could be a simple chart where you have to write down how many minutes per day you exercise and how many calories you ate. You could write the numbers in green if they met or exceeded the targets or in red if you did not. It's quick but effective communication to you (and others) about your progress.

- **Discipline 4: Create a Cadence of Accountability**

    On a weekly basis, 4DX says you should check in with others to report out on your progress with your lead measures and how that is moving the bar on your lag measure.[iii] At these W.I.G. Sessions, you discuss what might get in the way of your success with the lead measures for the coming week. For example, maybe it's your mom's birthday and you'll be going out to her favorite restaurant but you are dieting. You'll need to plan ahead how you're going to make healthy choices for the meal or indulge that night but add more exercise to counter balance so you can stay on track. This is a space of mutual vulnerability to lead to shared

---

[iii] There are many lag measures that can be monitored on a weekly basis (like losing weight), but many of the lag measures in schools have to do with student performance on yearly or infrequent assessments. If this is the case for you, you may not know until the end of the year or later if the W.I.G. was achieved. However, the best lead measures (actions) are those that are high leverage and therefore if you monitor success with the actions, the desired outcomes are apt to follow.

accountability. When someone makes their lead measures for the week, you celebrate and when they don't, you ask them about it in a supportive way to help them. For many, this can be the most difficult of the disciplines because of the public nature of the session. However, it is built on the idea that having these accountability partnerships helps to keep us honest and untrack to achieving the very thing that we have identified as being so important that if it wasn't achieved nothing else would matter.

Check out these links for more information about 4DX.

Videos
- https://cutt.ly/More4DX
- https://cutt.ly/4DX-Cartoon
- https://www.franklincovey.com/Solutions/Execution/

Articles
- https://cutt.ly/Forbes-4DX
- https://cutt.ly/4DX-Summary
- https://cutt.ly/4DX

Strategy 33: Read for Speed

In my kids' elementary school, every month in kindergarten they came home with a sight word list of about twelve to fifteen words that they were supposed to learn for that month. Though all three of my kids went to PreK before kindergarten, all of them struggled with learning to read—especially my youngest, Oliver. In fact, with factoring summer slide, by the time he started first grade, his reading level was that of a beginning of the year kindergartener. Needless to say, he didn't enjoy reading and he was frustrated. By first grade, there were no more sight words in isolation; he was expected to read the books in his take-home bag that were at his level. Both his teacher and I were committed to helping him, but getting him to read even the books that were at his level was not easy.

Watch Jim Wright talk you through how to create a Reading Racetrack here:
https://cutt.ly/Reading-Racetrack-Video

Around this time, I was doing some work in my district with Dr. Jim Wright, consultant, author of many books on Response to Intervention, and the man behind the comprehensive website www.InterventionCentral.org. At one of his presentations, he shared with us a strategy to help readers struggling with fluency, "Reading Racetrack." In this strategy, the adult identifies a set number of sight words for the student to learn. The adult plugs these words into the Reading Racetrack and the child reads the words as quickly and correctly as possible during the course of one minute. After the minute is completed, the adult indicates the number of words correct and incorrect and has the student practice the incorrect words. The racetrack is used until the student achieves ninety correct words in one minute or the racetrack has been used five times.

Read the step-by-step directions for Reading Racetracks and get access to the free templates here: https://cutt.ly/Reading-Racetrack

I really liked the idea of this strategy and was excited to try it with Oliver. The words I used were ones that I thought he was having trouble with. While I appreciated the practice that the strategy provided and that the words were limited to a certain number and then repeated throughout the racetrack, I wanted Oliver to learn that reading is done from left to right and not in a circle. Accordingly, I created my own strategy that I called "Read for Speed" (see Figure 6.19).

Figure 6.19: Read for Speed Steps

Materials:
- Selected sight words
- Read for Speed template filled out
- Timer

Preparation:
1. Adult identifies 6-8 words that the student is struggling with that are important for the student to learn.
2. Adult randomly fills in the Read for Speed template with the 6-8 words repeated.

Directions:
1. The adult provides the directions to the student. The adult tells the student that the goal is for the student to read as many words correctly within one minute as

> possible. When the student gets to the end of the page, the student should go back to the top of the page and keep going until the timer rings.
>
> 2. The adult points to each unique word and tells the student the word and has the student repeat the word for him/herself. The adult can also highlight some of the differences/similarities between the words.
>
> 3. The adult says to the student, "Ready! Set! Go!" and starts the timer (alternately, the student can press the button). As the student reads words aloud, the adult records and corrects any errors. The adult also notes the number of correct words. If the student hesitates for longer than 3 seconds on any word, the adult states the correct word, directs the student to the next word, and records the hesitation as an error. At the end of one minute, the student stops.
>
> 4. The adult prompts the student to tally the total number of words read correctly and shares with the student the number of errors observed. The adult or the student record both the number of correctly read words and errors on the back of the Read for Speed document. This should be done as a fraction so the student can see the denominator grow with subsequent attempts.
>
> 5. Repeat with the same list for a week.
>
> 6. Make a new list the following week using 2-3 of the words that need more practice and then 4-6 new words that the student is struggling with.

Figure 6.20 shows the physical layout differences between these strategies.

Figure 6.20: Visual Differences Between Reading Racetrack and Read for Speed

Reading Racetrack **Read for Speed**

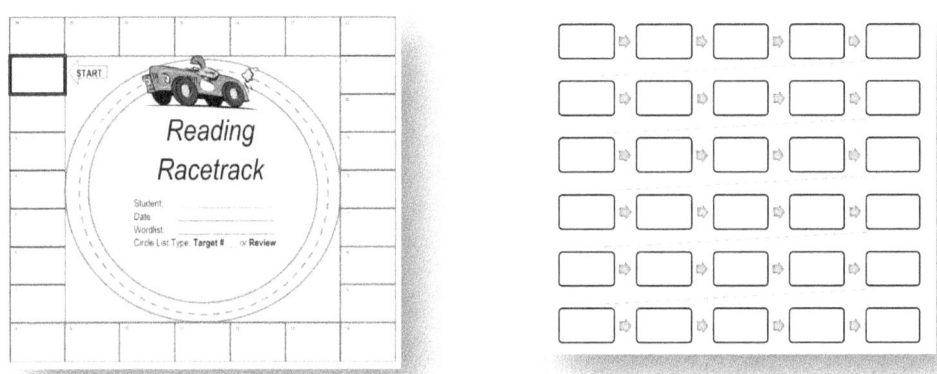

As well as the visual differences, rather than focusing on drawing the student's attention to the missed words at the end, I drew Oliver's attention to the words before

Access free editable Read for Speed templates here:
https://cutt.ly/Read-For-Speed

we started so that he had a chance to prime himself and notice the words before he started. "This word is 'the.' What is this word? Right! And do you see how 'the' looks like this word? This word has one more letter at the end of it though. This word is 'them.' What's this word? Right! 'Them!' and what's that word? Right! 'The!'" Both Reading Racetrack and Read for Speed last one minute and in both the students are trying to read as many words correctly in that time. Both end with a tally of correct words and incorrect words and both prompt the correct word when the child pauses for more than three seconds or gets the word wrong.

With Oliver, when he read books to me from his book bag, I would write down words he struggled with or ask him to tell me some words he wanted to work on. I also noticed that there were some letters he would mix-up, like lowercase Bs and Ds. I would then add those to his Read for Speed list. Every week he had about six to eight words that repeated on the list within the thirty spaces. I usually maintained two to four words from the previous week to really ensure automaticity and I would sometimes include one or two words from several weeks before just to check for retention. All of this was relatively easy because the Read for Speed document was created in Microsoft Word and I used the Find and Replace feature to type in the new word one and replace all the words that were being changed for that week.

This strategy is one that allows for personal goal setting. These "private victories" can actually be much more rewarding for students who are demotivated by more public displays of progress (like bulletin boards). Since Read for Speed and Reading Racetrack can be kept in a folder or a notebook that only the teacher and/or parent/guardian and the student see, the student is being held accountable while the progress is being monitored without any publicity to how many words the student knows or doesn't (yet). This same approach to privacy regarding progress can also be used for documenting progress on the acquisition of math facts, books, reading, etc.

Not only was I shocked by how quick and easy this strategy was (it was fewer than five minutes total each day between the priming beforehand, the one-minute reading, and then the tallying at the end), but I was also shocked with how motivated Oliver was to do it. He liked being able to press the timer button on my phone and to see his growth over the week. Most importantly, it worked! As his sight word fluency improved, his reading fluency did as well. He went from being a below-level reader at Christmas to being an above-level reader by the year's end. That cannot all be attributed to this strategy, of course, but the strategy certainly helped!

Chapter Summary

This chapter was about moving someone from the point of compliance to interest by changing the task. It seems self-evident that changing a task from something someone does not want to do to something they do want to do would garner increased engagement. However, the point of this chapter was to highlight possibilities to change tasks without losing the learning. When looking for ideas in how to change a task, remember that the destination (standards) should remain a constant and that the vehicle (the curriculum), the route taken to arrive at the destination (the instruction), and the GPS (the assessments) are variables that are able to be altered. When considering what variable you want to alter, I encourage you to think about how the people who are responsible for doing the task can have choice and voice in what they are doing. This will not only make the work more engaging for the person performing the task, it will make creating the task easier for the person assigning the task. Indeed, choice and voice are hallmarks of tasks that shift those doing it from compliant to at least being interested (if not absorbed).

Looking for even more strategies to
CHANGE THE TASK?
Please visit my website, www.LyonsLetters.com/learnmore, for print and digital recommendations including books, websites, videos, and more!

Thank you again Liz Buck and Nina Calarco for contributing Notice and Wonder, Molly DiPerro for contributing Esti-Myesteries, Which One Doesn't Belong, Can You Make It, and Strategy Share, and Susan Cyrulik for contributing Modeling—six strategies included this chapter.

Reflection Prompts

1. Think of a standard that you will be teaching in an upcoming unit. Brainstorm possible tasks that would demonstrate that students have learned that standard.

   _____
   _____
   _____

2. From the list above, star the three you think the students would be most engaged with. Give students the option to do any one of them.

   _____
   _____
   _____

3. Think of a standard that you will be teaching in an upcoming unit and the associated task. How can you ask students to explore opportunities to change the task but achieve the learning?

   _____
   _____
   _____

4. Name one thing you could do tomorrow based on what you learned from this chapter.

   _____
   _____
   _____

5. Tweet me @LyonsLetters to share an idea for a future reading or digital resource I should share on www.lyonsletters.com that would help someone who is compliant become interested.

Persistent Questions

1. What have you done so far regarding the three challenge questions from Chapter 1?

    a. **Three:** Find at least three people with whom to share your learning.

    b. **Two:** Find at least two ideas that change you.

    c. **One:** Apply at least one idea from your reading.

    _____
    _____
    _____

2. What have you learned so far, and how will you use it?

    _____
    _____
    _____

Chapter 7

Scheduling Strategies

"The key is not to prioritize what's on your schedule, but to schedule your priorities."
~Stephen Covey

Recognizing Your Thinking Before You Read...

1. What would you change about the schedule that you use now to improve learning outcomes for students?

   _____
   _____
   _____

2. What are challenges that would prevent those changes? What are selling points that would encourage those changes?

   _____
   _____
   _____

3. What stakeholders would need to be included to consider scheduling changes?

   _____
   _____
   _____

We're Going There

I have had the privilege to work in or for numerous schools—as a teacher, a staff developer, and as an administrator. Without exception, the schedule has been a limiting factor that impacts teaching and learning. The hope is that the schedule is designed to ensure the highest learning outcomes for students. In reality, the schedule is often created around factors that have nothing to do with learning. Anyone who has been in education for anytime already knows this. For example, the high school schedule is commonly designed to ensure that students are able to do one or more of the following:

1. Get home before younger siblings who need childcare.
2. Play sports.
3. Go to an after-school job.

We know now that the brains of adolescents are wired to sleep in and stay up later than the brains of their elementary peers. When high school students start later than the elementary students, both groups benefit. This is true and yet highly uncommon. Why? The schedule works for the teachers who are wired to get up earlier, it works for the status quo which would require oodles of changes (like parents needing to get afterschool care for elementary age children who would get home sooner than their secondary peers), it works for coordinating extracurricular activities, etc. It can be very, very difficult to change a practice that has appeared to work and does work if you're looking at metrics other than learning.

The start and end time of schools are not the only scheduling change that could benefit students. Many schools do not have systemic structures to allow students opportunities to benefit from additional support during the school day—again this is particularly true at the secondary level. Certainly students are encouraged to stay after to get help, but when staying after to get support is optional, that means that students can opt-out. This very issue is raised in Chapter 7, "Responding When Some Students Don't Learn" in the book *Learning by Doing*. Chapter 7 starts with a fictional scenario of a principal recognizing that his eighth grade teachers are approaching their instruction, grading, and assessments differently all of which have a negative impact on student outcomes. Ultimately the teachers and principal come to understand that "some students will not voluntarily take advantage of additional support. Because our mission is to *ensure* that all students succeed, students will not be given the option of failing. Interventions will be directive. Students will be required, not invited, to attend."[60] Finding time in the day for all students to get support beyond what would be expected in the classroom—both for students who are struggling and for students who are demonstrating the ability to extend their learning—can be quite difficult because generally speaking, adding time to the day is not possible.

Now What

At first, you might think that changing the schedule for academic reasons would achieve compliance, not interest. I disagree. If you recall Highlight 1 from Chapter 1, you will remember that the first question to ask regarding perceived non-compliance is whether or not the task they're supposed to be doing is within their Zone of Proximal Development. If the task is too easy or too hard, what appears to be non-compliance is really not lack of willingness to do the work, but a lack of skill to do it. This is why building in academic support for students who need it for both remediation and enrichment leads to interest—the problem was with the *task*.

This chapter is all about how to think about time differently. None of these strategies depend on adding more time to the day; they are instead focused on how to use the time you have differently. This is easier said than done, I know. With competing priorities and constituencies, changes in how time is used can be some of the most controversial changes a school can make. Yet, "schools must come to regard time as a tool rather than a limitation."[61] As you proceed with changes, remember that you might want to start small and/or give yourself ample time to plan—because planning for these changes takes a lot of lead time. Also consider what you *can* do, rather than what you can't. For example, even though it would be great to do these strategies school-wide, some of these strategies do not require mass implementation (meaning one teacher can decide to try it on their own). Here are six strategies to consider:

34. Intervention Block
35. Change Start/End Times
36. Flipped Classroom

37. Workshop
38. Student Led Conferences
39. Brain Breaks

Strategy 34: Intervention Block

One of the most frequent laments I hear from teachers at the elementary level is that the students who need interventions are being pulled from core instruction. At the middle school level, teachers protest because the students who need intervention are not getting it because the intervention time is paired with the music elective (band/orchestra/chorus) time—students who are musical either get interventions instead of being able to be in band/orchestra/chorus or they do not receive academic interventions because music trumps interventions. In short, there seems to be this competition for time.

So that we have a common understanding of Response to Intervention (RTI) (also referred to as Multi-Tiered Systems of Supports [MTSS]), this is a theoretical model which states that, 80 percent of general education students should only need the support of their classroom teacher to be successful. Instruction from the classroom teacher is called Tier 1 instruction. Within this model, about 20 percent of students will need assistance beyond what the classroom teacher can provide during the Tier 1 instruction. In addition to their Tier 1 instruction, these students would qualify for Tier 2 or 3 interventions which are generally provided by a specially trained teacher, like a Reading Specialist.

Regardless of what you call it—RTI, MTSS, or simply "My kids need help!"—when will this intervention happen? If there is not a block of time devoted to Tier 2, then the students are pulled from core instruction or they have to choose between interventions and interests. Thus, creating a schedule that includes an intervention block is crucial to supporting both the core learning and the supplemental instruction to ensure that students' needs are being met.

I used to describe building schedules as educational Sudoku—we have to use a pencil! Why? There is always so much that needs to fit in and there are always competing demands. If we want to be sure that we are meeting the needs of our students, then including an intervention block is critical to that aim. To do so, there must be a block of time of no less than 30 minutes that rotates throughout the day. During this time, students at the same grade level have access to the specially trained intervention teachers (see Figure 7.1).

Figure 7.1: Sample RTI Block Schedule[62]

Response to Intervention
Scheduling Elementary Tier 2 Interventions

Option 3: *'Floating RTI':Gradewide Shared Schedule*. Each grade has a scheduled RTI time across classrooms. No two grades share the same RTI time. Advantages are that outside providers can move from grade to grade providing push-in or pull-out services and that students can be grouped by need across different teachers within the grade.

Anyplace Elementary School: RTI Daily Schedule

Grade	Classroom 1	Classroom 2	Classroom 3	Time
Grade K	Classroom 1	Classroom 2	Classroom 3	9:00-9:30
Grade 1	Classroom 1	Classroom 2	Classroom 3	9:45-10:15
Grade 2	Classroom 1	Classroom 2	Classroom 3	10:30-11:00
Grade 3	Classroom 1	Classroom 2	Classroom 3	12:30-1:00
Grade 4	Classroom 1	Classroom 2	Classroom 3	1:15-1:45
Grade 5	Classroom 1	Classroom 2	Classroom 3	2:00-2:30

Source: Burns, M. K., & Gibbons, K. A. (2008). Implementing response-to-intervention in elementary and secondary schools: Procedures to assure scientific-based practices. New York: Routledge.

www.interventioncentral.org

Jim Wright, author of several books on RTI and the www.InterventionCentral.org website, supports this model stating:

> One advantage of the floating-RTI scheduling option is that classroom teachers can take on the role of providing Tier 2 (supplemental, group-based) intervention services. Students would be grouped by need across different classrooms within the same grade. Some classroom teachers could work with small groups of students during the RTI period while those children in their class not requiring RTI services go to other classrooms for appropriate review or enrichment activities.

Another advantage of the floating-RTI scheduling model is that supplemental intervention providers such as reading teachers can move from grade to grade, providing push-in or pull-out Tier 2 intervention services during each grade-level's RTI period—allowing these professionals to work more efficiently and with fewer potential scheduling conflicts.[63]

While this model would require finding the time in the schedule to devote to the intervention block, doing so not only helps those students who need more support because they are behind, but it also provides support to those students who are ready for more by giving them time to explore learning that may not be possible during the Tier 1 instruction. In this way, students who would otherwise be compliant in the learning environment have a chance to go deeper with what they need now.

> **A Word Of Caution**... Honestly, creating the time in the schedule is not the hardest part of this strategy. That does not mean that it will be easy to build a schedule where you have an intervention block. After all, most school do not lengthen a day to create the time—they have to take time away from other things to do it. However, creating an intervention block is a waste of time if teachers do not commit to practices like viewing the students as "our" students since the block of time is meant to be shared so teachers can regroup students according to need rather than by homeroom. If classroom teachers do not create opportunities for students to have access to enrichment/extension as well as re-teaching and teaching differently, then an intervention block becomes something much closer to worksheets of drill and kill or a guided study hall. Therefore, if this is a strategy that you are considering, please focus on *how the time will be used* in addition to *when could this happen*.

> *Alternative Use:* In some cases, recreating the schedule to add time for interventions is not possible and/or students need more than one intervention, so they are already being pulled during the intervention block but still need to be pulled for another intervention. In cases like this, I recommend using a staggered pull-out model that is most commonly used for students who participate in pull-out instrumental lessons.

> Just like a music teacher may see all the students who play flutes at the same time and all the students who play trumpets at another, these schedules tend to move the time when the students are pulled so that they do not miss the same course each time. With that, for week 1, the flute players are pulled during first period, week 2, they are pulled during second period, and so forth. The same staggered pull-out model can be used with students who need interventions. For example, students in the fifth grade who qualify for Tier 2 interventions may be pulled from 9:00-9:30 during week 1, 9:45-10:15 week 2, and so forth. This would minimize the amount of Tier 1 instructional loss for any one content area while still allowing the students to receive their inventions.

Strategy 35: Change the Start/End Times

In his 2018 book, *When: The Scientific Secrets of Perfect Timing*, Daniel Pink explains the impact of timing on learning. Among other points Pink makes, he shares that there are common patterns of sleep/wake rhythms. Specifically, he says that from birth through about age 14, people are wired to wake and go to bed earlier. This pattern will become the routine again around 25 and actually most of us are and will remain "larks" for the rest of our lives. However, from 14-24 people turn into night owls due to physiological changes.

> This is one reason why for teenagers and college students, school typically starts way too early. In fact, the American Academy of Pediatrics in 2014 issued a policy statement that said, please do not start school for teenagers before 8:30 in the morning. Unfortunately today, the average school start time to teenagers is 8:03 AM, so most schools are operating directly in contravention of the recommendation of the nation's pediatricians.[64]

I know what you're thinking. *We can't change the start time to be later! What about the students who have jobs? Watch their younger siblings? Play sports? What about the buses? The union contract won't allow it.* There are a million reasons why this is challenging. Challenging, however, doesn't mean impossible. What's more, perhaps the choice is not to change the time completely or we don't change it at all.

Maybe the better question is, what are small things we can do if we can't change everything? Here are some ideas to consider.

1. If you already have a tiered bussing system, is it possible to have the elementary start earlier and the secondary start later?
2. If you can't do an overhaul, can you make minor changes by pushing back the start time at the secondary by even 15 minutes?
3. If you can't even push back the time, can you put less rigorous classes at the start of the day? For example, make study halls first or second period and make it optional for students to attend those?

The point here is to look for opportunities, however small, to go from the current state to the desired state in a pursuit of changing when the task (of going to school) is done.

Strategy 36: Flipped Classroom

When I was in school, I did my homework at home. If I did it in school, it was because the teacher finished the instruction early or because I happened to have a study hall (or, that I forgot to do my homework the night before and I was scrambling to get it done that day). With advances in and integration of technology, the model of instruction has greater flexibility. Enter the flipped classroom which turns the traditional framework of teaching and homework on its head. In this approach, the instruction occurs at home via videos and the homework takes place in the classroom with the teacher. By having students watch prepared videos of the lessons outside of the class, the teacher is free during the class time to provide support to students. According to Kim Garcia, former Computer Science and Web Mastering teacher, "When the content is delivered at home, the classroom can be used to explore extension activities, conduct small-group learning exercises, and provide homework support for students who most need it."[65] The graphic in Figure 7.2 summarizes how the flipped model works and the benefits of the model. Student engagement increases because students are able to get real-time support when they apply the learning rather than struggling in isolation or needing to wait until the next time they see the teacher.

Figure 7.2: The Flipped Classroom Model[66]

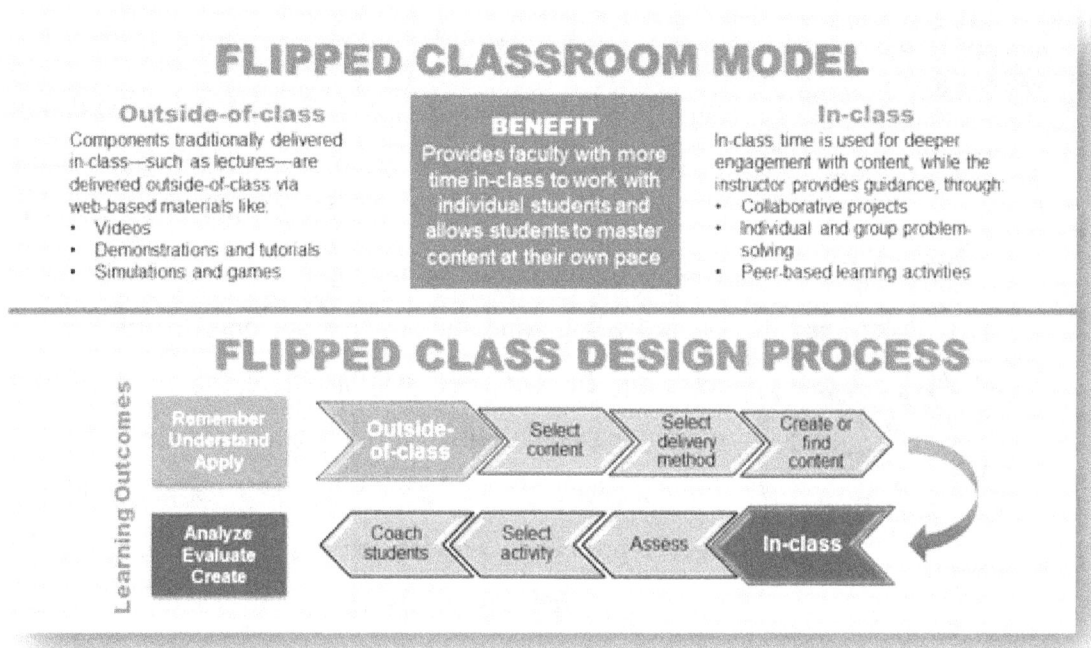

In order to create a flipped classroom, teachers must either find videos of the content being taught and share those videos or record themselves delivering the content. Ideally these videos are mini-lessons, meaning the content is relatively brief. There may be some questions about the content that the students have to answer based on what they learned. This could also come in the form of an entry ticket into the classroom.

For many teachers, the idea of creating videos is so intimidating that it is a deal-breaker. The best way to overcome this hurdle is to start small. There is no need to do this for every lesson every day, especially for a beginner. Try it for one class for one day and see what happens. Do not be discouraged by the time it may take in the beginning since everything is more time consuming when you are doing it for the first time.

If you're interested in learning more about flipped classrooms, I encourage you to visit the Rochester Institute of Technology website here:
https://cutt.ly/flipped

It is true that to accomplish a standard flipped classroom students need access to devices and internet outside of the school. If this isn't possible, a low-tech flipped classroom can be fashioned with hardcopy materials that students have to read. This will not be as interesting but the intention of the flipped classroom is less about integrating technology, and should really focus on providing time in-class for students to apply their learning. In fact, one way to think about a flipped classroom, is to think of it like a lab setting in which the students demonstrate and employ their learning with the teacher present to provide real-time, as-needed support. This structure reduces errors in learning and application because, unlike in the standard approach to learning applied outside of the classroom, the teacher is available for questions.

A Word Of Caution... If learning new content is "homework" to be done outside of school, we have to assume that a percentage of our students will not do it. Certainly, for some students, the reason for not doing the work is due to non-compliance. However, for other students, those reasons are beyond students' control. Remember, the first question you need to ask when you see that someone is non-compliant is whether or not that person has the ability to do the task in the first place.

Alternative Use: The flipped model is not just for teachers and students; it can also be used for administrators and teachers. Ideally, faculty/staff meetings are more than just information sharing—they are opportunities to work together. Therefore, if there is background information needed in advance of the collaborative work, the information could be made available to the faculty/staff prior to the actual meeting to allow the time during the meeting to focus on the collaborative work. This is all

> dependent on the structures and culture that exists in your building. For example, you may need to subtract the time spent watching the information outside of the meeting from the meeting time. For those who may be concerned about people not watching prior to the meeting, that speaks to non-compliant behavior that is likely associated with (a) a handful of people and therefore those people should be addressed rather than the option being eliminated, it speaks to (b) a non-compliant culture, or (c) a lack of trust. No matter the reasoning, this would be an issue of non-compliance and I would suggest going back to the strategies in Section I on non-compliance.

Strategy 37: Workshop

If you teach language arts, you are probably familiar with a workshop approach where teachers see their role as the person who provides brief instruction to students during the "mini-lesson" which lasts no more than about ten to fifteen minutes (or about 25 percent of the instructional time). The bulk of the remaining instructional time is devoted to students applying the lesson (or previous lessons) to their own independent reading and/or writing. The class ends with about five minutes of sharing by the students and/or teacher to reflect on what was accomplished, learned, or demonstrated during the class. During the independent time, the teacher confers with students one-on-one or in small groups based on similar need. This is the opportunity for the students to get real-time, as-needed instruction based on their unique needs. Figure 7.3 shows how the time in a workshop approach would be allocated.

This approach differs from traditional instruction where students are either listening or watching the teacher throughout whole group instruction for

Figure 7.3: Time Allocations in a Workshop Model

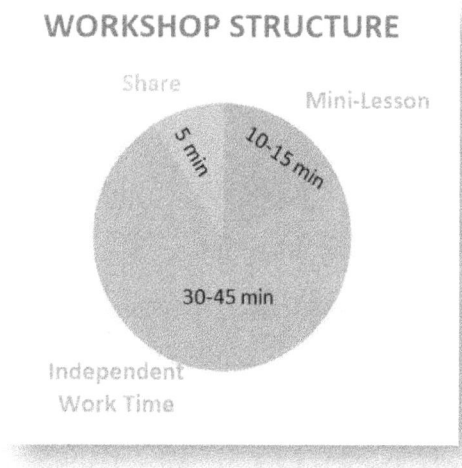

most of the lesson and then left with only a small fraction of time to work independently and/or where the students are all doing the same work during the application portion of the lesson. Further, with the workshop model, since students are able to work at their own pace on tasks that are within their Zone of Proximal Development and likely devised by the students, engagement is increased.

While it is true that this approach is a staple of many language arts classes, there is no reason why it could not also be used within any discipline. I worked with an art teacher, Julie Bridge, who approached art instruction in a very traditional way. She showed the students step-by-step what they were going to make and all the students made the same project. As we worked together and discussed how she could use a workshop approach, she gradually began to make changes. Eventually, Julie did a mini-lesson at the start of each class to show the students a technique that they may want to try with their projects. Julie credits the organization TAB, Teaching for Artistic Behavior, for her use of workshop in her art classes. TAB advocates for choice-based art education. Specifically, using the workshop teaches students to think like real artists and see the classroom as their studio where they own their authentic learning. As a result, students choose what to work on, how to work on it, and how long to work on it (within reason). Obviously, this makes the learning completely developmentally appropriate and differentiated.

There are some challenges, of course. Julie would tell you that assessment can be tricky. This is why she utilizes resources and techniques like including:

- Differentiated rubrics while planning with the artist.
- Regular self-assessment and peer-assessment (which helps students take more responsibility for their own learning).
- The book *Student Thinking: The Real Benefits of Visual Arts Education* by Lois Hetland, et al., which provides TAB teachers with a framework for assessing authentic artwork.

More specifically, after Julie's initial mini-lessons, students used the rest of the class to practice the techniques. After a few classes, the students then created proposals of projects they wanted to work on. They had to describe what they would do, what they would learn, what materials they would need, etc. Julie then met with each student one-on-one to review the proposal and push their thinking. Once the projects were approved, the students got to work. Julie would still start the lessons with a mini-lesson, but the students may or may not apply that lesson for that day or that project. As the students worked, they would voluntarily sign-up to conference with Julie and/or she would circulate and give the students feedback. The lessons would end with the share time so the students could share what they did or learned and/or Julie would share observations. This is an example of how the workshop model can work outside of a language arts classroom.

The same thing can happen within any content area. In a math classroom for example, the teacher could provide some direct instruction to the students about the concept for the day. The students could then go back and work on their application of the learning for the majority of the time as the teacher circulates and provides feedback. As the teacher sees that there are a handful of students demonstrating the same error, the teacher can form a small group and provide some additional intervention with just those students as the rest of the students move along.

Figure 7.3 shares some safeguards against common pitfalls regarding the workshop model.

7.3: Safeguards Against Common Pitfalls Regarding the Workshop Model

Pitfall	Solution
"Winging" the mini-lesson	Because the mini-lesson is so concise, it is critical to maximize what you do during that time. That requires planning.
Many times our examples are too long	Have your model ready. Use only enough of the mentor text/writing/problem/artwork/etc. to get to the point—you don't need all of it
Mini-lessons become maxi-lessons	It is very easy to have your ten-minute mini-lesson turn into a twenty-five minute maxi-lesson. When this happens, the time for the students to do their independent practice is compromised. Keep the mini-lesson mini. Time yourself. Stop yourself. Move on. If you can't teach it in the allotted time, you're probably trying to teach too much.
Neglecting to take notes	Don't rely on your memory with regard to the conferences you're having with students. Take a moment and jot down what each students is showing you they know and can do. That will allow you to form better groups and create better instruction.

Skipping the share	Students should have the chance to learn from each other. That is what the share is about. Whenever possible, give students the stage when it is share time.
Starting conferences before routines are in place	Since students will need to work independently while the teacher is conferencing with students, the teacher must first teach students what to do if they need help when the teacher is working with other students. These routines and procedures must be in place before starting student conferences for the workshop will be successful.
Giving students instructional level work	The work the students are doing independently must be at their independent (not instructional) level. If the work is too hard, the students will not be able to complete it and be off-task; if the work is too easy, the students will get bored and off-task.

Strategy 38: Brain Breaks

I am living proof that the Couch to 5K app works. I not only was able to go from a person who was never a runner to running a 5K (3.1 miles), but I have since used the app to build up to a 10K and even up to running 10 miles. The app works by building up the runner's stamina through interval training. In the version of the app I use (Run Double), the first interval has the new "runner" go through eight intervals of sixty seconds of running and ninety seconds of walking. This means the runner is only running for a total of eight minutes. The runner repeats each interval three times during the week with each weekly interval getting progressively longer and harder. After ten weeks, the once couch-sitter is now a 5K runner. Interestingly, if you were not a runner and wanted to become a runner, you probably would not think that you only needed to run thirty total runs to demonstrate such sizable improvement—from not running at all to running a 5K (3.1 miles). This concept emphasizes that finding the proper intervals of running is just as important as understanding that your body needs to rest in order to successfully perform.

Even though some people call the brain a muscle, it's an organ. Learning to do new cognitive tasks is quite similar to learning to do new physical tasks, meaning working in intervals of ever-increasing stamina works well for improving thinking as it does for improving running. As well, the brain needs both activity and rest in order to function well and grow. Cue brain breaks.

As reported by neurologist and professor, Judy Willis in the *Edutopia* article "Using Brain Breaks to Restore Students' Focus":

> For students to learn at their highest potential, their brains need to send signals efficiently from the sensory receptors (what they hear, see, touch, read, imagine, and experience) to memory storage regions of the brain. The most detrimental disruptions to traffic along these information pathways are stress and overload.
>
> Brain breaks are planned learning activity shifts that mobilize different networks of the brain. These shifts allow those regions that are blocked by stress or high-intensity work to revitalize. Brain breaks, by switching activity to different brain networks, allow the resting pathways to restore their calm focus and foster optimal mood, attention, and memory.[67]

The amount of time and the frequency of the brain breaks varies depending on the age of the students. However, Willis advises "brain breaks should take place before fatigue, boredom, distraction, an inattention set it in…As a general rule, concentrated study of 10 to 15 minutes for elementary school and 20 to 30 minutes for middle and high school students calls for a three- to five-minute break."[68] In this way, brain breaks offer strategic rests to enhance focus and interest; what looks like disengagement may actually be fatigue or distraction.

Brain breaks can be accomplished through quiet and calm practices like attentive breathing or meditation. These mindfulness practices are wonderful to teach students so that they may employ them as-needed without requiring formalized, teacher-directed breaks; this can increase student autonomy and self-awareness. Brain breaks that employ physical movement are also very beneficial. Allison Posey, author of *Engage the Brain*, recommends "options to move, such as stretching, standing, walking, or playing" in order to

Watch this short video called "The Science Behind Brain Breaks:"
https://cutt.ly/BrainBreaks

"increase oxygen intake and help keep the brain fueled with energy."[69] Sensory brain breaks (like playing with playdough), skill-building brain breaks (like writing spelling words on someone's back with your finger), and brain break games (like a scavenger hunt) are also examples of possible ways to temporarily shift focus in order to reset the brain.

Chapter Summary

This chapter was about moving someone from the point of compliance to interest by changing the schedule, or thinking about the use of time differently. One of the biggest obstacles regarding changing schedules is that schedules are often viewed as unchangeable and static so that everything else must work around them and not the other way around. This is simply not true. Getting to the point at which people are open to considering changes to schedules is difficult, but even then, there are still obstacles that interfere with change. In reality, the schedule you currently have to work with is likely equally bad for everyone but when you change it to improve outcomes for one group, another group may feel like they are being negatively impacted. This is why when it comes to making changes to schedules, it is important to remember that the goal of the schedule is to ensure the best learning outcomes for students. All other outcomes are a distant second. When considering how the use of time works (or does not) in your school and what changes might improve student outcomes, it is wise to plan this work well in advance of any change since there will likely be many meetings and voices to listen to along the way.

Looking for even more strategies to USE TIME DIFFERENTLY?

Please visit my website, www.LyonsLetters.com/learnmore, for print and digital recommendations including books, websites, videos, and more!

Thank you to Julie Bridge for her input to Workshop—a strategy included this chapter.

Reflection Prompts

1. In what ways are you maximizing your current schedule to maximize student learning outcomes?

   _____
   _____
   _____

2. Many teachers find that students are reluctant or adverse to doing homework at home. If this is a challenge for you, how can you use time differently regarding homework assignments? If this is not a challenge for you, what advice would you give to someone else regarding this concern?

   _____
   _____
   _____

3. Name one thing you could do tomorrow based on what you learned from this chapter.

   _____
   _____
   _____

4. Tweet me @LyonsLetters to share an idea for a future reading or digital resource I should share on www.lyonsletters.com that would help someone who is compliant become interested.

Persistent Questions

1. What have you done so far regarding the three challenge questions from Chapter 1?

    a. **Three:** Find at least three people with whom to share your learning.

    b. **Two:** Find at least two ideas that change you.

    c. **One:** Apply at least one idea from your reading.

    _____
    _____
    _____

2. What have you learned so far, and how will you use it?

    _____
    _____
    _____

Section III: Absorption Strategies

The next five chapters address strategies to achieve absorption which happens when the relationship with the task is at the highest level and the reason for doing the task is intrinsically motivated. Both the students and the adults in schools should have the chance to experience what that feels like. However, it is not the expectation that absorption should or could happen for everyone in every class every day.

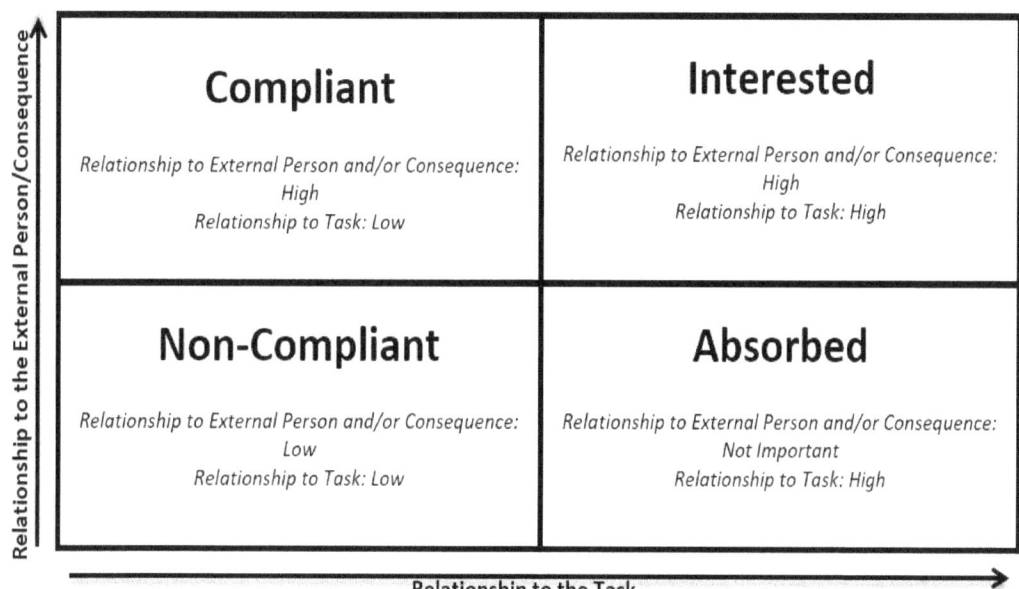

Chapter 8 addresses strategies that focus on building culture, values, and beliefs that support intrinsic motivation. Chapter 9 focuses on strategies to rethink how students are graded. Chapter 10 includes strategies to expose students to tasks that they might not have known before or those that they can dive into deeper. Chapter 11 has strategies that hook students into the learning. Finally, Chapter 12 shares strategies for engaging students through projects. By the end of Section III, you will be able to identify actions that can shift someone to absorption.

Chapter 8

Culture, Values, and Belief Strategies

"Actions prove who someone is; words just prove who they want to be."
~Unknown

Recognizing Your Thinking Before You Read...

- What are your beliefs about learning and how do you put those beliefs into action?

  _____
  _____
  _____

- What does the culture in which you currently work value about teaching and learning? How do you know?

  _____
  _____
  _____

- Share an example where someone's words and actions are not in sync. What impact does this contradiction have?

  _____
  _____
  _____

Getting on the Same Page

Absorption is the highest level of engagement. When you are absorbed, you do tasks because you are intrinsically compelled to do them. This means that the task you are doing is so engaging that you would choose to do it even if you didn't have to. I want to remind you that this is the goal for everyone, but this is not the goal for everyone in every class every day. Human beings are not wired to be absorbed in everything we do (see Highlight 9 in Chapter 1 of this book).

So what does absorption look like? *In Engagement is Not a Unicorn (It's a Narwhal)*, I wrote about three manifestations of absorption:

1. **Novice:** We feel smitten towards activities we are just "trying on" to see if we really like them; these can be a passing phase or may deepen into engrossment.

2. **Enthusiast:** We feel engrossed towards activities that are a long-term commitment of time and resources, fill our free time, and become a part of our identity.

3. **Addict:** We feel obsessed towards activities that result in the neglect of our responsibilities and other people.

What's important to remember if you want to create opportunities for absorption is that the tasks that people find truly absorbing are those with the appropriate level of challenge; absorbing tasks are not easy (see Highlight 10 in Chapter 1).

This chapter is about creating a culture that puts into practice the values and beliefs to support challenge and risk. After all, risk does not occur in environments that condemn failure since if I get it wrong the first time, I probably don't even have a second chance to get it right. In conditions like this, rather than creating absorption (which embraces challenge and risk), we end up creating compliance (at best). If this sounds familiar, it's because that's happening in schools daily.

Actions and Words

We have all heard the saying, "Don't just talk the talk, walk the walk." When people's words and actions are not aligned, we notice because our "actions speak louder than words." These are clichés, of course, but they are clichés for a reason. Specifically, behaviors show us on the outside what we believe on the inside.

Some people value meal times so they make sure that a certain number of nights per week the family shares a meal. Imagine if the parents said that they value meal times, and that the family should eat dinner together daily. However, one or both parents routinely scheduled work conflicts so they missed dinners with the family. This created an environment where there was no predictable routine or schedule. Meals were haphazard. Do you think the children in that family would think that meal time was truly important to the parents?

If we were friends, you would know that I am known to swear. However, I am not friends with my kids, so they don't know this about me. In my house, my husband and I live by our values that it is not appropriate to swear around children or for children to swear around adults. Since I cannot control what other people say or do, when we used to watch TV or a movie and there was foul language or when we have friends over who swear, I would tell my kids, "I cannot control what you hear, but I can tell you what is acceptable for us to say. That's not it. You know it and so I expect you to meet that expectation." Now that they're older and this is all they know, I don't even have to have the conversation anymore.

With regard to engagement, we have to not only make our invisible expectations visible, we have to commit to those expectations. This means, if you want to have people become absorbed in tasks, we must create thoughts and actions that support doing the tasks you love to do for reasons that fuel intrinsic motivation. This creation doesn't just happen. It cannot be relegated to words without actions or actions that undermine the words. Both are required. When words and actions are misaligned, things like this happen:

- We tell students "do your best" and then do not give students the chance to re-do or revise their work based on feedback.
- We say "the learning is the most important thing" and then give students extra credit for bringing in boxes of tissues.
- We declare that an assignment is late so the grade is reduced even though the grade now does not reflect the students' content knowledge.

- We preach to students about a future where there is a "the real world" but create an arbitrary world for them where the adults are monarchs (at best) or dictators (at worst).

Tried and Failed

At this level of engagement, there will be failure by those doing the tasks since absorbing tasks are challenging. The goal when doing absorbing tasks is not to produce a product that is perfect, and if perfection is achieved at the first try, the task was not at the correct level of difficulty to sustain the highest levels of engagement for long. The goal when doing absorbing tasks is to learn through the process of doing—and doing includes failure. In the real "real world," that's how learning happens. Scientists repeatedly have ideas and test them only to discover their original ideas were not quite right. Athletes attend hours and hours of practices and drills and games and yet a .300 batting average is good for a professional baseball player. Unfortunately, not every patient will be cured by every doctor. Failure needs to be seen as one of the best methods to learn, not a flaw and certainly not something to be avoided.

We have created a culture of engaging failure with video games. No one wants to play a video game that is too easy. This is why video games are designed to operate within the player's Zone of Proximal Development (ZPD). The game's first level is often the exemplar of how the game works. It is extremely easy and designed to get you feeling interested and make you believe you can be successful. The next level is much more difficult because it is the first "real" level. You do not expect to beat this level the first time. As you play, you acquire skills that are sufficient to progress into but not enough to master the next level the first time you try. In other words, people play video games with the knowledge that they *must* fail. Because it is so important, let me repeat that: people play video games with the knowledge that they *must* fail.

> In other words, people play video games with the knowledge that they *must* fail. Because it is so important, let me repeat that: people play video games with the knowledge that they *must* fail.

So if people know that in video games they must fail in order to ultimately succeed, what do people know about school? In school people know they must *not* fail in order to succeed. The fact that we have debates in schools about whether or not a student should be able to retake a test or redo their homework is astounding. The culture in most schools is clear: Do it right the first time because that's the only chance you've got. Then we wonder why students give up or drift towards compliance.

> The culture in most schools is clear: Do it right the first time because that's the only change you've got. Then we wonder why students give up or drift towards compliance.

Human beings are wired to seek mastery and driven towards success. Don't believe me? Go to a hospital nursery and watch babies. They do not start their lives crawling, let alone running. They do not know how to talk or feed themselves. They are helpless. Now go to a nursery school and watch the infants who are repeatedly failing to learn to walk, talk, and feed themselves. Do we grade them? Nope. Do we lament that they didn't "get it" the first time. Certainly not. Do we tell their parents that infants are not trying hard enough? Please! So what do we do? We cheer them on. We celebrate the approximation. We give them time and space and do not panic if they need more time. This is a culture of risk-taking that celebrates failures because failure is the first step to success. This belief is what we need in every classroom in every school every day.

Now What

The next three strategies are designed to help build a culture for absorption. I cannot overstate that it is not enough to build a façade that looks like it will support absorption; if you want those with whom you work to become absorbed, you must be absorbed in creating the conditions of safety for others to take risks.

39. Who Do You Want to Be
40. The Learning Pit
41. Morning Team Time

Strategy 39: Who Do You Want to Be

When people who do not spend time with kids encounter kids, there are a series of about five go-to questions that they ask because, for reasons unknown to me, people who do not spend time with kids become awkward around children. In this list of questions you will hear:

1. So, how old are you?
2. How's school?
3. Do you have a pet?
4. What's your favorite color?
5. What do you want to be when you grow up?

It's this last question that I want to focus on here. As Adam Grant wrote in the *New York Times*, this question

> forces kids to define themselves in terms of work. When you're asked what you want to be when you grow up, it's not socially acceptable to say, "A father," or, "A mother," let alone, "A person of integrity." This might be one of the reasons many parents say their most important value for their children is to care about others, yet their kids believe that top value is success. When we define ourselves by our jobs, our worth depends on what we achieve.[70]

In other words, we're asking the wrong question. Furthermore, no matter what the age is of the child that you're asking, undoubtedly, there will be not just jobs—but entire fields of work—that will exist in the future that do not exist now. We need to help children (and adults) see that rather than a profession they want to be, kids should be focusing on dispositions and conditions that they are drawn to or exhibit.

Therefore, the right question (or at least better question if we're talking about creating culture) is to ask *who* do you want to be—and I'm not referring to a specific person like Wayne Gretkzy or Spiderman (which could be an answer depending on the age of the child). I'm also not referring to a job title like President of the United States or a YouTuber. "Who do you want to be" is meant to be answered with adjectives that describe the type of characteristics the child would want to embody as an adult. I suppose another way of phrasing this question would be, "How do you want people to describe you?"

Asking a question like this would be a way to open the door to teaching children about ideas like legacies, values, and living a life of purpose. You could talk about the behaviors that would align with those descriptions. The school's mission and vision (or better yet, your classroom's mission and vision and even better than that, *each student's* individual mission and vision statement) could be a springboard for the conversation by saying, "If we agree that as a class we will [mission statement]…then, who would we want to be if we were acting/living/behaving in ways that would *show* others *these beliefs* are what we aspire to be?"

Furthermore, you could ask your students, "If you want to be described as someone who helps others, what are ways that you could do that as an adult *and* what are ways that you can practice that now?" In fact, it is this last part (practicing that now) which is the real motive for this strategy. Phrased differently, the follow-up question would be, "Who do you need to be now to get there?" Keeping with the idea of wanting to be an adult who helps others, you can show students that they are capable of practicing those skills and behaviors already. They are capable of connecting with people who are doing that today. They can learn about a multitude of professions that lend themselves to those traits which broadens their future professional options. In short, when the focus is on *who* rather than *what* you want to be, you don't have to wait until some unknown future. The time to start becoming or celebrating who you want to be is now. This shifts students' focus from talking about the work they would do, to working now to define themselves.

Strategy 40: The Learning Pit

The college course I teach is called "EDU 645: Curriculum Planning, Design, Implementation, and Evaluation" (I didn't name it). In creating my syllabus, I decided to include a thematic question that we focus on from the first night and revisit throughout the course. This question is also one that I have the students ask themselves, their co-workers, practicing administrators, and guest speakers to the class. What's the question? *"Who is curriculum for?"* I don't ask them to ponder about "what" curriculum is. The "what" question has a right and a wrong answer. That question is simply one that requires opening up a dictionary or glossary of a book. No. I do not want them to wrestle with *what curriculum is*, but *who curriculum is for* because the question is not easy to answer.

My desire to ask this specific question came after being introduced to James Nottingham's book, *The Learning Challenge: How to Guide Your Students Through the Learning Pit to Achieve Deeper Understanding*. As John Hattie acknowledges in the book's Foreword:

> Learning involves being on the edge of knowing and not knowing. It involves acknowledging what we do not yet know but could with effort and strategy. It sometimes involves reorganizing what we already think we know into something different and giving up some previous and sometimes precious knowledge to reach a deeper and more flexible understanding. As Piaget famously said, it involves *disequilibrium*. That is, learning occurs when there is an imbalance between what is understood and what is encountered. When our equilibrium is imbalanced, we have the possibility to grow and develop.[71] (emphasis in original)

To achieve this, Nottingham provides the reader with a visual to show the journey from the start to finish of the learning pit process (see Figure 8.1).

The Learning Pit journey essentially has five markers, beginning with being confronted with a "concept" that at least some of the students would think they understand already. In my class, that was the concept of curriculum. In the image of the journey you can see that learners start on the figurative edge of the pit because once leaners really start to mull over the concept, they finds themselves falling into the pit. This is because during the "challenge" phase of the journey, learners start to see nuances and inconsistencies with the concept. In my class, this is when students saw that when they asked the question, "Who is curriculum for," to different people, the answers were inconsistent.

Find free Learning Pit graphics at:
https://cutt.ly/Free-Pits

In the "cognitive conflict" point of the pit, students try to seek out answers to the new questions that have arisen related to the concept. In my class, the students hear inconsistency and want to make their worlds tidy again. So they question who they agree with and why, which causes them to look for other resources to resolve the dissonance. This is the deepest portion of the pit; not only do you feel like you don't know the concept anymore, you question if you ever knew it at all.

Figure 8.1: The Learning Pit[72]

The good news is that the next step, "construct," begins to bring you out of the pit. Here, students begin to feel like they have made some traction on their understanding because they start to notice patterns through organizing ideas. My students, for example, began to broaden how the question could be answered based on what they learned from each other and the various resources in the course. The idea that the concept could be answered in a nuanced way was originally not even considered.

Upon reaching the other side of the pit, the students have a better understanding of the concept than they had going into the pit, which is represented in Figure 8.1 by showing that the cliff on the right (point of exit) is higher than the cliff (point of entry) into the pit. When you exit the pit, you are excited about your progression. My students shared with me that going through the Learning Pit was not only impactful for the course, but also for helping them frame for themselves and their students how we have to get comfortable with being uncomfortable in order to learn. They said that the experience of using the Learning Pit gave them a concrete understanding of how their learning was going to progress and that was reassuring to them because otherwise they might have been even more uncomfortable when they didn't have a concrete answer to the question. As well, they started to see that this process of concept, challenge, cognitive conflict, construct, and eureka was one that was applicable any- and everywhere and kept them absorbed in the learning; they were driven to come to some resolution.

Watch a video of James Nottingham narrating an animation of The Learning Pit here:
https://cutt.ly/LearningPitAnimation

How can you create a learning challenge? First and foremost, you have to develop a really strong question. Admittedly, for me, this was the hardest part. I went through several iterations before I decided "Who is curriculum for?" was the one I was going to use. I found it extremely helpful to explicitly teach my students the Learning Pit using the visual and some excellent videos found at Nottingham's website, www.challenginglearning.com. I also had to celebrate (yes CELEBRATE) and validate their journey into, struggles in, and ultimate exit from the pit. When they would say, "Wait! I'm confused. Last week

I thought X and now I'm thinking that's not right," I'd exclaim, "Yes!! This is great!! You're in the pit!!" My job was not to get them out, but to let them know that it was okay for them to be there and that I had confidence that, with time, they would get *themselves* out. Was it messy? Sure. Did I sometimes have to bite my tongue? Of course. Was it worth the struggle? Absolutely!

Strategy 41: Morning T.E.A.M. Time

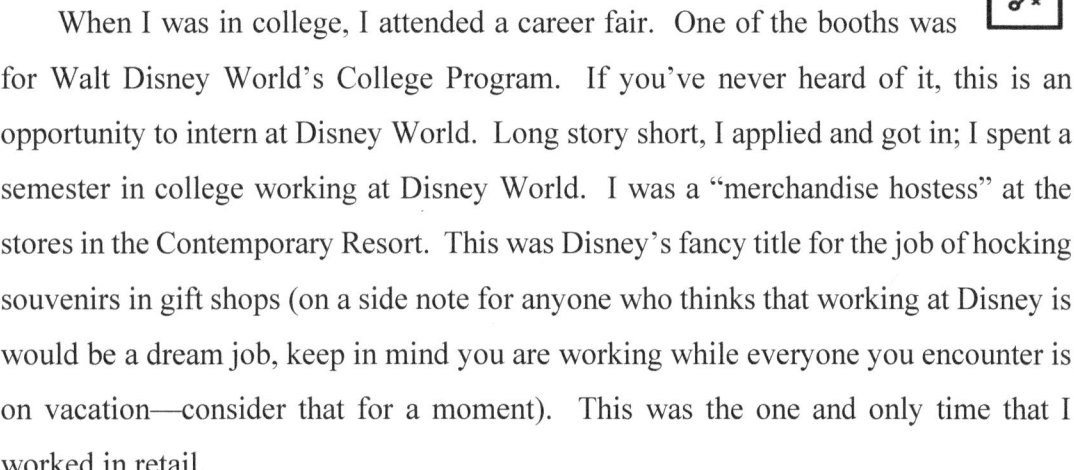

When I was in college, I attended a career fair. One of the booths was for Walt Disney World's College Program. If you've never heard of it, this is an opportunity to intern at Disney World. Long story short, I applied and got in; I spent a semester in college working at Disney World. I was a "merchandise hostess" at the stores in the Contemporary Resort. This was Disney's fancy title for the job of hocking souvenirs in gift shops (on a side note for anyone who thinks that working at Disney is would be a dream job, keep in mind you are working while everyone you encounter is on vacation—consider that for a moment). This was the one and only time that I worked in retail.

Before the shift started, we often gathered in the hallway for a short informational meeting. During these meetings, we would spend time doing things like learning about new products, discussing upcoming events, and being shown the latest photos and plots of known shoplifters or credit card scammers with the Be On the Look Out (BOLO) sheets.

If you have ever watched the show *Say Yes to the Dress*, you have seen a pre-shift informational meeting. On *Say Yes to the Dress*, a show that documents women finding their wedding dress, the meetings focus on topics like how to handle a bridezilla, what to do if the mom is unhappy with the bride's choices, or how to help a bride who doesn't have time to order a dress because her wedding is less than a month away. Each meeting is brief and directed to a specific situation.

It was this type of short and targeted meeting that I wanted to replicate when I was the Head of School in a previous job. It thought it was a great opportunity for people in the school to get to know each other even though they did not work directly with everyone. These meetings, which I called "Morning T.E.A.M. (Together Everyone Achieves More) Time" felt like a way to ensure that I was in contact with everyone daily to message and shape the culture to align with the mission and vision of the school. Finally, it was a chance to model a circle for the adults in the building so that they might be able to use that strategy with their students.

In the school, there was planning time at the start of the day before students arrived. I built in ten minutes daily during that time for the entire staff to come together and stand in a circle in a common area of the school. In the beginning, I planned the questions and topics. Of course there were times when these meetings were a chance for me to share some information or take a quick pulse on something that I needed input on. However, I strove to keep those types of interactions to a minimum. Therefore, most of the time we responded to prompts like these:

- Share an example of how you or your students live the school's mission?
- What is something we can do next week to spotlight our mission in action?
- In our next assembly, what are some ways that we can model our beliefs about our students and their families?
- Between now and tomorrow's T.E.A.M. Time, take a look at our website and come back ready to talk about how we can make improvements to reflect the school's values.
- Tomorrow is our first parent-teacher conference day. Turn and talk to the person next to you about something that you've planned that will highlight your beliefs about your students.
- Turn and talk to the person next to you about a book that you read that impacted your beliefs about teaching and learning. What was the book and why was it so impactful?
- It's so good to see everyone today. We believe in a culture of celebration. I'm wondering what we can celebrate. Please shout out something amazing that has taken place or a special event that we should acknowledge.
- We believe in a culture of celebration. When we come together tomorrow, I want you to be prepared to talk about something that you saw today that a student did that was awesome.

Eventually, I enlisted others to lead the meetings including every member of the adult school community from administrators to teachers to assistants to aides.

By the way, when you add up those ten minutes per day, that becomes fifty minutes per week or 200 minutes per month or 2,000 minutes per year. That is a lot of time to build culture and create deep levels of engagement in the school's mission and vision.

I know that there are many schools and districts that do not have even ten minutes per day to do this. If you cannot do ten minutes per day, could you get ten minutes per week? Is it possible to get ten minutes per team rather than the whole building? Are there people who would be willing to do it if you cannot mandate that it's done? If you want to try this, think about the ways to make this work rather than the ways that it will not work for you.

Alternative Use: This strategy works just as well with students to establish and reinforce culture, values, and beliefs. In fact, with students you could use this when studying different cultures in social studies, reading books in language classes, and even when learning about different work that people might do in the sciences by asking students to take on the role of someone who they are studying. For example, a teacher might say, "We have been learning about the beliefs of the Puritans in New England in the 1600s. As we answer our Morning T.E.A.M. Time question each morning this week, I want you to answer it as a Puritan in the 1600s might." A science teacher might say, "As we are looking at the differences between these rocks, I will ask a question each morning and I want you to answer from the perspective of a geologist."

As well, Morning T.E.A.M. Time is similar to Strategy 5, "Community Building Circles." Here, the purpose is to establish and reinforce the culture, values, and beliefs of the participants, whereas Community Building Circles are to establish community. The same group of people might be in a community building circle one day and in a Morning T.E.A.M. Time the next and they may not even know the difference.

Chapter Summary

This chapter was about moving someone from the point of interest to absorption by focusing on the culture, values, and beliefs. When thinking about what it means to be absorbed—to be compelled to do a physically or cognitively challenging task for the intrinsic benefit of doing the task—we know that work like this is neither easy nor without risk; failure is a part of absorption. Given this, even if someone is intrinsically motivated to do the task, they will be less likely to do it if the extrinsic conditions do not permit struggle. Creating environments that foster and even reward risk-taking are the focus of this chapter. Doing so requires more than lip-service. If the words and the actions from the person assigning the task do not match, the person doing the task will catch on and possibly check-out. In truth, as humans, we want to work at the top of our Zone of Proximal Development and are comfortable with failure if we are allowed and encouraged to approximate the desired outcome and persist without negative consequence.

Looking for even more strategies to
BUILD CULTURE, VALUES, AND BELIEFS?
Please visit my website, www.LyonsLetters.com/learnmore, for print and digital recommendations including books, websites, videos, and more!

Reflection Prompts

1. In your own words, how do culture, values, and beliefs impact engagement?

   _____
   _____
   _____

2. What is something specific you explicitly say and do with those with whom you work (children or adults) to improve agreement regarding your shared culture, values, or beliefs?

   _____
   _____
   _____

3. How do you currently respond when a student is struggling and what does that tell you about your hidden beliefs about struggle?

   _____
   _____
   _____

4. Name one thing you could do tomorrow based on what you learned from this chapter.

   _____
   _____
   _____

5. Tweet me @LyonsLetters to share an idea for a future reading or digital resource I should share on www.lyonsletters.com that would help someone who is interested become absorbed?

Persistent Questions

1. What have you done so far regarding the three challenge questions from Chapter 1?

    a. **Three:** Find at least three people with whom to share your learning.

    b. **Two:** Find at least two ideas that change you.

    c. **One:** Apply at least one idea from your reading.

    _____
    _____
    _____

2. What have you learned so far, and how will you use it?

    _____
    _____
    _____

Chapter 9

Grading Strategies

"If school put learning instead of testing and memorizing as the top standard, then the letter 'F' would not stand for 'failure;' it would stand for, 'find another answer.'"
~Prince Ea

Recognizing Your Thinking Before You Read...

1. What is the purpose of grades?

2. What should happen to a student's grade if the student turns in work late?

3. In your experience, in what circumstances do you see students embrace or avoid academic risk-taking?

Will You Marry Me

In the interview I did on the Lasting Learning Podcast hosted by author, administrator, and educator, Dave Schmittou, Dave shared with me an analogy about engagement that I never heard before. He said, "Engagement in the classroom is sort of like engagement in the real world… If you want to know if a woman is engaged, just check out her social media because she is telling everyone about it. She's showing off her ring. She's shouting it from the rooftops."[73]

Watch the video of the Lasting Learning Podcast with Dave Schmittou here:
https://cutt.ly/Lasting Learning

I love this because he's right! When people hear the term "engagement" in isolation, they are likely to think about someone getting down on one knee and wedding planning. People do not first think "students in classrooms" when hearing the word engagement. Yet, when talking about the highest level of engagement in classrooms, it is helpful to think about the energy and emotion that those who are planning to get married exhibit. Engaged students should be showing off what they're learning and shouting about it from the rooftops in the same way. This is why I couldn't agree more with Dave when he said, "The best place to measure engagement isn't always in the classroom. It's in the hallways and lunchroom."[74] These are places where the students can talk about anything—so if they're talking about what they are doing in their classrooms, then you know that they are absorbed in that work.

You Can't Stop Me

The strategies in every chapter in this section of the book are designed to help students become truly absorbed in what they are doing. Remember, when people are absorbed, time passes by differently. An hour can feel like ten minutes and you feel like you are just on the verge of mastery. Implicit in that statement is that there is some level of challenge and failure since those who are absorbed are in a struggle between what they are capable of now and what they are trying to achieve. This struggle, however, is not just challenging; it is rewarding and motivating. When people are absorbed, you have to tell them, often repeatedly, that they are out of time. The bell rang. Put the book away. Turn the lights out. We have to go. In response, absorbed people say things like, "Can I just have one more chance?" or "Oh, I didn't hear the bell," or "Please can I have just a few more minutes."

What else happens when people are absorbed? They think about the work they are doing even when they are not doing it. They are mentally rehearsing and revising. They are tinkering in their heads even when they cannot physically touch or do the work they are away from. Absorbed people also talk about what they are working on without being asked. They are zealots and driven; they get excited when describing what they have accomplished and what they want to do next.

One Size Fits All

How often do you assign students different tasks for the same standard? Sometimes? Often? Never? I know when I was in school my teachers would have answered "never" if they were being honest. We all read the same chapter for social studies and answered the same end of chapter questions. We all did the same labs in science. We all read the same books in English. We all made the same drawing in art. Did the same activities in P.E. Did the same problems in math. Need I go on? This was true not just in grade school but in middle and high school and even in college. Schools are more or less factories of learning. This is fine if all the students are the same, but obviously they are not.

However, when we have students do the same work—most of which is a regurgitation of what they have been told or read—the students become demotivated to learn and the task becomes getting the work done. Conditions like these promote cheating via copying since students focus on work completion rather than learning. The completion will get the grade; the learning is irrelevant. This can be a reason why students might perform well on homework and not on assessments. After all, if students didn't have to think much to do the formative learning and they were dependent on others to get the task done, when it comes time to be independent during a summative learning assessment, students will struggle.

We make tasks of learning high stakes by giving students grades rather than looking at it as practice. When learning tasks are viewed as practice, they are not graded because the point is to learn. The grade comes when it is time to show what you have learned—after the practice. During the learning process when students are practicing the learning, they need ample feedback to know what they are doing well and how to improve. This is similar to sports practices versus the actual games. Athletes go to practice to improve their skills needed to do well in the game when they get a score. Scores are reserved for the games, not the practice.

Know Your Audience

I have been on more report card committees than I can count. Given this, I know now that the place to start report card change conversations is with the question, "Who is the primary audience of the report card?" This question is critical because it impacts every step that comes next. I would argue, particularly at the elementary level, the primary audience is the parents. Given this, why on earth would we ever use percentage grades for elementary students? The percentage highlights the percentage of what a student got right or wrong. If we are in a place of learning, isn't it more important to speak to what a student knows yet or doesn't, which is best communicated in a narrative, not a number.

At a secondary level, the primary audience might be the students. If that's the case, why on earth would we ever use a percentage? So often at the secondary level students are not actually graded based on their content knowledge in isolation, but rather on some arbitrary combination of knowledge of content plus behaviors towards learning plus some other nonsensical, unrelated things like if the heading was right or wrong or if the student turned in the assignment late. Tell me this, if a child turns in an assignment late and the assignment is supposed to be a reflection of the standards, what does a percentage off of the grade tell you about the student's content knowledge?

What's in a Name

Have you, as the adult, ever turned in paperwork to the office late? Maybe you took attendance late one day (or you have a pattern of doing it late). Or perhaps your supply order was late or you accidentally forgot to submit your report card grades on time. What happened to you? I'm guessing, at worst, you got an email asking you to make sure that this didn't happen again. Your paycheck was likely never docked.

Given how we respond to adults who are late with submissions, here's the question. If a student turns in an assignment late, should points be taken off? The grade attributed to that assignment is meant to name (describe) the acquired learning of that *content*. If the assignment was submitted on-time, the grade would be X. If you take off points because the assignment is late, the grade is X minus Y (i.e., the value deducted for being late). Does the grade in the late scenario describe (a) the student's content knowledge or (b) the value of the student's content knowledge *and* the student's behaviors related to learning? Would it matter if there was a death in the family or if the student had a pattern of turning in assignments late for no reason? Your gradebook and the student's report card would not be able to tell the difference.

Now What

These four strategies start with the most important of all of the strategies, "Focus on the Learning" because this is the strategy that distinguishes the difference between getting the job done (compliance) and learning from the job (engagement).

42. Focus on the Learning
43. Goal Setting
44. Standards-Based Grading
45. Withholding Grades

Strategy 42: Focus on the Learning

I began working in a district that adopted a new Language Arts program and the teachers were told to use the materials faithfully. Unknown to the teachers or administrators at the time, the program was designed for flexibility. In other words, to use the program with fidelity meant that the teachers would have to make some choices about the resources based on their knowledge of the content and the students who they were teaching at the time. That understanding of the program was not quickly understood and when it was, the first message of fidelity overshadowed the second message of flexibility. Thus, even though teachers and students both felt that blindly following all aspects of the program was disinteresting, they did it anyway. The focus was not on the learning, but on the activity.

Here is an example of what it looked and sounded like when there was a focus on the activity rather than a focus on the learning. I walked into a classroom where the students had a packet of about four pages of the same graphic organizer that was similar to a double-column entry. For this task, the students were given a specific passage of the text in the left-most column, then in the remaining two columns they had to (a) summarize the text and (b) give two to three details from the text. This task was four-pages long and the students had repeat the process 22 times! It was mind-numbing. What's more, what was the *learning*? In other words, what was the purpose of the task? I'm sure to both the students and the teacher, the focus was on completing the task. Yet, when I look at the assignment itself that was created by the publishers of the program, there are not even written directions on the top of it, let alone learning outcomes. The teacher materials list the Common Core Learning Standards of RL 4.1-3, 5 as the learning outcomes. Though I would support the standards as the learning outcomes, nowhere in the standards does it talk about quantity. So, if we're focused on the learning, we are focused on the *quality*; students do not need to complete all 22 rows to demonstrate a command of the learning.

All tasks should be in service to the standard and this is why backwards planning or an Understanding by Design® (UbD) model that begins with the end in mind is so helpful. Before teaching the students, the teachers have to be clear on what the students are expected to know and be able to do as a result of the learning and that needs to be connected to the standards for the course.

When instruction is designed to focus on the learning, the teacher and the students are able to articulate the purpose of the task as a vehicle to access the learning. That may not necessitate a different task, but a different purpose for the task. For example, take these two explanations for doing the graphic organizer described above.

- Example 1: *Over the course of reading this book, you're going to have to complete this graphic organizer. I expect all rows to be filled. At the end, you'll turn this in and your grade will be based on completion of the graphic organizer, so be sure that each one is done. Any questions?*

- Example 2: *Over the course of reading this book, I want you to learn how to notice how the author uses specific language to help us understand how the character feels and changes over time. We'll be able to use details from the book to do this. This graphic organizer will help you keep track of these details. I'm going to show you how to do this and then we'll do a couple together because I want to make sure that you've got it before you do it on your own. Once I'm sure—and that might be different for each of you—I'll check in with you again. The goal again is to learn about how the author uses specific language to help the reader understand the character's feelings and growth. My expectation is that all students will be at least proficient when they finish this learning opportunity. So, once you're able to demonstrate that you have achieved the learning goal, the graphic organizer will go away, meaning most of us will only need the graphic organizer for a little while and there is a chance no one will need to use all of the rows.*

Obviously, there is a difference in length between the two examples. The point is not to use more words (again quality versus quantity), but to focus on the learning. That can be challenging without a thorough explanation which generally does mean more words. More important than the length is the intention. The intention in Example 1 is to do the task. Did you notice there is no formative assessment in Example 1? The graphic organizer is turned in at the end and is assessed based on completion. The intention in Example 2 is to do the learning with formative assessment so students who have shown mastery with feedback can move on and those who still need time and help will get it.

When the students and the teacher know what the learning is meant to be, the curriculum, instruction, program, and tasks become tools to use to achieve the intended learning. That doesn't just happen. It takes thought and it takes revising and/or letting go of tasks that are not really aligned to the intended learning. Just because you have always gone to the apple orchard in September and make stamps by carving apples or applesauce or apple pie, etc., doesn't mean that you have to keep doing that. On the other hand, it doesn't mean you can't. It just means that the only reason for any task is because it serves the learning.

The best way to know if a task is serving the learning is to identify the intended learning at the start of your planning and to use that as your north star when planning your lessons. To do this, consider the Seven Tenets of Understanding by Design®[75] in Figure 9.1.

Figure 9.1: The Seven Tenets of Understanding by Design ®

The Seven Tenets of Understanding by Design®

1 Learning is enhanced when teachers think purposefully about curricular planning. The UbD framework helps this process without offering a rigid process or prescriptive recipe.

2 The UbD framework helps to focus curriculum and teaching on the development and deepening of student understanding and transfer of learning (i.e., the ability to effectively use content knowledge and skill).

3 Understanding is revealed when students autonomously make sense of and transfer their learning through authentic performance. Six facets of understanding—the capacity to explain, interpret, apply, shift perspective, empathize, and self-assess—can serve as indicators of understanding.

4 Effective curriculum is planned backward from long-term, desired results through a three-stage design process (Desired Results, Evidence, and Learning Plan). This process helps avoid the common problems of treating the textbook as the curriculum rather than a resource, and activity-oriented teaching in which no clear priorities and purposes are apparent.

5 Teachers are coaches of understanding, not mere purveyors of content knowledge, skill, or activity. They focus on ensuring that learning happens, not just teaching (and assuming that what was taught was learned); they always aim and check for successful meaning making and transfer by the learner.

6 Regularly reviewing units and curriculum against design standards enhances curricular quality and effectiveness, and provides engaging and professional discussions.

7 The UbD framework reflects a continual improvement approach to student achievement and teacher craft. The results of our designs—student performance—inform needed adjustments in curriculum as well as instruction so that student learning is maximized.

You will see that Tenet 4 specifically mentions three stages in effectively planned backwards design:

1. Identifying Desired Results
2. Determining Acceptable Evidence
3. Guiding Questions

Figure 9.2 describes each of these stages in more detail.

Figure 9.2: The 3 Stages of Understanding by Design ® Planning[76]

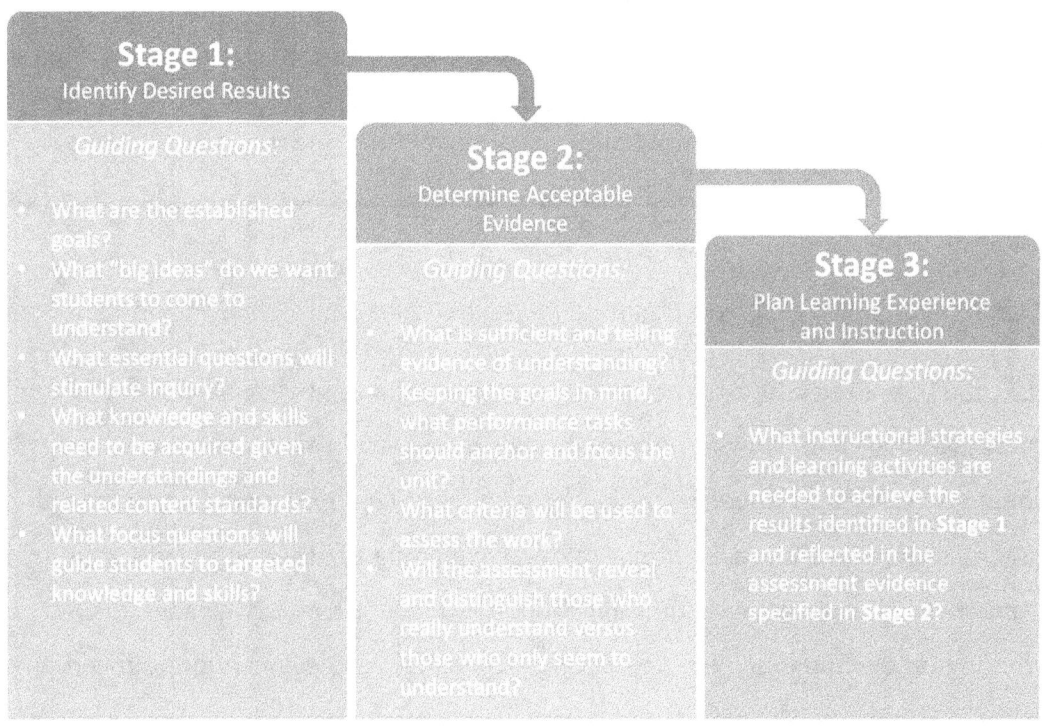

Notice how the tasks/activities are not determined until Stage 3—after the learning is determined in Stage 1 and the assessment(s) is determined in Stage 2.

It is important to note that grading is connected to the learning as well. The learning is about the content, not about the behaviors associated with the student. Think about it this way…when a student takes a high-stakes test like a final or state assessment, the score the student earns has nothing to do with whether or not the student handed in the homework late, talks back in class, or even if the student is a dream to have in class.

These are personality traits, not evidence of content or skill knowledge, i.e., they are not evidence of learning. The kindest student who always turns in homework on time can fail a final due to lack of content knowledge while the very rudest student who never does any work and skips class can pass a final with flying colors. Why? Because that assessment tests the learning, not the behaviors associated with the learning.

> *Alternate Use:* Faculty meetings and professional development for adults parallel student opportunities for learning in a classroom. Educational leaders could approach these experiences using the same backwards planning that teachers use with their students. Begin with the end in mind and determine what the learning is, how the teachers will demonstrate their learning, and then plan the tasks that would best meet those desired outcomes.

Strategy 43: Goals

I've done a lot of work in my career regarding goal-setting. This is true in speaking about both student and adult goal-setting (and this is, in part, why I wrote about goal-setting in *Engagement is Not a Unicorn [It's a Narwhal]*). Even with my experiences related to goal-setting, my understanding of it grew when working with Dana Britt, a consultant with Education Elements (EE). My school district was working on our strategic plan and partnered with EE, an organization founded on the belief that because we are all connected, our work together is as important as the individual work we do. Thus, EE works with schools and districts to help them grow in the areas that matter most to the school or district.

In my district's updated strategic plan, we identified that we wanted to develop a common understanding of what student success would look and sound like. This included that students should be setting and achieving their own goals. Certainly, no one can argue that goal-setting is a life-long and life-changing skill. In order to increase student engagement, we can target the students' sense of ownership over what and how they are learning. But as many teachers who have tried to promote student ownership before know, it can be a bit like teaching a child to ride a bike. Plopping the child on a bike and expecting immediate success is a recipe for disappointment. When we first learn to ride a bike, we generally struggle initially, resulting in a crash and a scraped knee. We must first start with training wheels. When the child wants to learn to ride without training wheels, someone holds onto the bike while the child pedals. Only when the child demonstrates effective pedaling and the ability to maintain balance independently, does the adult let the child go. At that point, both the child and the adult celebrate.

For our strategic plan, EE advocated that before diving straight into strategies to increase ownership and student agency, we need to try building first towards habits of goal-setting and reflection. Goal-setting is a simple way to help students understand and feel in control of the "what" and "why" of learning. Reflection strategies will help them understand their progress towards their goals. Once those skills have been mastered, you'll find your student is ready for the strategies for ownership and agency.

You'll find a continuum of action steps and resources for goal-setting, reflection, and ownership in the charts on the following pages. The most important aspect of goal-setting with regard to absorption is that the goal should be created and owned by the person who the goal is for. This seems obvious, but is often not the case. Most commonly, in classrooms, goals are created by the teachers and given to the students. In order to be absorbed, however, the students have to have intrinsic motivation to achieve the goal which is unlikely (if not impossible) when the goal is created *for* the student. Also, the purpose of the goal is not to achieve the goal, but to embody the behaviors that create the result. In this way, the goal isn't to finish a book; it's to be a reader. The goal isn't to write a report, but to become a writer. It's not to run the 5K, but to become a runner.[77] This is because if you are really absorbed, the task is your identity, i.e., you are an enthusiast. Even children as young as Pre-K can set goals since they may want to learn to tie their shoelaces, ride a bike, learn to write their name, etc.

Figure 9.3: A Continuum of Goal Setting Behaviors

GOAL SETTING

Description

EMERGING	DEVELOPING	ADVANCING	SUSTAINING
Teacher supports students in setting their own simple learning goal. • Do I provide opportunities for my students to set their own learning goal with my support, as needed?	*Students begin to set their own learning goals.* • Do I provide opportunities for my students to set their own learning goals, with little to no support from me?	*Students consistently set, track, and evaluate their own learning goals. Students continuously reflect on their own data and academic performance to boost growth.* • Do my students consistently monitor their progress to their learning goals? • Do I provide opportunities for my students to reflect on their performance or data?	*Students consistently set, track, and evaluate their own learning goals; student goals direct student activities. Teacher meets with students on a frequent basis to provide mentorship and support.* • Do I align student goals to classroom learning activities? • Do I frequently meet with my students in either a small group or 1:1 setting to provide guidance toward their goals?

Teacher Action Steps

EMERGING	DEVELOPING	ADVANCING	SUSTAINING
• Reflect on 3-5 opportunities for students to set goals within a week that can either be academic based or behavior based. • Provide a goal-setting sheet to students (monthly or weekly).	• Teach a mini-lesson on SMART goals • Identify major areas for student feedback around goal setting. • Provide students opportunities to set both behavioral and academic goals. • Provide whole or small-group feedback to students on their goal setting.	• Use an individual tracker sheet for each student • Provide weekly time for students to fill in tracker sheet • Provide reflection sheets for exit slips 1-2 times per week • Increase the frequency of giving student reflection slips to 3-4 times per week. • Provide daily time for students to fill in tracker sheet. • Provide students with choice of learning activities in order to meet their goals.	• Provide time at the end of opening framing for students to set a learning activity goal • Group students based on similar goals • Make a plan to meet with students at least once weekly in small group setting • Plan to conference with students individually 1-2 times/month • Allow students to create for themselves the learning activities that will best meet their goals.

REFLECTION

Description

EMERGING	DEVELOPING	ADVANCING	SUSTAINING
Teacher provides students with foundational knowledge on the process of reflection.	*Students use a tracker to monitor their own data and use simple means to reflect on their learning*	*Students monitor their own data and reflect on their learning in a variety of ways (journal, blog, share with a partner, etc.)*	*Teacher monitors student reflections on their learning and meets with students on a frequent basis to provide mentorship and support. Teacher works with students to reflect on their progress over time*
• Do I explicitly teach my students how to reflect on their learning?	• Do I provide a tracker for my students to use to monitor their own data and reflect on their learning?	• Do I provide opportunities for my students to monitor their own data in a variety of ways? • Do I provide opportunities for my students to reflect on their learning in a variety of ways?	• Do I frequently meet with students to review their reflections and provide support? • Do I work with students to reflect on their progress over time?

Teacher Action Steps

• Plan a mini-lesson on reflection • Provide opportunities for students to practice reflection as a do now or exit slip • Increase the number of opportunities for students to practice reflection. • Utilize a common tracker across grade level and subjects • Model quick and easy feedback (smiley faces)	• Provide an individual tracker or reflection tool for each student (notebook, digital reflection, etc...) • Provide weekly time for students to fill in tracker sheet • Provide reflection time 1-2x per week for students • Incorporate partner/peer feedback • Increase the opportunities for students to reflect and track progress	• Introduce an additional tool to monitor data aside from tracker sheet (anonymized data wall, Google spreadsheet, Reflection Journal) • Give students an additional reflection tool (reflect on behavior, reflect on participation, etc.) • Increase the different tools and ways for students to interact with reflection and data analysis • Increase the frequency of reviewing benchmark data against bigger goals.	• Provide students with tool to connect reflections to progress • Teach students how to lead their own conference conversation • Make a plan to meet with students at least 1x weekly in small group setting to discuss reflections • Plan to meet with students individually to discuss reflections (1-2x/month) • Adequate time "uninterrupted time" to reflect on data w/students

OWNERSHIP

Description

EMERGING	DEVELOPING	ADVANCING	SUSTAINING
Teacher provides students with some form of choice with the content. • Do I allow my students to have some choice in content?	*Teacher provides students with choice in the process- prioritization of tasks or path to complete assignments* • Do I provide my students with opportunities to select which learning task they complete? • Do I provide my students with opportunities to choose the order they complete assignments?	*Teacher provides students with more authentic and autonomous choices with the content and process* • Do I provide my students with opportunities to initiate learning tasks? • Are students able to work through the learning assignments autonomously with little teacher direction?	*Teacher allows authentic and autonomous choice with the content, process and product* • Do give students opportunities to make authentic choices on content, process and product?

Teacher Action Steps

EMERGING	DEVELOPING	ADVANCING	SUSTAINING
• Provide students with 2-3 choice activities aligned to objective for the day (1 weekly) • Increase the number of choice activities or the number of days where students have choice.	• Plan a playlist of learning tasks with a "May Do" side where students select a learning task of their choice • Provide a playlist of activities and allow student choice over order of completion • Increase the frequency or the number opportunities to select learning tasks in a week. • Provide opportunities for students to talk through expectations (rubric use, instructions, standards/skills, outcomes, etc.) of choice board	• Provide independent work stations that allow students to make choices over content, process or product at their appropriate level • Provide a set amount of time each week to allow students opportunities to select what they'd like to work on • Design student-teacher debrief sessions to do "temp checks" for monitoring student progress	• Provide daily opportunities for students to choose to work individually or collaboratively • Provide daily opportunities for students to select a topic of interest they would like to research • Provide frequent opportunities for students to choose a project they'd like to work on

Strategy 44: Standards-Based Grading

Though standards-based grading is not new, it is more commonly used at the elementary level for report cards. This is why I was so excited when I attended a New York State Association for Computers and Technology in Education (NYSCATE) Conference in November 2019, and heard Angela Messenger and Nicole Mucica share how they use standards-based grading in their ninth grade algebra classes in the East Irondequoit Central School District. Along with their colleague, Jessica Colavecchia, these three teachers have developed an impressive approach to teaching and learning that helps students focus on what they are learning rather than what grade they have scored. Everything in this strategy comes from their amazing work.

"What can I do for extra credit?" "Can I have all my missing assignments?" "I'll take the zero." Sound familiar? Without meaning to, schools have created a system where students are more focused on their grades rather than the learning. At the end of the marking period, many students find themselves frantically trying to make up any work they had missed or even do extra work to try get their grades up. Unfortunately, the effort students were putting into their work was focused on getting enough problems correct to boost their grade to a magical number that they had predetermined was satisfactory for the course. The structure of schooling had inadvertently taught students that the grade was more important than the content and the learning standards. In order to engage students, it is important for students to take ownership of their learning. Using a standards-based grading model is one way to create a student-centric classroom.

What Does a Standards-Based Grading Classroom Look Like?

Standards-based grading shifts the focus from the grade to the learning. Traditionally, many teachers focus on direct instruction of a specific skill or new content. After direct instruction, students move on to practice the newly taught skill during class or at home. The next class period, the instruction shifts to the next skill. This cycle continues for the duration of the unit, and then at the end of the unit, students take a unit exam.

After the exam, many educators spend their due diligence looking at the results to determine what skills students still need to practice. Time is set at the end of the year for review of these topics. Prior to the test, most teachers can make a prediction about which skills their students need to work on more. Even with best efforts, the pacing chart is still what drives many educator's teaching practices. In these situations, teaching is teacher-centered rather than student-centered.

One method of shifting the focus to student–centered learning is to use a standards-based grading framework. By using this cycle (see Figure 9.4), they are still ensuring that they teach skills, but the timeline is not as rigid, and students have multiple opportunities to show growth and re-assess their learning.

Figure 9.4: The Standards-Based Grading Cycle

In this model, the new skill is briefly introduced through some form of direct instruction. After this brief introduction, students take a pre-assessment to determine their current levels of understanding. Students are scored based on 1-4 rubric (see Figure 9.5), a rubric modified from *Rethinking Grading: Meaningful Assessments for Standards Based Learning* by Cathy Votterot.

Figure 9.5: Standards-Based Grading Rubric

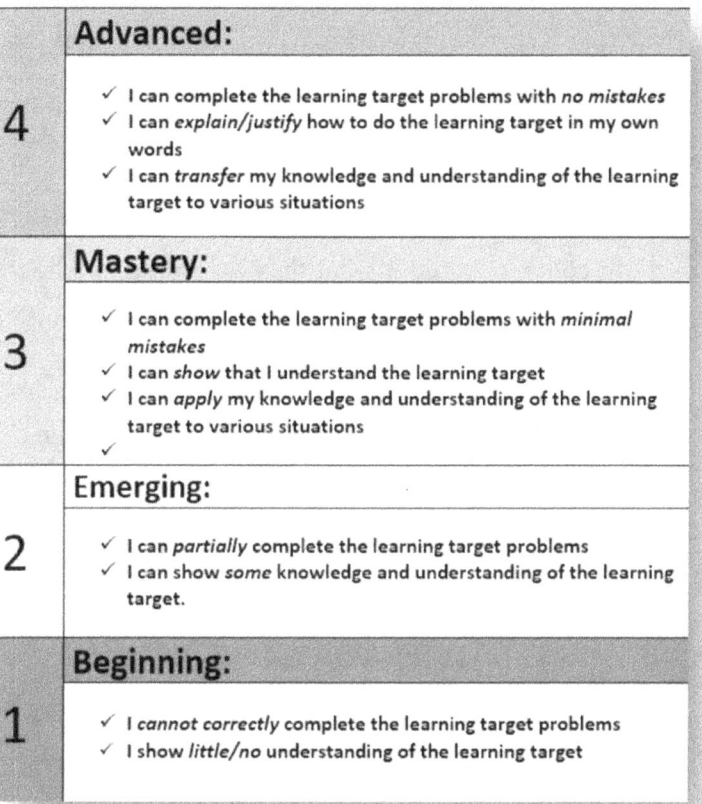

Based on the results of this pre-assessment, students receive leveled practice that allows opportunities for student choice. This could include leveled worksheets with varying levels of scaffolding, creation of a product based on the understanding of the learning target, and/or use of digital resources with direct and immediate feedback to students. Figure 9.6 shows a digital board with two to four choices in each colored square. Students are assigned a color based on the results of their pre-assessment and then can choose which activities to complete on the board. They

Figure 9.6: Example of a Digital Choice Board

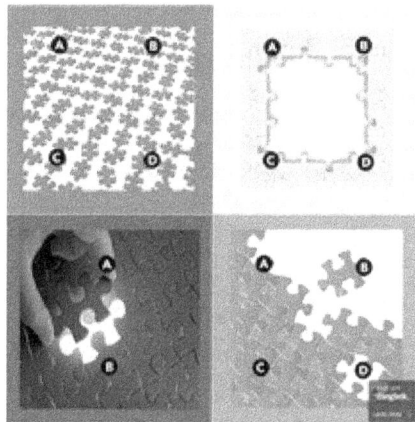

can see the activity by holding their cursor over the letter in the square.

A key feature of this type of classroom routine is continuous feedback. Each time a student completes practice of the specified learning target, the teacher provides feedback, *not a grade*. Teachers may write what the student did well, what needs to be fixed and suggestions for improvement. Based on this feedback, the student can try another practice exercise in the same level of the rubric or may choose to adjust and pick an activity in a different level of the rubric. This shows the students that the teacher is more concerned about what they are doing and how they are doing it, rather than always giving a task to assign a grade for the gradebook.

After students have had an opportunity to practice at their current level of understanding, students would have the opportunity to re-assess. The new score on the re-assessment would replace the previous score. Employing a system of replacement grading shows students that they have continuous opportunities to learn and demonstrate their current level of understanding.

> **Employing a system of replacement grading shows students that they have continuous opportunities to learn and demonstrate their current level of understanding.**

In this system, it is imperative for students to track their own learning. Instead of using traditional review packets, students design their own review. When it is time to review for the unit test, students use their tracking sheets to determine what skills they should spend more time reviewing (see Figure 9.7). The review is designed to provide student choices of what material to review and how to review the material. For example, if the unit has eight learning targets, the teacher can have a list of two to three opportunities to practice each learning target. Some of these can even be recycled from learning opportunities that were used previously in the unit. Students are able to look at their tracking sheets, and determine the learning targets they had the lowest score on and then choose the review activities listed under that learning target.

Figure 9.7: Tracking Sheet Example

Unit 3C Learning Target Reflection & Score Tracker

LT1: **I can solve a multi-step equation algebraically using the properties of real numbers**	**Prior Knowledge**		
	Understanding of Targets (After Lesson):		
	Understanding of Target (At Uniest Time)		
1st Score:	**2nd Score:**	**3rd Score:**	**Unit Test Score:**

Physical Structure of the Classroom

In order to make this work in a classroom, learning targets must be clearly visible and displayed in the classroom. The learning targets should be printed on class notes, worksheets, and assessments. Students need to begin to "own" the learning target so that each time they complete an activity, purpose of the assignment and what they should be able to do after they complete that assignment are explicit and understood.

The classroom should be set up in groups rather than traditional rows. This allows students to work cooperatively with one another, and also shows the students that the classroom is a collaborative environment. Grouping of students may change based on the day. Students should not become comfortable sitting in the same seat each day because they may need to work in different groups.

Some days the teacher may chose to use homogeneous groups where the students are working with other students who currently have the same level of understanding of the learning target. In this set up, the teacher reviews the students' assessments from the previous class and comes up with the groups before class. When the students walk into the room, the teacher would assign them groups. This would avoid having to make an announcement such as "everyone who scored a 1 can sit in this group." In addition, since the work is fluid, the groups would change regularly. Therefore, students only know what score the other students in their group received and not everyone in the class. Students can choose to work together on the same activities and when the teacher works with each group, the teacher can provide mini-lessons to the entire group that focus on the skills students in that group all need to work on.

Other times the teacher may choose to use heterogeneous groups and have students with mixed levels of understanding of the learning target working together. Students can rely on peer support before calling the teacher over for help.

In both scenarios, the teacher moves freely through the room working with groups of students and is not always seen at the front of the classroom. Switching the groups regularly and for each learning target also avoids the stigma students may have for being in the "low" group. Since the groups change regularly and fluidly, students are never labeled as always being in one group.

In this type of learning environment, there is constant movement and it can best be described as "organized chaos." Students may need to move around the room to check answer keys or get materials for various activities. The teacher is also moving from group to group. The classroom may be louder than the traditional classroom because students are talking to one another rather than working independently on each task. However, the benefit of this environment is students feel comfortable in the classroom, are free to ask questions, and most importantly are engaged in the learning.

Example of Process: Graphing Quadratic Functions

The following will walk through an example of a standards-based lesson for graphing quadratic functions. Figure 9.8 displays the process.

Figure 9.8: Standards-Based Lesson Example

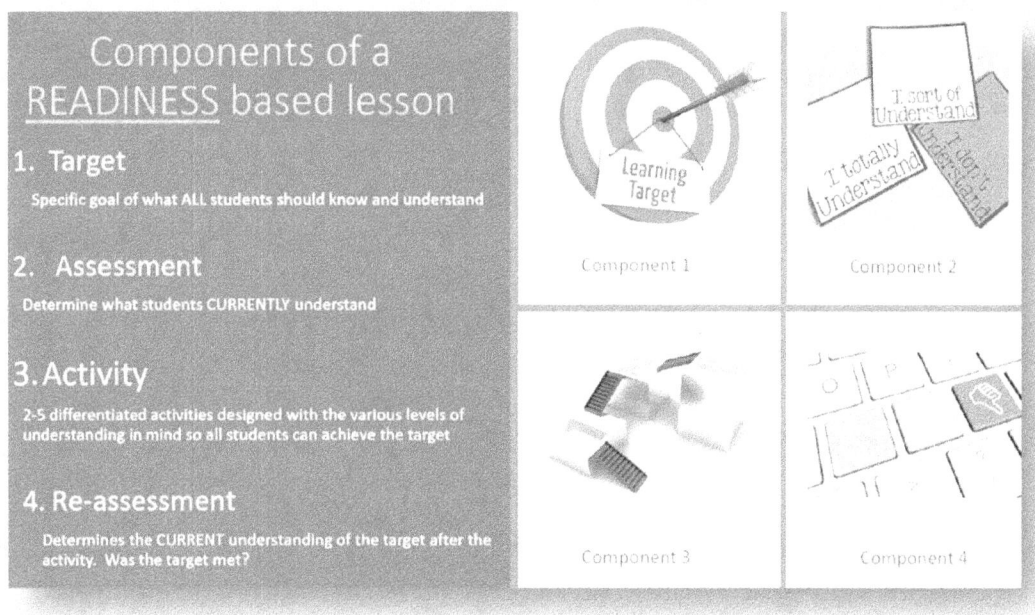

1. **Learning Targets**. This process always begins with a learning target. For this classroom design to work, educators must take some time to take the standards that are aligned with the course and create "I can" statements, which re-write the standards in student-friendly language so the student takes ownership of the learning. For example, "Standard: HSF-IF.C.7 - Graph function expressed symbolically and show key features of the graph, by hand in simple cases and using technology for more complicated cases: a. Graph linear and quadratic functions and show intercepts, maxima, and minima" becomes the I Can Statement, "Learning Target: I can graph a quadratic function." The teacher is aware of the standards that needs to be taught but all printed material and classroom displays will have the learning target rather than the standards.

2. **Teach**. The next step is to pre-teach the material. Pre-assessments are important, but depending on the subject and course, students may have no prior knowledge of the material and therefore the pre-assessment is a waste of time without a brief introduction to the material. The teacher should spend no longer than ten to fifteen minutes to briefly introduce the learning target. This may be through direct instruction of notes, a discussion board where all students respond and then the teacher leads the conversation, a video, or any other type of teaching material the teacher may found useful for this topic. For this example, guided notes were used to introduce the topic as shown in Figure 9.9.

Figure 9.9: Guided Notes Example

NB-U6-1-L1: Graphing Quadratic Functions

LT3: I can graph a quadratic function

Given the polynomial function $f(x) = x^2 - 5x - 3$...

    a. State the DEGREE →   b. What **shape** does this function make?

    c. What specific name can we give this function?

Buttons to press to graph quadratic functions:

1) Press [Y=] and type the function in (use [X,T,Θ,n] for the variable)

2) Use [x^2] to make an exponent of 2

   (**Pressing this ONLY does the exponent of 2...NOT the variable!!!!)

3) Press [2nd] [GRAPH] (table f5) to view the table of points

---

1) Graph the quadratic function $f(x) = -x^2 - 2x + 8$

    Does this *parabola* open upward or downward?

2) Graph the quadratic function $f(x) = x^2 + 2x - 3$

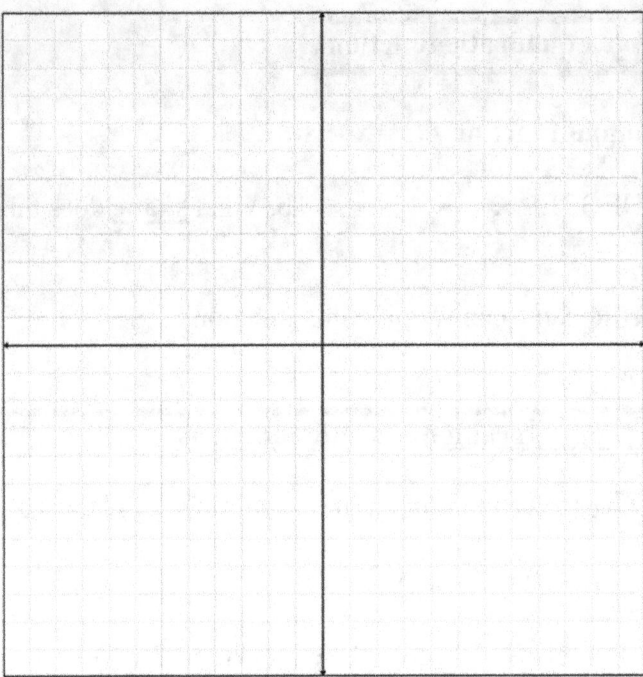

Does this *parabola* open upward or downward?

What "shape" does a QUADRATIC function graph?

What makes the graph of a quadratic function...
- Open **UPWARD:**

- Open **DOWNWARD:**

3. **Pre-Assessment**. After the introduction to the topic, the students will be pre-assessed on the material (see Figure 9.10). This should only include one to two thoughtful questions that would allow for showing full understanding of the learning target. Students will receive a score of 1-4 based on the rubric. The purpose of the pre-assessment is so that the teacher can then provide students with appropriate leveled work, either remediation or enrichment. This builds student confidence because they know they will receive work that is tailored to them, and therefore they will be more engaged in the material. While it might seem obvious, it logically follows that a teacher is not going to require the same out of students who are at a level 1 versus students who are at a level 4; the purpose of this pre-assessment is to know what students need for their instruction and so there is an expectation that the instruction will need to be different.

Figure 9.10 Pre-Assessment Example

PA-U5-LTI & LT2 Pre-Assessment

LT1: I can graph a quadratic function
LT2: I can label and state the key features of a quadratic function

1. On the set of axes below, graph the following quadratic function
$$f(x) = -x^2 - 4x + 12$$

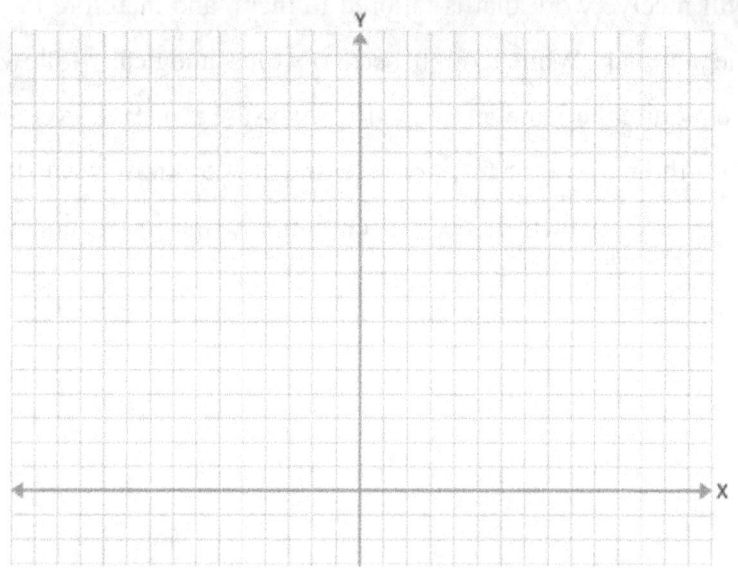

a) Label and state the vertex of the function.

b) State whether the vertex represents a maximum or a minimum point for the function. Explain your answer.

c) What is the equation of the axis of symmetry?

d) Label and state the zeros of the function.

U5-LT1 Score:	U5-LT2 Score:

4. **Remediation/Enrichment**. When students are ready to begin practicing, teachers may need to regroup students based on readiness. In some cases, the teacher may allow the students to choose their seats and work independently or with other students, and other cases the teacher may chose to create mixed ability groups. The key is flexible seating and modifying the classroom environment based on the learning at hand. Another key component of the remediation/enrichment part of the cycle is differentiation. Activities are differentiated by readiness based on the pre-assessment, but then students also have choices of activities that are differentiated by learning style and interest.

One way to make the creation and distribution of materials easier is to use technology whenever possible. Technology provides autonomy and immediate feedback. The teacher can pre-create answer keys that students can access online through QR codes or learning management systems. Some programs and software also provide built in feedback so the students can receive immediate feedback even when the teacher is not available. The teachers who created this standards-based approach, Angela, Nicole, and Jessica, like to use https://www.thinglink.com/ to create interactive, technology-integrated methods for students to work through. This approach allows students to learn at their own pace and with work that matches their individual needs as shown in Figure 9.11, where there are four different pathways to achieve the learning depending on each student's readiness level.

Figure 9.11: A ThinkLink.com Example

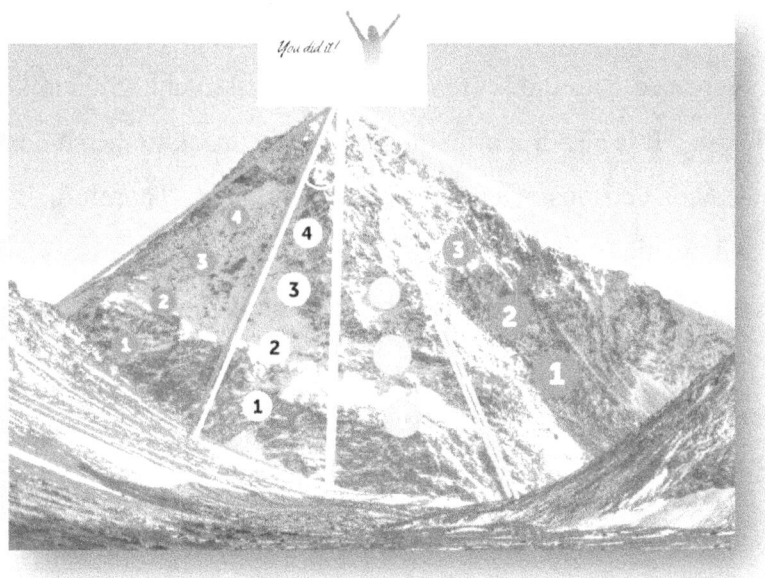

When used in this way, technology allows for teachers to be free to work with small groups or individual students who are in need to support while also allowing other students who do not need support to have meaningful and challenging work to complete.

For this example, the students are grouped based on readiness. Each group is assigned a different color on the mountain, and the students choose activities to complete that are found in the color they are assigned. For the students who need the most support, the activities are scaffolded so they can start at the bottom and work their way up. Students who may not need as much support can choose the activities in their section of the mountain and complete them in the order they want to. Students who find they are struggling or excelling in their section of the mountain, can easily move up or down to another color without drawing attention to themselves because everyone is working on the same digital board. There are also many choices for students to complete, so this avoids students saying "I'm done" or "I'm bored. There is nothing to do." Students always have work to do and classroom management is easier because behavior issues that result from students finishing work too early are minimized.

This link will take you to a live ThinkLink example from Angela, Nicole, and Jessica.
https://cutt.ly/SBG

5. **Assessment**. After students have had an opportunity to practice, they are given an opportunity to take another assessment. The score the students received on the pre-assessment is replaced with the score on the new assessment. Students are scored on the same 1-4 scale. It is also important to provide feedback to the student. It is a good idea to have a couple versions of a re-assessment available. Therefore, if students want to go back and practice more, they can do that and then re-assess when they are ready. Students realize they always have an opportunity for growth and the learning never ends.

In Figure 9.12, the assessment was designed to re-assess on four different but related learning targets at once. This helps the students see how all of the learning

Grading Strategies 241

targets are tied together. Notice the boxes on the top right of the example. The scores in these boxes are important because they show the students that they will continue to have practice until they have mastered the standards and know which standards they are mastering.

Figure 9.12: Standards-Based Grading Assessment Example

Unit 5 – LT 1-4 Assessment	US-LT1 Score	US-LT1 Score	US-LT1 Score	US-LT1 Score

Name: _____   Class Color: _____

LT1: I can graph a quadratic function.
LT2: I can label and state the key features of a quadratic function.
LT3: I can calculate the average rate of change for a quadratic function.
LT4: I can apply the key features of a quadratic functions to real world scenarios.

1) a. **LT1:** On the set of axes below, draw the graph of $y=x^2 - 4x - 1$

TABLE OF VALUES

b. **LT2:** State the *coordinates* of the *vertex*

c. **LT2:** State the *equation* of the axis of symmetry.

2) **LT2:** The zeros of the function $f(x)=x^2 - 5x - 6$ are

(1) -1 and 6   (2) 1 and -6   (3) 2 and -3   (4) -2 and 3

3) **LT2:** In the function $f(x)= -(x-2)^2 + 4$, the minimum value occurs where x is

(1) -2   (2) 2   (3) -4   (4) 4
(5)

4) The height of a rocket, at selected times, is shown in the table below.

Time (sec)	0	1	2	3	4	5	6	7
Height (ft)	180	260	308	324	308	260	180	68

   a) **LT4:** Based on this data, what was the height, the rocket was launched from?

   b) **LT4:** Based on this data, at what time did the rocket reach its maximum height?

   c) **LT3:** What is the average speed of the rocket from 2 second to 6 seconds? Be sure to include units.

5) The height, H, in feet, of an object dropped from the top of a building after t seconds is given by
$H(t) = -16t^2 + 144$.

   a) **LT4:** How many seconds does it take for the object to reach the ground? Explain how you arrived at your answer.

   b) **LT4:** How many feet did the object fall between one and two seconds after it was dropped? Justify your answer.

   c) **LT3:** What is the average rate of change for the object between 1 and 3 seconds?

6. **Review/Reflection**. A final piece of this cycle is review and reflection. At the end of the unit, students should have an opportunity to review all the learning targets in the unit and reflect on the skills they did well on and those needing additional practice.

Figure 9.13 shows a Padlet where students determine what areas they need to review the most and complete the review that is designed for those skills first. Then, they can move on to other skills.

Figure 9.13: Review/Reflection Padlet Example

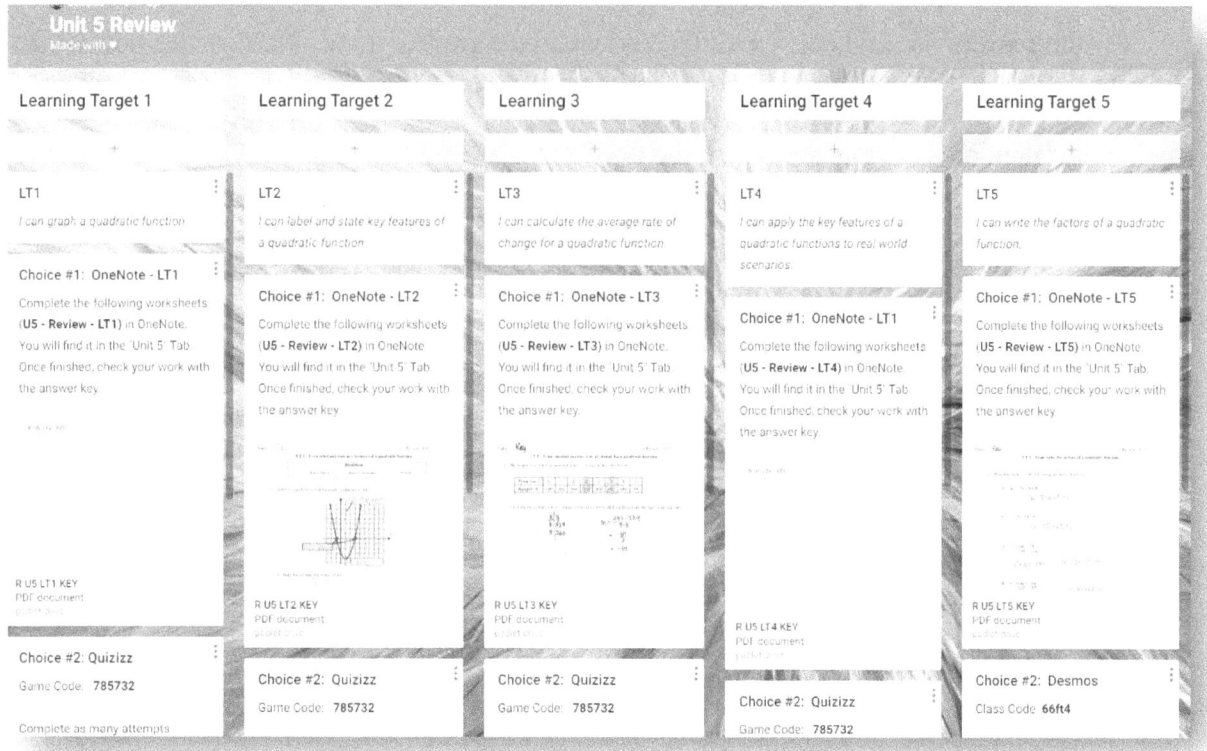

The key to making standards-based grading successful and increasing engagement is that none of this work is graded. Instead, the teacher or the digital tools provide regular feedback to the students. The only "grades" that students receive are on the one-to-four rubric so students can regularly see their growth of understanding of learning targets.

Many schools still require averages on report cards and progress reports, so teachers may need to find creative ways to move their rubric scores to a traditional grade format. However, if the work is done in the classroom, students will quickly become more focused on learning and less focused on that final grade, which in turn increases student engagement.

Strategy 45: Withholding Scores

Though I am an administrator by day, I have had the wonderful opportunity to teach part-time. One of the best changes I have made to how I grade from my early years as a teacher in the classroom until now is that I used to give my students their grades on their papers when I gave the papers back. I do not do that anymore. Here's the reason why: when I gave the students their grades, it wouldn't matter how much feedback I gave them about what they did and where they succeeded and how to work through areas that demonstrate the need for growth. The grade was what mattered to them and the feedback was lost.

The question about how to time feedback with grades is not new. Jeffery Schinski and Kimberly Tanner's 2014 article, "Teaching More by Grading Less (or Differently)" cites the work of Butler and Nisan from 1986. In their work, Butler and Nisan compared the impacts of evaluative feedback, descriptive feedback, and no feedback on student achievement in problem-solving tasks and in "quantitative" tasks (e.g., those requiring quick, timed work to produce a large number of answers). They found that students receiving descriptive feedback (but *not* grades) on an initial assignment performed significantly better on follow-up quantitative tasks and problem-solving tasks than did students receiving grades or students receiving no feedback. Students receiving grades performed better on follow-up quantitative tasks than students receiving no feedback, but did not outperform those students on problem-solving assignments. In other words, providing evaluative feedback (in this case, grades) after a task does not appear to enhance students' future performance in problem solving.[78]

I did not need to read this to know that it was true because I saw it play out repeatedly in my classroom when I was a classroom teacher. What's more, the same thing happens when I provide teachers with their observation feedback and scores; the focus is on the scores.

Susan Brookhart, author of *How to Give Effective Feedback to Your Students*, wrote, "the grade 'trumps' the comment; the student will read a comment that the teacher intended to be descriptive as an explanation of the grade. Descriptive comments have the best chance of being *read* as descriptive if they are not accompanied by a grade"[79] (emphasis in original). I agree. This is why when I have feedback to give, I will not give the grade until the student comments on my feedback. There is no doubt that this is more time-consuming for me because I have to write down the grade somewhere so I don't forget it before I give it to the student. It also means that I have to wait for the student to respond to my feedback. However, the work that the students completed was undoubtedly better as a result of this process. It wasn't that I just withheld the grade, but I had the students explain what grade they thought the work they submitted earned and why. This metacognitive task forced the students to really think about their work in comparison to the directions for the task. It also forced me to explain the expectations for the task. This was especially powerful given that there was a repeating task of writing reflections on the assigned readings.

Though it is likely not possible to do this for every task every day, withholding grades is a very powerful way to shift attention to what you want the students to focus on: the feedback.

Alternative Use: Prior to post-observation conferences, I ask teachers to self-evaluate and share the scores they have identified for the observed lesson. I compare the teacher's self-assessment to the scores I identified based on the lesson. I then provide the teacher with a copy of the rubric where I highlight the components (along the far left) where the teacher and I differed by more than one point. For example, if the teacher scored a component at a level 4 and I scored it at a 2, I would highlight that score. When we met for the post-observation conference, I would ask the teacher to share the evidence that they used to determine the score. This process helped me to better understand the teacher's work and helped the teacher to better understand the rubric.

Chapter Summary

This chapter was about moving someone from the point of interest to absorption by altering practices related to grading. The problem with traditional grading practices is that they focus on the grade as the outcome rather than the learning. When we focus on the learning and not the grades, students not only learn more and do better, but they enjoy the process of learning in ways that are healthy and productive. Students who are focused on the learning are not given identical assignments, have options about what assignments they do have, and do not copy their friends' answers because that would not foster their learning. Furthermore, teachers who are focused on the learning do not take off points when assignments are late or give extra credit for tasks unrelated to the knowledge of the content since the grade the student earned should reflect the knowledge the student has about the content. Learning allows students to get feedback during the learning process and a score later when the students are ready for the application of the learning. This is parallel to athletes when they practice versus when they have a game.

**Looking for even more strategies to
IMPROVE LEARNING VIA GRADING?
Please visit my website, www.LyonsLetters.com/learnmore, for print and digital recommendations including books, websites, videos, and more!**

Thank you again to Dana Britt for contributing Goals and to Jessica Colavecchia, Angela Messenger, and Nicole Mucica for contributing Standards-Based Grading—two strategies included in this chapter.

Reflection Prompts

1. How do grades undermine student learning?

   _____
   _____
   _____

2. What is one way you can improve either student feedback or student goal setting?

   _____
   _____
   _____

3. Write about a time when you were a student and the negative impact that grade had on your engagement OR a time when you were a student and goals or feedback (not grades) has a positive impact on your engagement.

   _____
   _____
   _____

4. Name one thing you could do tomorrow based on what you learned from this chapter.

   _____
   _____
   _____

5. Tweet me @LyonsLetters to share an idea for a future reading or digital resource I should share on www.lyonsletters.com that would help someone who is interested become absorbed.

Persistent Questions

1. What have you done so far regarding the three challenge questions from Chapter 1?

    a. **Three:** Find at least three people with whom to share your learning.

    b. **Two:** Find at least two ideas that change you.

    c. **One:** Apply at least one idea from your reading.

    _____
    _____
    _____

2. What have you learned so far, and how will you use it?

    _____
    _____
    _____

Chapter 10

Exposure Strategies

"Experience is the teacher of all things."
~Julius Caesar

Recognizing Your Thinking Before You Read...

1. Think of a hobby you had when you were a student. How did you learn about that hobby?

   _____
   _____
   _____

2. Why is it important for students to have access to extra-curricular experiences?

   _____
   _____
   _____

3. What do you *pay* to do in your spare time? What makes those tasks enjoyable?

   _____
   _____
   _____

I Want To Be Like Mike

Do you know what Michael Jordan said as he left the arena after winning his sixth NBA Championship in 1998? Before I tell you, remember that Michael Jordan loves basketball. If you watched the 2020 docuseries, *The Last Dance*, you would have learned that Jordan was someone who was compelled to be the best at basketball. He's the first one to arrive and last player to leave practice. He will continue playing until he wins. He will trash talk and taunt players on the other team and his own teammates if he thinks that they are not doing their best. He retired from basketball and came back to win three additional championships and would have continued with the Bulls if management would have renewed coach Phil Jackson's contract. Yet, after winning his sixth championship in eight years, Jordan said this as he was getting onto the bus, "It's still daylight. We might be able to get some golf swings in."[80] Sure, Jordan was engaged in basketball, but he wasn't looking to play more basketball at the end of the day—he wanted to play golf.

What's going on here? If we're lucky, we get paid to do something that we're engaged in. However, if we're lucky, we also have enough money to pay to do things we cannot get paid to do. The tasks we pay to do are those that we are absorbed in. Jordan got paid to play basketball and he paid to play golf.

Who Am I

As I wrote about in *Engagement is Not a Unicorn (It's a Narwhal)* and pointed out at the beginning of Chapter 6, there are at least three manifestations of absorption: (1) novice, (2) enthusiast, and (3) addict. Obviously, I am not going to share strategies about how to become an addict. This chapter focuses on how to create experiences for students that give them an introduction into tasks that they might not otherwise be exposed. This is really important since most of the tasks that we try on are ones that only take us as far as being a novice but not enthusiast.

The rejection of possible absorption tasks is actually a perfectly healthy and important behavior. After all, it would be very unhealthy if people continued to do things they did not like doing in their free time. As well, learning what you do not enjoy is just as important as it is to learn what you do enjoy. In other words, just like in your dating life where it is important to kiss a lot of frogs before your find your "prince(ss)," it is critical to try on a lot of different tasks before you find your true loves.[81]

It's also possible that something we once were enthusiastic about we can outgrow. When you were a child, you may have wanted to be a superhero. You may have had a closet of costumes to choose from, asked for comic books for your birthday, and had a Superman backpack or lunchbox that you loved. As we grow, the things that we love to do change.

Who Do I Want to Be

The strategies in this chapter are designed to expose students to experiences and tasks that they may not have the chance to explore on their own. They may also be opportunities that can take students outside of the class and into a non-academic setting. After all, schools are more than just places to learn about others; they are places to learn about yourself. While it is wonderful when academic content offers that chance, schools should also offer options outside of the classroom for students to become absorbed. Schools can be places where we find our "people"—those who make us feel like we belong. We can become actors, athletes, or debaters. We can learn that we are journalists, artists, or musicians. These titles may be titles that we want to pursue for our careers, but they don't have to be; we also need to find titles that describe who we are when we are not working.

Now What

The next three strategies are ones that will provide opportunities for students to explore new tasks. As well, they may be a chance for the students to dive deeper into tasks they already know about and enjoy. These are likely the tasks that students will decide they want to pay to do now or later in life.

46. Field Trips
47. Clubs
48. Internships

Strategy 46: Field Trips

The value of field trips cannot be underestimated. A 2011 large scale, randomized control study on the educational value of field trips found that field trips have a statistically significant impact on students. This research studied almost 11,000 kindergarten through twelfth grade students from 123 schools who visited the newly opened Crystal Bridges Museum of American Art in Northwest Arkansas. The students "received a one-hour tour of the museum in which they typically viewed and discussed five paintings. Some students were free to roam the museum following the tour, but the entire experience usually involved less than half a day."[82] The results of this experiment were clear. As shown in Figure 10.1, all students benefited from the field trip but rural and high-poverty students benefited the most.

Figure 10.1: Impact of a Day at the Museum[83]

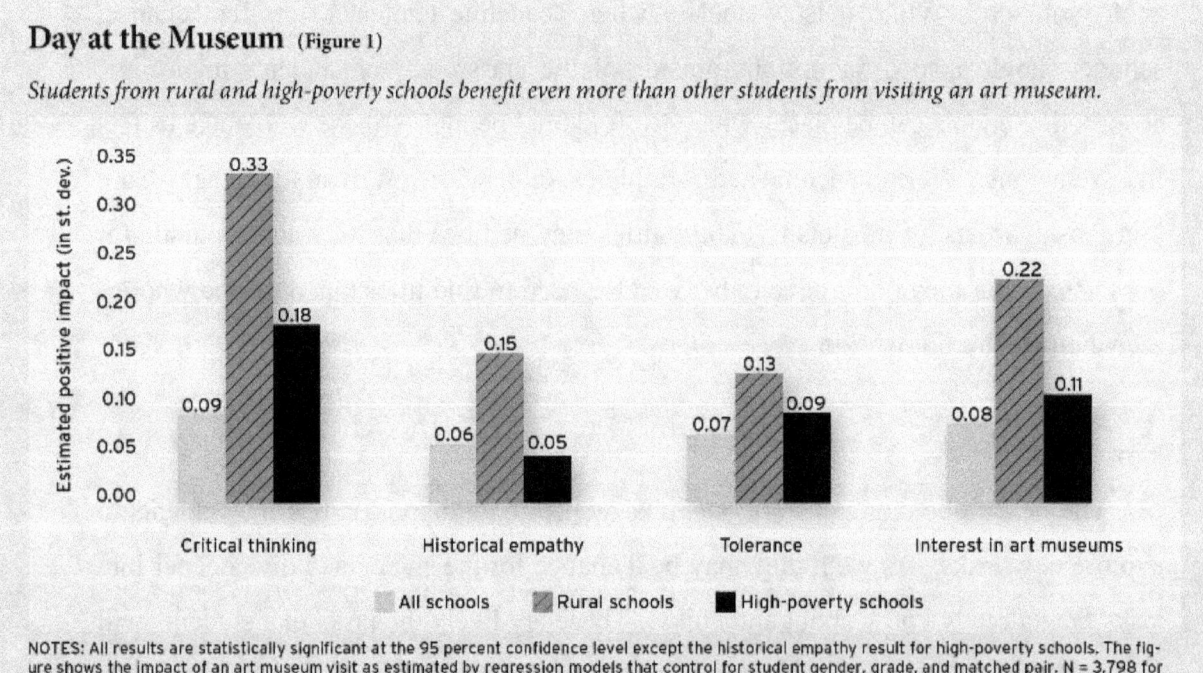

Empirically, field trips have benefits too. Steve Berer from musexplore.net, highlights a list of eight of these.[84]

1. Students are energized by the excitement and anticipation of leaving the school environment.
2. The transportation to and from the museum/site is often a pleasant open-social time.
3. Students have the opportunity to see new things and learn about them in a more unstructured way.
4. Students have the opportunity to determine what they learn and how they learn it. Said differently, student learning can be interest-driven, not teacher and curriculum driven.
5. Students will experience a more holistic, integrated picture of the information that, in the classroom, may have only been presented in a textual and abstract way.
6. Museums and many other kinds of field trips are multimedia experiences; therefore, learning is enriched and reinforced with superimposing sensory and intellectual inputs.
7. Most museums are designed to stimulate curiosity and actively engage the visitor, so you have a very professional partner working with you to help your students learn.
8. In some museums you can arrange for your class to meet with a museum educator, often in a private classroom, to facilitate directed learning and/or provide a question-answer session.

What's more, students almost always love field trips because the learning becomes experiential (not to mention the benefit of a change in their routines). Unfortunately, live field trips are expensive—between the price of admission to the location to the busses, etc. As well, there are many places that are impossible for people to visit directly, but even more so when talking about younger students. Perhaps, when taking a German language course in high school, students might visit Germany, but fourth grade students reading *Number the Stars*, Lois Lowry's book about the Holocaust, will not go to visit Denmark. In fact, unless those students live around Washington, D.C., they probably wouldn't even be able to visit the United States Holocaust Memorial

Museum. Then there are trips that are literally impossible with traditional means. For example, though there theme parks (like Colonial Williamsburg) or reenactment sites, no students are ever going to go into space when studying the solar system or travel through time when learning about something historical. This is the true advantage of virtual field trips (VFTs).

Since live field trips are not new and I dare say all of us have gone on one as a student and/or a teacher, I will simply say that they should be a part of any teacher's repertoire who is aiming to achieve student engagement. With regard to VFTs, I'll spend a little more time since these are a more recent addition to a teacher's toolbox.

There are many pre-made VFTs that teachers can choose from, some free, some at a cost. There is also the possibility that teachers can create VFTs by curating different websites to personalize the experience for the students based on the explicit learning in the specific classroom. Scott Mandel notes in "Why Use Virtual Field Trips,"

Access the Common Sense Education list of VFT websites and apps here:
https://cutt.ly/VirtualFTs

> The choice between using a packaged or a personalized field trip is similar to the choices made in the planning of a real-life excursion. For instance, if students go to a museum and are required to take a predetermined tour supplied by that museum, with no alterations or changes based on their classroom curriculum, that would be considered a real-life packaged field trip. However, if the teacher talks to the museum personnel and has the tour tailored to meet the specific curricular goals of the class, that is a personalized field trip.[85]

In short, there are times when a packaged VFT would be appropriate, just like a standard tour for a live field trip would be. Then there are times when you want something more personal.

If you're not sure where to start with VFTs, I strongly recommend reviewing Common Sense Education's list of VFT apps and websites. It is divided into user-friendly categories of (a) Virtual Reality Experiences, (b) On-the-Ground Reporting and Journalism, (c) On-Line Museums, and (d) Other Tools and Resources. As well, for each app or website, they provide a summary, the applicable grades, the cost, a button to read reviews, and a link to the website/app. Equally appealing, most of the apps listed are free.

Strategy 47: Clubs

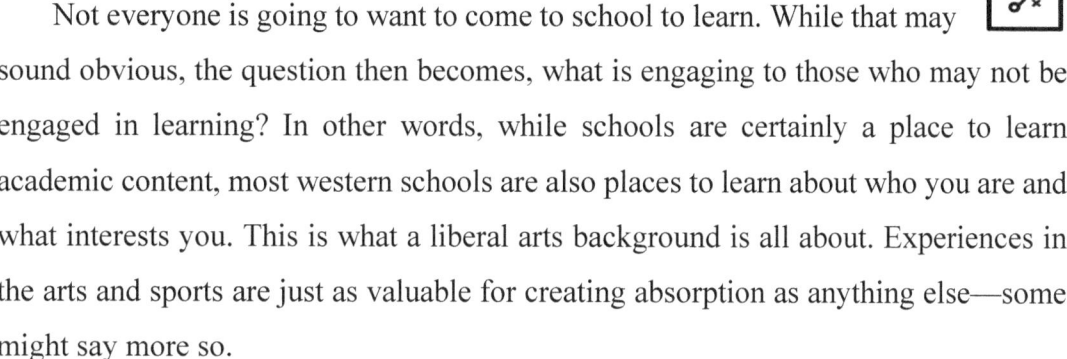

Not everyone is going to want to come to school to learn. While that may sound obvious, the question then becomes, what is engaging to those who may not be engaged in learning? In other words, while schools are certainly a place to learn academic content, most western schools are also places to learn about who you are and what interests you. This is what a liberal arts background is all about. Experiences in the arts and sports are just as valuable for creating absorption as anything else—some might say more so.

Most schools have intramurals, clubs, and extracurricular activities in addition to elective vocal and instrumental learning experiences during the school day. I cannot say enough about how important these experiences are to absorption because they provide opportunities for students to sample a variety of experiences to see what might stick.

For the purposes of this strategy, I am not going to tell you about how to include intramurals, clubs, and extracurricular activities afterschool because this is so common. Instead, I'll tell you about a creative way to do this during the school day. In a K-8 school I worked in, over ninety percent of our students qualified for free or reduced priced lunches, meaning they were considered impoverished according to the federal government's guidelines on socio-economic status. As such, it was not possible for many of these children to participate in activities outside of the school due to the cost of the activity and the inaccessibility of transportation. In line with cliché, if you can't bring Muhammad to the mountain, bring the mountain to Muhammad, we created a thirty minute time in the day when all students participate in clubs.

At the start of the school year, each teacher was asked what club they would like to run. The teachers created the title of the club, the grades the club was for, and a brief description of the club. These ranged from things like a Chess Club to Spanish Club (which would be called the Dora Club if it was targeted for younger students), to an Art Club to a Basketball Club, and there was a Writing Club and a Harry Potter Club. These descriptions were compiled into a Club Catalog that was circulated to students in the first couple of weeks of school. For the youngest students, teachers would review the choices with them, but this could have easily been sent home for the parent to review and make the choices with/for the children. All students indicated their top three choices and then one or two administrators would go through the selections and make the groups. The clubs lasted for one marking period, at which point the process started all over again.

If I were to do this again, I would see if there were any student-run clubs that students might be willing to facilitate with a faculty-member advisor. I would also seek student-recommendations for clubs in addition to teacher-generated clubs. Either way, the point remains that you want to create opportunities for students to engage in experiences that they enjoy. Not only will students benefit from the skills needed to be successful in chess, Spanish, and so forth, they will also gain valuable soft skills around communication, teamwork, and perseverance. Creating these opportunities will draw in students to school even when/if there are other times when the learning is less engaging.

Strategy 48: Internships

In the book *Rest: Why You Get More Done When You Work Less*, author Alex Soojung-Kim Pang shares that the term "follower" is from the idea that students used to literally follow around their teacher as the teacher waxed philosophically. Pang writes, "Walking and thinking have been amiable companions since ancient times. The connection is reflected in the fact that we refer to members of a philosophical school as 'follower.'"[86] In this way, the learning was done not by sitting in desks and taking notes, but by shadowing.

We can all envision medieval apprenticeships where the young, inexperienced person worked alongside the experienced professional in order to acquire the skills of the craft. In the teaching profession, student-teaching is a critical time in which the book-smart, eager pre-service teacher has the opportunity to observe a seasoned teacher who will model how to teach with the goal of allowing the student-teacher to take over.

With regard to American K-12 schools, internships are not common unless students are in specific programs of study including marginalized career-preparation vocational schools or exclusive college-preparation programs found in magnet or charter schools. At the same time, who would not find value in exploring a potential career by having the opportunity to learn from someone who is currently doing that work? This will not only provide important information about the content knowledge needed, but will surely assist students in building their soft skills—something that is important no matter what field they ultimately select.

Adults in elementary schools may want to think about leadership roles for students that are within the school itself. For example, could you have students "intern" with the librarian and learn how to check-in and shelve books? Could you have students "intern" with the person who does the announcements and learn how to write the "copy" and run the process? Could you have students "intern" at dismissal to assist with students who are walkers? There are endless possibilities that are only limited by the students' interests, the adults' imagination, and the willingness of the adults to hand over the wheel.

Middle school is a great time to have students dip their toes into career possibilities outside of the school through career exploration. Teacher, George Haines created "micro-internships [which] are single day, full-emersion [sic] one-on-one experiences with prominent tech companies where the kids would be able to shadow executives and start-up teams in their intimate working environments. They'll get to see everything from product development to the sales process."[87] Of course, not everyone works in an environment that has access to tech companies. That's okay. What do you have access to? If you see the world through a lens of possibility, your students will too. If you can't bring students to a site, how can you replicate the site in the school? What experts can you bring to the students? In the 21st century, consider virtual tours or expert guests. For example, maybe rather than visiting a location that may not be conducive to having students en masse like an engineering laboratory, have the engineers come to the students. The engineers could bring models, photos, etc., and even show videos to students. As well, the engineers could share some questions or challenges they have faced and ask the students to see how they would approach the task.

The possibilities grow exponentially at the high school level. Indeed, there are existing programs like Big Picture (www.bigpicture.org) and NAF (www.naf.org) that provide the structures and expectations around internships. Big Picture, for example, has students attending school three days per week and their internship (during school hours) two days per week. NAF, on the other hand, has students participate in paid summer internships.

The high school itself is always a place to consider for internships. In *Engagement is Not a Unicorn (It's a Narwhal)*, I shared how Burlington High School in Massachusetts has a student-run help desk where students provide tech-support to their peers using the Apple Genius Bar as a model. This is actually a course the students take and so there is a curriculum that is taught by a certified teacher. At the same time, they

> expect students to be self-driven, independent and capable of managing multiple projects, just as they would be if they were in the workplace. We encourage them to take initiative and devise an independent learning path centered on technology. Help desk students do this by developing an individual learning endeavor (ILE), our version of a 20-percent time Genius Hour project.[88]

This is one small but powerful example of how relevant internships can be created within a school.

If you are a school that has no internships at all, then the advice I would give you is to start small. Are there some students who would be a good first-cohort? Can all students create a resume and practice interviewing even if not all students would be able or interested in an internship? What are the small entry points that could lay the foundation for a larger goal? What could you focus on in the short-term? My guess is that if you are the person who is interested in running this, you are absorbed and your passion for this could become contagious.

Chapter Summary

This chapter was about moving someone from the point of interest to absorption by exposure to tasks that are new, ones they already like, or tasks that they might grow to love. These tasks may or may not be academic in nature, and that's not only okay, but important. It is unreasonable to expect that 100 percent of people would be absorbed in 100 percent of what they do; humans are just not wired like that. It is nevertheless important to provide opportunities for others to learn about what they do and do not enjoy. One of the important aspects of school should be for students to learn about what they are studying, obviously, but also for students to learn about themselves. Schools are places where we find not only people who are different than we are, but also people who connect with what we're connected to—those people who are absorbed in the things we are absorbed in even if that takes place outside of a classroom. After all, even those people who we think of as stars of their fields have unrelated hobbies they enjoy in their free time. This is not to say that people do not connect to or get absorbed in learning; it's simply to say that in addition to learning about academics, schools are designed to be places where students can have the chance to learn about themselves and the world in which they live.

Looking for even more strategies to BUILD EXPOSURE?

Please visit my website, www.LyonsLetters.com/learnmore, for print and digital recommendations including books, websites, videos, and more!

Reflection Prompts

1. What is something you learned to love through exposure when you were in school?

   _____
   _____
   _____

2. What are you or your school currently doing to ensure that students have exposure to opportunities that develop or enhance students' knowledge of absorbing tasks?

   _____
   _____
   _____

3. Besides the strategies listed in this chapter, what other ideas do you have to expose students to tasks they could become absorbed in?

   _____
   _____
   _____

4. Name one thing you could do tomorrow based on what you learned from this chapter.

   _____
   _____
   _____

5. Tweet me @LyonsLetters to share an idea for a future reading or digital resource I should share on www.lyonsletters.com that would help someone who is interested become absorbed.

Persistent Questions

1. What have you done so far regarding the three challenge questions from Chapter 1?

    a. **Three:** Find at least three people with whom to share your learning.

    b. **Two:** Find at least two ideas that change you.

    c. **One:** Apply at least one idea from your reading.

    _____
    _____
    _____

2. What have you learned so far, and how will you use it?

    _____
    _____
    _____

Chapter 11

Hook Strategies

"Opportunity may knock only once, but temptation leans on the doorbell."
~Oprah Winfrey

Recognizing Your Thinking Before You Read...

1. How is the presentation of a task linked to the engagement someone might have in doing that task?

   _____
   _____
   _____

2. How do you attract others into tasks that you want them to do?

   _____
   _____
   _____

3. How do you ensure that you are drawing others into the task and not just into being engaged with you?

   _____
   _____
   _____

You Can't Eat Just One

When given the chance to eat one potato chip or none at all, you probably should opt for none at all. In many instances, abstinence is easier than self-control. Food manufacturers know this and design their seasonings to trick your brain into wanting more. For example, in a study on why chips are so contagious that won the IgNobel Prize in 2008, participants were given chips to eat while wearing headphones to change the volume at which the crunching of the chips was perceived. The study found that, "the louder the participants heard the crunch, the more they perceived it as crispier and fresher and, as a result, more desirable. While this addictive cue is subconscious, sound plays a big role in our overall enjoyment of everything we eat."[89] The point here is that our perceptions influence our experiences.

In his book *Blink: The Power of Thinking Without Thinking*, Malcolm Gladwell writes about the power of first impressions. In chapter 5, Gladwell hones in on Louis Cheskin "one of the great figures in twentieth-century marketing."[90] Upon interviewing Cheskin, Gladwell learns of countless marketing manipulations that convince sellers that they are getting something special—or at least something that they want—even though the consumers do not have conscious awareness of what is happening. For example, margarine used to be white and consumers turned their noses up at it. Cheskin staged an experiment disguised as a "luncheon" where the attendees were served butter and yellow-colored margarine to ensure that visually there was no difference between the two options. When rating the food afterwards, everyone "thought the 'butter' was just fine."[91] Then, in side-by-side comparisons of the same margarine—one wrapped in fancy foil with a fancy name and one without either—taste-testers rated the fancy-named and foil-wrapped choice as tasting better. Again, this was the *exact same* margarine with the exception of how it was packaged and presented.

I watch my fair share of cooking shows and cooking competitions. In most of them, the way the food looks, known as the "presentation," is factored into the final score. This is because how food looks influences how it tastes. After all, "we eat with our eyes first."

Whet My Appetite

The cafeteria is not the only place in a school where first impressions matter. In classrooms every day, there are some teachers who find ways to pique students' interest in the learning by figuratively coloring the food to make it look better, putting some special foil on the outside to make it fancier, and giving it a special name. These are the teachers who will dare to transform their rooms into jungles or the moon, speak in an accent while teaching students about the French and Indian War, or play songs from the 20s and have the students dress as flappers while reading *The Great Gatsby*. Whatever the students are studying in those teachers' rooms is the same content with the same standards as the teacher down the hall or in a different district. The difference is not in the destination (go back to the differences between standards, curriculum, instruction, and assessment on pages 121-122), but in the vehicle used to get there.

Now What

This chapter has strategies that are designed to ignite students' attentions in order to connect them deeper into the learning. Again, the goal here is *not* to get students' absorbed in the bells and whistles, but to use the bells and whistles as a lure into engaging the students into the work. You'll miss your target every time if you focus on the hook and lose sight of the intended outcome: the learning. The three strategies in this chapter are designed to keep kids coming back for more!

49. Reel Them In
50. Be The Tiebreaker
51. Student Gamification

Strategy 49: Reel Them In

I have to confess that as an adult, Halloween or Spirit Week were the only times I ever dressed up in a costume and went to school. The idea of doing it on any other day for any other reason never occurred to me. That is, it didn't occur to me until I read the book *Teach Like a Pirate: Increase Student Engagement, Boost Your Creativity, and Transform Your Life as an Educator* by former teacher, author, consultant, and publisher Dave Burgess. One of the major themes of this book is that students engage when their teachers are engaged. Further, engaged teachers are not afraid to employ techniques that "hook" students—like dressing up as a pirate. In fact, Burgess uses pirates as a symbol of people who:

> are daring, adventurous, and willing to set forth into uncharted territories with no guarantee of success. They reject the status quo and refuse to conform to any society that stifles creativity and independence. They are entrepreneurs who take risks and are willing to travel to the ends of the earth for that which they value. Although fiercely independent, they travel with and embrace a diverse crew.[92]

While you do not actually need to dress up like a pirate to embrace the spirit of being a pirate, teaching like a pirate is something that can transform your classroom.

Hear Dave Burgess talk about *Teach Like a Pirate* here:
https://cutt.ly/Pirate

Specifically, Burgess breaks down his approach to teaching like a pirate into three areas which he represents as a three circle Venn Diagram shown in Figure 11.1. He believes that most teaching and professional development focuses on techniques/methods to improve the learning through content. Though these techniques/methods are important, not enough attention is paid to the presentation aspect of teaching. The goal of focusing on the presentation aspect of teaching is to design lessons students would pay to attend.

An effective way to focus on presentation is to use a "hook." In *Teach Like a Pirate*, there are literally dozens of hooks. It would be both foolish and criminal to reproduce them here. Instead, I'm going to highlight a couple to give you a taste of what a hook is and encourage you to go straight to the source (the book) and to think about what your own hooks could be. The notion here is that you can take what you are already doing to a level that is both very unique to you and also very intriguing to others. This is your chance to make designer instruction out of off-the-rack lessons.

Figure 11.1: Dave Burgess' Venn Diagram on Effective Teaching

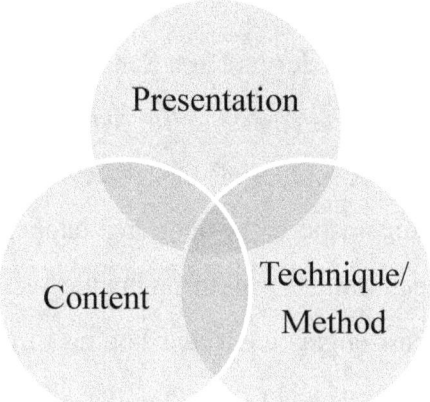

The hooks shared below come directly from *Teach Like a Pirate* and are meant to be a small sampling of what a hook is and the wealth of ideas shared in the book.[93]

- **The Kinesthetic Hook: Use Movement**
    - Can we get up and act something out?
    - What kind of simulation can we do that would allow them to reenact a part of this lesson?
- **The Picasso Hook: Use Art**
    - What can my students draw or make that would help them understand and retain this information?
    - Can they make some kind of non-linguistic representation of the material? (A photography project or 3-D art, for example?)
- **The Hobby Hook: Use Student Interest**
    - How can I incorporate the hobbies and outside interests of my students into this material?
    - How can I harness the power of connecting my content to what students are *already* interested in?
- **The Backwards Hook: Use Time Differently**
    - How can I gain an advantage or increase interest by presenting this material out of sequence?

- Can I tell them the end of the story and let them figure out and discover the beginning and middle?

Andrew Marotta is a principal at Port Jervis High School in Orange County, New York, and the author of the books *The Principal: Surviving and Thriving* and *The Partnership: Surviving and Thriving.* One of the secrets to his success is his commitment to being in classrooms where the learning happens. In his district, administrators conduct ten to fifteen minute walkthroughs they call, "snapshots." On these visits, he's always looking for engagement and hoping to provide his teachers with feedback to lead to administrator-teacher dialogue. He shared with me a couple examples of teachers using hooks that he witnessed on during snapshot visits. Remember, these were teachers who did not know they were going to be visited by the principal—meaning, what Andrew saw was how these teachers hook their students on any given day.

Andrew recalls when a World Languages teacher reeled in her students. Danielle Brand, the teacher, had Pitbull playing as she greeted students walking into the room. There was a short story on their desks with a "Do Now" on the board to read the story and write down two to three points about Pitbull and his music. After their warm-up, Mrs. Brand had a variety of activities for the Spanish 1 students to do, including, but not limited to:

- On the board, they all wrote one point they learned about Pitbull.
- They were then broken into small groups by birthdays and asked to listen to the Pitbull song with closer attention, while having the lyrics in front of them.
- Each group was tasked with a different assignment:
    - Writing all the Spanish words (translating) he sang.
    - Noting the references to Latin culture and to making money.
    - Documenting the number of dance moves throughout the video (they were watching YouTube at this point).

Mrs. Brand played the video twice for them, checked in on their groups, had a timer going, and then had each group share out verbally and in written form in Spanish. She did a short wrap-up about what they learned asking questions and checking for understanding, reviewing each content poster the groups created. Of course, then the class ended with a dance contest with members from each group in a dance off.

Mrs. Brand's reeled them in using several hooks. First, there is the novelty of the class—it was loud, exciting, and had something for everyone. Andrew points out that the novelty was only of value because through the presentation of the lesson, the students were able to become absorbed in the learning. Let's remember, throughout the lesson, the students were collaborating around reading, writing, listening, and speaking in the target language. Did Mrs. Brand have to use Pitbull's music to achieve the learning target? No. Did using a unique and student-centered approach improve the students' learning? Absolutely! Andrew also remembers vividly Danielle's infectious smile and laughing along with the students. Everyone enjoyed the lesson, and most importantly, they were all thoroughly engaged.

A second example of a good hook in action comes from the classroom of Cory Ferguson (@wrestlingwmath and Ferguson Tutoring Center on Facebook). When Mr. Ferguson started his lesson, Andrew could tell something was up. Mr. Ferguson humorously grabbed his cell phone and pretended to take a call. Mr. Ferguson couldn't believe it! It was Howie Mandel on the other line! "I'll be right there," Mr. Ferguson told Howie as he stepped into the hallway.

The kids were buzzing about what was happening and where did their teacher go? Minutes later, Mr. Ferguson entered the room as Howie Mandel (see photo), complete with a bald wig, a different shirt, and the briefcases for the gameshow "Let's Make a Deal." He turned a regular math activity into an amazing lesson full of engagement activities for the kids playing Deal or No Deal. Everyone was dialed in as Mr. Ferguson stayed in character the whole time, and truly engaged the kids.

Mrs. Brand's and Mr. Ferguson's hooks provided variety and change from the mundane. Will the kids remember the concept taught that day years from now? Maybe, but the hooks used by the teachers certainly increased those odds. As well, they will also remember fondly that their teacher was willing to break the mold, act silly, and be creative in the classroom. Ironically, in the moment, the students probably forgot they were in school even though they were learning more than they would have under more traditional presentations of content. By reeling in students and embracing the pirate-mindset, teachers see their role as the person who intentionally creates an environment to tap into students' natural curiosity so learning is creative and interesting.

> *Alternate Use:* Not to be outdone, former teachers and school administrators, Shelly Burgess and Beth Houf wrote an equally stimulating book, *Lead Like a Pirate: Make School Amazing for Your Students and Staff*. This book shares pirating strategies for those who are educational leaders. As well, the hooks in *Teach Like a Pirate* would be just as valuable with faculty meetings and/or professional development as they are in a classroom with students.

Strategy 50: Be The Tiebreaker

Student engagement has been an education buzzword for decades and continues to be one of the largest struggles for educators around the globe. Yet, have we ever stopped to really think (...really think...) about teacher engagement? Think about your colleague next door or down the hall, why do they teach? How engaged are they in the true *art* of teaching and do they have the stamina to endure education for thirty or more years? And, what about *you*? Can you say that you are truly engaged in education for the long haul? What does teacher engagement really look like?

Rebecca Gibboney, the author of *The Tiebreaker: A Scouting Report on Building A Culture of Gamification in Professional Learning*, spent her time as an Instructional Coach focusing on how she could engage her colleagues in the workplace, because, ultimately, she realized that if the teachers were bored, the students were bored. If the teachers were having fun, the students were having fun. To Rebecca, fun is one means of engagement. Rebecca coached with the mentality of Kevin Carroll, the author of *The Red Rubber Ball*. There should be no difference between work and play. Bystanders (students, community members, etc.) should not be able to tell if we are working or playing, because work should be play.

With this mindset, Rebecca introduced her colleagues to the idea of gamification. Again, like engagement, this education buzzword—gamification—has been floating around education for decades, yet, once again, with a focus on students. Why couldn't we practice gamification with adults? After all, aren't adults just big kids at heart? Couldn't we find a way to get those non-compliant educators interested? Perhaps, even absorbed?

Rebecca acknowledges that gamification has been around forever, and, quite frankly, it is not necessary to recreate the wheel. What is necessary is to take those games everyone loved (Monopoly©, Jenga©, etc.) and transform those games to align with the keys to victory and engage your colleagues. In Rebecca's book, she hands over the game plan and outlines what she has defined as the four quarters of a school year. Within each quarter, she draws up the plan for gamification. For example, Figure 11.2 details a gamification that Rebecca used with her colleagues in the first quarter of the season.

Figure 11.2: A Sample of Adult Gamification

LTMS Tailgate Challenge

Are you ready to kickoff another amazing school year?!

In order to kickoff another school year, we will be competing in our LTMS Tailgate Challenge. Like in the past, grade-level teams will be competing against one another (mini-course and related arts teachers will be assigned a team and special education teachers will be with their grade level).

Purpose:
- Build community within our building
- Understand Bloom's Taxonomy and Webb's DOK
- Integrate critical verbs and Collin's Writing into Bloom's and Webb's

How does it work?

- Certain points will be allocated to each team when a team member makes a "big play" (aka completes a task).
- Points will be updated once the 'big plays' are reviewed
- Winning team gets a surprise!

How do I accumulate points for my team?

QUARTER 4

Fumble recovery – 1 point
- Complete a Collin's Writing (any Type)
- Integrate a critical verb in a question stem
- Complete a low level DOK (1 or 2) or Bloom's (remember/understand)
- Take a 'team picture' with your best 'game face'.

Safety – 2 points
- Use a new app or website in your classroom.
- Write someone (a student or coworker) a pep talk and make their day. This should be thought provoking and meaningful! Show your proof by emailing me (rleid@loyalsocklancers.org) the note with a signature of the person who received your talk. *Extra point: act out the pep talk and really dramatize it! Send the proof (a recording) of your performance to me!*
- Complete a DOK (3 or 4) or Bloom's (Apply, analyze, evaluate, create)

Field goal – 3 points

- Share with a colleague an activity how you integrated all three (Webb's or Bloom's, critical verbs, and Collins) that <u>you tried out in your classroom.</u> Discuss if it was a success or something you need to adjust for future use. Email me evidence!
- Choose an area of focus and invite a colleague to visit your classroom to give you feedback.
- Email me 3 ways you connected or learned something new about your students in your Lancer Period.
- Give your Lancer Period a pep talk

Touchdown – 7 points
- Invite the coach to come in and check out critical thinking in action.
- Reflect with a coach about creating questions and create an activity or worksheet for the classroom using questioning strategies.
- Develop a low-level question and scaffold the question to eventually complete a high level question
- Create a lesson that encourages critical thinking in your classroom. Share with a co-worker and then make copies for your colleagues!
- Make team shirts for a dress down day. Everyone must wear them!

Interception – 7 points and deduct 3 points from any team
Complete a full BDA with a coach.

For Rebecca, the game began around 2013 when she questioned her own engagement and her potential as an educator. The struggle was real, and she knew she needed to level up her own game if she was going to thrive in education for thirty more years. She, herself, was living in the compliant world when, really, she was an absorbed-kind-of-girl. Unfortunately, she was in a building where administrative shifts were common and culture and morale were at an ultimate low. The game had to change and it was up to Rebecca (and the new principal) to be the Tiebreaker.

She had to create the fun, engage her colleagues through innovative ideas, and bring her "A-game!" Among her colleagues, there were the outliers who were absorbed, and a sprinkle of interested colleagues; and, while there were some non-compliant colleagues (we all have them), the majority of her colleagues were compliant, including herself. Yet, she knew deep down that she was an absorbed educator. She just had to find her niche—gamification. It was her niche that challenged her to engage her colleagues in their work and encourage competitive, fun play. To shift those non-compliant to compliant, compliant to interested, and interested to absorbed, would be a victory. In order to do that, Rebecca knew she had to start with the culture.

As The Tiebreaker, many of Rebecca's gamifications revolved around sports, because she found that to be appealing to her staff. Throughout this gamification, Rebecca found a way to reinforce their vision by adding tasks aligned to their literacy initiatives, as well as some morale boosters. She listened to her dream team, as they continuously gave her feedback regarding what was working and what was not. As a result of that specific feedback, she was able to balance teacher tasks and realistic outcomes. After all, gamification should be fun! It never should feel like one more thing for educators. At the conclusion of the tailgate challenge, Rebecca always reflected on teacher challenges with her colleagues and refined the gamifications so that they were bigger and better for the upcoming year; and, of course, Rebecca went hard when it came to the rewards! The winning team received their favorite tailgate snacks, a marching band surprise, and an escape lunch to Panera.

In Rebecca's book, *The Tiebreaker*, she outlines the five keys to victory that will help build a culture for gamification.

1. **Investing and valuing ALL staff.** Simply put, in order to engage colleagues they must feel invested and valued. How do we do that? How do we get our colleagues to feel part of the team? They won't play for your team if at first they don't feel part of the team.

2. **Driving your vision.** Every gamification has a purpose. After all, any competition you play for a purpose—a victory. In the education setting, you have a purpose—to impact your students inside and outside of the classroom. Our initiatives, programs, and instruction are usually aligned to building level goals. Gamification should also be aligned to these goals. By aligning this process, you are streamlining efforts and really pushing professional development to professional learning.

3. **Recruiting your dream team.** The coach is only as strong as the team. The team you create to help move closer to victory needs to be honest, balanced, and committed. You must value their input, take their advice and allow them to also be creators! After all, they are the voice and can help you plan the perfect gamification to engage all players.

4. **The Xs and Os.** It is always important to keep in mind all parts of the game—the Xs and the Os. In the book, Rebecca defines the Xs as your players and the Os as you, the coach. This might look like being strategic with how much one can handle, including you. This may look like being intentional with gathering data and resources. In order for the play to be executed correctly, you must consider how to take care of the Xs and the Os.

5. **The Regen Effect.** To perform at your full potential, athletes need to regenerate. In the world of education, this term is uncommon, but the idea has been around for a while. Rebecca encourages educators to practice their own version of regen at the conclusion of each gamification. Educational regen, according to Rebecca, is the practice of rewarding, reflecting, and refining. Reward the winners (go big or go home), reflect on the ups and the downs, and then refine the challenge (or your practices) to make it better in the future. In order to have growth, regen must happen, and it is up to you, the Tiebreaker, to make it happen!

It won't always be a victory. In fact, there will be many failures along the way. That is how we grow and that is what makes us human. The beauty of the regen effect is that the process makes us vulnerable and gives us all a level playing field. It allows us to support one another and grow in the process, together, and united under the same vision.

Rebecca challenges you to be The Tiebreaker. Create a culture of gamification, bring the fun, and re-engage your colleagues. After all, if we want to engage our students, we first must engage our teachers.

To get you started, here are some ideas in how you might approach gamifying your environment.

- Adult Seasonal Examples:

- You could create a tailgate challenge during football season in the fall for a staff cookoff.
- During March Madness you could have the staff try an engagement tournament with brackets for different types of strategies.
- In baseball season you might have a "homerun derby" where staff recognize each other for doing something that "hit it out of the park."

> ***Alternative Use:*** This strategy also works great with kids. Here are some kid-friendly seasonal examples you could use with students.
> - For football season you could have students create a fantasy draft of their favorite books, experiences from school for the year (if it's towards the end of the season) or the prior years (if it's in the beginning of the year and you want to get to know them).
> - During March Madness you might have students create brackets for doing presentations or pitting different historical figures against each other and having students vote on who would win.
> - If it's a year with Olympics, you might ask the students to select their favorite Greek myth or create different academic games and award medals.

Strategy 51: Student Gamification

Gamification is the application of game design elements in non-game contexts. It is the act of borrowing from games to make other endeavors feel playful. It is observing that games understand engagement, and looking under the hood to better inform our instructional design. There is no external economy here—people don't play games as a means to an end. People play games because they want to play games, and as educators, we want to see those parallels in our classrooms. We want to see students who are immersed in task and topic, not just muddling through because they are afraid to not comply, or because they want to be paid in candy and grades.

Mike Neumire is currently an instructional technology specialist and formerly an English teacher, but his roots in gamification can be traced back to high school, where instead of pursuing the gamification of learning, he gamified his study halls, free periods, and "bathroom breaks." He claims credit for inventing three games his senior year: Book Ball, Danger Ball, and FireBall. This penchant for game design began with Book Ball, a version of ping pong where the paddles and net are made of... books. For an extra twist, the table has a few books spread out to create an uneven surface, resulting in a little random chaos. The next two games Mike and his friends created are not ones that either of us would endorse others play, but are nonetheless examples of how when people are given the opportunity to design, the process can be absorbing and the results can be impactful. Specifically, Mike told me about Danger Ball, and game that brings together elements of dodgeball and laser tag. In it, players lock themselves in a dark room, armed with racquet balls, and their goal is to be the last player untagged by a racquet ball (a vicious game, certainly). The final game, Fire Ball, required accuracy, patience, and the ability to respond to feedback. To play, participants lined up at a consistent distance (for them it was the length of a tennis court), and throw racquet balls at a fire alarm. Obviously, being the "winner" in this game is a complex title to bear, as it almost definitely comes with a visit to the principal's office. They only played it once, but he still remembers it over fifteen years later.

Do You Wanna Play

The gamification of learning has some common trademarks. First, there's autonomy, and it comes from the realization that games are malleable systems and the rules aren't edified recipes for someone else's idea of fun. You could play the game, or you could play *with* the game. You get to make choices that impact the experience. What happens when you change to 20-sided dice in Monopoly? Is it more fun? Less fun? Does it break the system? Then, there's challenge. Changing or borrowing from a game to fit within a new system is a deeply creative exercise, that requires drafts and revisions, testing and tweaking, and constant reflection on the original goal. Finally, there's an audience. Mike's games were created to be played by bored seniors in study halls (this was a time before smartphones) and the more ridiculous and odd they were, the more dedicated a following of bored seniors they gathered. There was no grade for these creative efforts, and honestly got him in trouble several times, but it was absorbing.

Briefly, according to Kendra Cherry writing for the website www.verywellmind.com, Self-Determination Theory is a psychological term that:

> is an important concept that refers to each person's ability to make choices and manage their own life. This ability plays an important role in psychological health and well-being. Self-determination allows people to feel that they have control over their choices and lives. It also has an impact on motivation—people feel more motivated to take action when they feel that what they do will have an effect on the outcome.[94]

Autonomy, challenge, and social context are foundational to SDT. These traits are easy to spot in games and game design, but not always in the classroom. In games, players get to make meaningful choices about strategies, teamwork, etc. that amount to an in-game identity. They get to test and adjust their choices, and while doing so, become comfortable taking risks. Most games, especially video games, also adjust the difficulty based on player performance, and scaffold the skills they need to get better at playing the game. In doing all of this, players are usually celebrated for milestones, are able to develop unique strengths under the game's umbrella, and might even go so far as to create a YouTube channel to impart their hard-gained experience on others.

When classwork is passive, students disengage because they don't get to make any meaningful decisions, the level of difficulty is aimed at the middle, and the only attention their efforts earn them is from the teacher. Gamification at its best is more than just slapping a point-system and a leaderboard on class work. It works with your instruction, not just around it. It challenges students to consider a variety of paths, and doesn't feel like a punishment when a path doesn't pan out. It relies on creativity, both from teachers and students.

Game On

To be clear, there is a difference between game-based learning and gamification. Playing Monopoly would be game-based learning, but applying game mechanics to overall game type structure in the classroom is gamification. Here are five steps you can take to gamify your classroom no matter if you choose game-based learning or gamification.

1. **Remix the classics.** Games are our mentors on this journey, and they offer so many valuable mechanisms we can borrow and repurpose instructionally. Let's start with Monopoly® and the idea of "residual income." One of the more engaging aspects when playing Monopoly® is that you can acquire properties that continue to bring you income throughout the game, like a fisherman pulling up a lobster trap or YouTube star checking on their video views. It's this idea that you can put something out there that will collect for you. This mechanism can be repurposed in the classroom too.

A strategy you can try right away to get students building on each other's ideas is to treat the ideas like properties. Let students roll dice to see which idea they land on, and let them build from there. Maybe instead of an idea, when students land on an "unowned property," they have to craft a question to successfully purchase the property. Maybe they have to answer several other students' questions to build enough equity to put hotels on their property. While Monopoly® is a good example to help teachers contextualize gamification, it might not be your students' first choice in games to model after. A good first move is to survey your students about the games they *choose* to spend their valuable time playing. What is it about Fortnite that keeps them coming back? Most likely it relates back to those three foundational pieces: (1) autonomy, (2) challenge, and (3) social context.

2. **Get by with a little help from your tech.** Once you've begun to deconstruct games and pull from their designs, you'll find that technology can help structure your playful experience. For example, a learning management system might provide the discussion boards you need to open up your brainstorming game from one class to all your classes. Or maybe a student can use block-based coding to build you a leaderboard. Encourage your students to brainstorm ways to "recycle" common technologies for gamification purposes.

A strategy you can try right away involves a mystery box and a Google form. Each week, fill a box with a mystery item and seal it. Invite students to explore the box as best they can without opening it. Shake it, observe the weight, etc. In science class, this might help students notice characteristics. In English class, this item might connect to setting or impact a character's development in a story. As students explore the box from the outside, encourage them to submit all the guesses and theories they can come up with to a Google form. Add conditional formatting to the spreadsheet where your students' answers collect. If they use certain buzzwords, their answer box will change color. This can be an indication to the student of a right answer, or just a clue that they're on the right track.

3. **Playtest.** Gamification comes with a myriad of benefits and opportunities, not the least of which is the opportunity to turn your classroom into a laboratory. As the teacher, your gamification efforts will not be perfect the first time. It's easy to trash a gamified lesson after a bad first run, but if you frame it as a design process in which your students are the focus group, it quickly becomes a collective effort of trial and tweak until you have something truly fun for all parties. Talk about student ownership! In this way, you also get to model a growth mindset and create a safe space to take risks. An easy way to establish this culture of feedback and revision is to start with something small and consistent, like vocabulary.

A strategy you can try right away is a vocabulary guessing game using only yes/no questions. The goal of the game is to guess a vocabulary word using only yes/no questions to learn more about it. Is it a place? Is it a thing? Is it safe to eat? Is it larger than a human hand? While the goal of this game stays the same, there are a million ways to structure the rules. Is everyone shouting out questions to the teacher? Do you create two teams and arm each with a vocab word? Do you slow-play it and have students submit yes/no questions to a question box throughout the day? Chances are the best structure will differ for each class, and this creates an opportunity for you to think out loud. "I worked hard on this game, but it won't be perfect without feedback from you all, so we'll play it and then talk about what can be improved."

4. **Linger on the learning.** Learning shouldn't end when the game does! A gamified lesson creates a rich experience full of teachable moments that may not be apparent in the blur of the action, but provides lightbulb moments during a well designed extension activity. As the teacher, you have the opportunity to guide transfer. You can help students make connections between the skills that make them successful in the game and ones that will make them successful in school and beyond, like problem-solving, collaboration and much more. You can help them pull those skills from the neat, closed loop of the game, to more open-ended problems by providing scenarios for them to work through.

If you're interested in learning more about gamification in the classroom, you can start with Mike's website: https://cutt.ly/Gamify

A strategy you can try right away is to identify the thinking skills that went into playing your game-like experience. Did students have to do any kind of analysis? Did they have to prioritize, or allocate resources? Did they have to determine an item's value, or convince other players to do something? Using a jigsaw structure, have students reflect on a game by identifying these skills and placing them in real world contexts.

5. **Empower students to create the next Book Ball.** Trust your students to be part of the process! When students are in charge of creating, they have to get metacognitive and reflect on what they actually enjoy, and why they enjoy it. This self-awareness could have an impact that ripples out beyond your classroom. Whether they're making little widgets for you on Scratch or designing and printing their own 3D board game pieces for a game about spending money, students might have more creative energy to spend than you, and you will have given them a much more authentic audience than just a teacher with a red pen.

A strategy you can try right away is to have students survey your school about their game preferences. Then, using that data, host a "Shark Tank" where students pitch you game ideas, or better yet, pitch their game ideas to an authentic audience like the owner of a toy store, the school board, or digitally on Twitter.

Chapter Summary

This chapter was about moving someone from the point of interest to absorption by eliciting engagement through a hook. Hooks are essentially the presentation of the task. Though the hooks may lure someone into the task, the way to make the task absorbing by ensuring that the task has intrinsic value to the person doing it. In other words, the goal is not to hook students into the hook, but to capture their attention with the hook and keep their attention with the learning.

> **Looking for even more strategies to**
> **HOOK OTHERS INTO LEARNING?**
> Please visit my website, www.LyonsLetters.com/learnmore, for print and digital recommendations including books, websites, videos, and more!

Thank you again to Andrew Moratta for contributing to Reel Them In, Rebecca Gibboney for contributing Be The Tiebreaker, and Michael Neumeir for contributing Student Gamification—three strategies included in this chapter.

Reflection Prompts

1. Think of an upcoming unit. What hook can you create that will draw in students to the learning?

   _____
   _____
   _____

2. Think of an upcoming assignment. How can you add gamification aspects to the task?

   _____
   _____
   _____

3. Name one thing you could do tomorrow based on what you learned from this chapter.

   _____
   _____
   _____

4. Tweet me @LyonsLetters to share an idea for a future reading or digital resource I should share on www.lyonsletters.com that would help someone who is interested become absorbed.

Persistent Questions

1. What have you done so far regarding the three challenge questions from Chapter 1?

    a. **Three:** Find at least three people with whom to share your learning.

    b. **Two:** Find at least two ideas that change you.

    c. **One:** Apply at least one idea from your reading.

    _____
    _____
    _____

2. What have you learned so far, and how will you use it?

    _____
    _____
    _____

Chapter 12

Project Strategies

"Projects are determined by missions; the project is great if it has a great mission"
~Anton Pavlovich Chekhov

Recognizing Your Thinking Before You Read...

1. What was a project you were tasked with as a student? How engaged were you with that project?

   _____

   _____

   _____

2. What is the difference between student-centered and student-driven tasks?

   _____

   _____

   _____

3. Think of a project that you have assigned to students in the past. Who decided what the students would do and who the audience would be of that project?

   _____

   _____

   _____

See What I Can Do

Even if you were asking a primary-aged child, you would be hard-pressed to find one who has not done a project for school. When my own children were in both kindergarten and first grade they were asked both years to create an "All About Me" poster. I think in kindergarten the poster was a pre-designed one that the students colored in and the parents added text and photos. If I recall, there was one student per week who had the task of completing the poster at home and then the student would share out to the class everything on the poster. (I thought about including an example here, but these are so ubiquitous that you already know what I'm talking about or you can just google "All About Me Poster" and see one for yourself.)

When my kids were in second grade, the tradition in the school was to have the second-graders transform a pumpkin (or gourd) into the child's favorite book character. When my oldest, Nolan, was in the second grade we somehow settled on Captain Underpants—though I'm pretty sure that Captain Underpants wasn't his favorite book character. I think I convinced him that Captain Underpants was the most doable character of the ones he might have been interested in at the time. Two years later when it was my daughter Lilia's turn, she (okay, we) chose Thing 1 and Thing 2. When my youngest, Oliver was in the second grade two years later, he (okay, I) chose Pikachu. With Nolan's, I did the project and let him do the outline of the diaper after I painted it. I think I let Lilia be in the room with me when I made Thing 1 and Thing 2 gourds. I let my husband help me with Oliver's because he's the one who spray painted the pumpkin yellow. I think Oliver held the ears in place where I told him they went so I could glue them. Figure 12.1 shows photos so you can admire my handiwork.

Figure 12:1: Photos of Projects I Did For My Children

Captain Underpants   Thing 1 and Thing 2   Pikachu

If you think that I am the only parent doing her kids' projects with (for) them, you are not a parent or an educator. It obviously makes sense that children of a certain age are not independently able to do certain tasks all by themselves. However, what is that age and why are children assigned tasks they cannot do? Furthermore, how do we help both parents and children understand what appropriate assistance is and when it crosses the line? If a parent (like me) is literally *doing* the project, then whose work is the teacher assessing?

It's Not You, It's Me

In pre-service teacher preparation programs future teachers are told about the benefits of having students do projects. In fact, they are probably assigned projects to research and learn more about how to have students do projects in schools. In classrooms every day, students are assigned tasks that are projects because the teacher believes that the project is a better alternative to a paper-pencil task. Projects can be tasks like group assignments or long-term research papers, creating posters or making a slideshow.

There are pitfalls associated with projects that we often fall into not because we are bad, but because we are going through the motions. Here are just a few.

1. Obviously, the first pitfall is what I described on the previous page—the parents are really the ones doing the work.
2. Assigning a project to a group but not really knowing who did what or how to fairly assess and evaluate the work of individuals within the group.
3. Believing that all projects will lead to student engagement. They won't. This is especially true if there is no choice or voice regarding what they will do. All students create an All About Me Poster is not really a project.
4. The teacher choosing the project that the students will do even when there is choice and voice.

Since this chapter is about projects that will lead to student absorption, the projects shared here are of a different caliber; these are designed to have students not just have opportunities to learn more about a topic that is interesting to them, but to develop a deeper understanding of themselves—how does the *student* like to share their learning, what are the conditions under which the *student* likes to learn, what are the ideas that the *student* finds compelling, etc. These are projects that:

- Are messy, iterative, and student-driven.
- Ask the teacher to guide and listen, and ask the student to drive and lead.
- Have an audience beyond the teacher or the classroom.
- Are long-term because they take time to create, tackle, and execute.
- Impact the student beyond that unit, year, or experience.

In other words, these are projects that focus on the development of *the students*, not the content or the teacher.

This probably sounds far-fetched if you feel tethered to certain standards or curriculum. I cannot deny or minimize the challenge in creating projects like the ones I've described here if you have never done this before. However, the biggest challenge once you start will be that your students will beg you to do them all the time. Really. No, really. Your students will be driven to want to work on these projects as much as they can. Use that to your advantage. Since they *want* to work on their projects, you will not need to make time for them to work on it in class because they will be more than willing to do it on their own time. You will need to find time to check-in and confer with the students regularly to give them feedback. As you do so, make sure to position the student as the one who is steering the conversation so that *the student* is the person who is directing the teacher about what they want feedback on.

Now What

This chapter has five strategies that are designed to position students as the designers of their tasks.

Here are the five strategies found in this chapter:

52. Service Learning Projects
53. Problem-Based Learning
54. Golden Lasso Moments
55. FedEx Day
56. Room to Breathe

Strategy 52: Service Learning Projects

I want to point out that the first strategy, Service Learning Projects, is a unique example of a task that has the potential to shift students from non-compliance to absorption because it is designed to direct students' attention to others rather than to themselves. I say this because creating a shift of engagement of this magnitude is rare and unexpected. Though non-compliance can be associated with the extrinsic consequences we receive for the task, generally speaking, the roots of the non-compliance are connected to a lack of relationships and connections to the task. Service Learning Projects create a sense of purpose for the doer—particularly if the doer is able to select and design the project. As a result, participants become absorbed in the project.

Service learning projects create opportunities for both character development and authentic learning that is "disguised as fun." In the process, non-compliant behaviors melt away, as students become fully absorbed. What is behind this shift? To understand, let's look at the quadrants on the bottom of The Engagement Matrix: non-compliant and absorbed (see Figure 12.2).

Figure 12.2: The Engagement Matrix

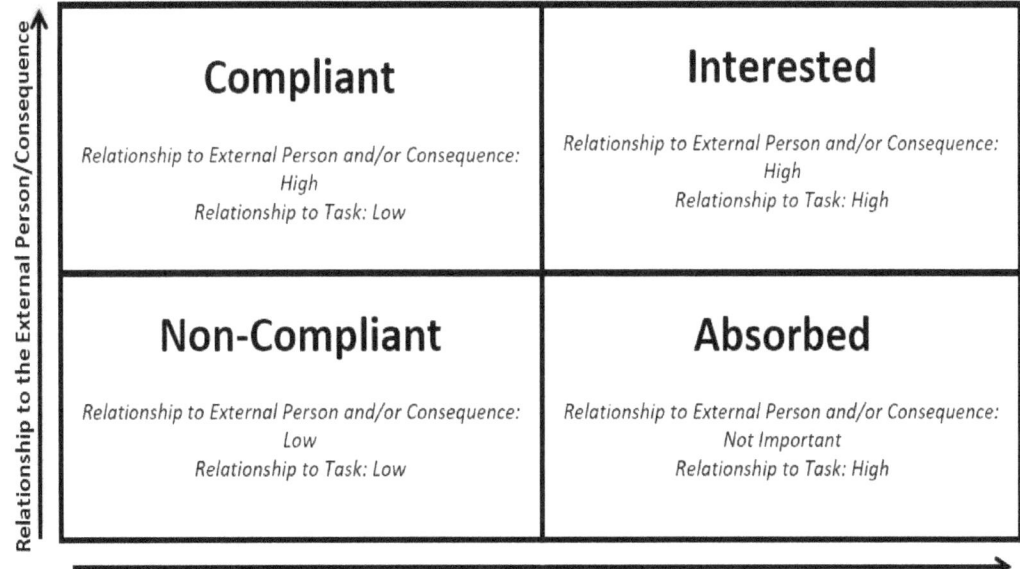

By making the task more meaningful and relevant, the connection to the task increases and moves student engagement from non-compliance to absorbed. When the focus shifts away from whether the student is engaged in an assigned task or not, to looking beyond themselves, to consider the needs of others, the power struggle that often accompanies non-compliance is neutralized.

Service learning projects nourish the universal human need to be generous. Sally Berman, author of *Service Learning for the Multiple Intelligences Classroom*, explains it this way:

> Service learning strengthens students in many different ways. Students who learn to do for others, rather than "being done for" by others, become more self confident and develop more self-esteem. They feel that they are useful members of the community who can identify problems, propose solutions, act independently in implementing solutions and open themselves to new experiences and roles as they do so. Students gain self-respect as they develop the real-life skills of being on the job on time, having good attendance, and doing the work they have promised to do.[95]

As students carry out a service learning project, empathy for others in the community is increased because students take on the perspective of others, to understand the need.

Stages of Service Learning Projects that Elicit Strong Student Engagement

Summarized below are recommended stagtes to get the maximum benefit from student participation in service learning projects from *The Educator's Guide to Emotional Intelligence and Academic Achievement*.[96]

- **Preparation** involves identifying a need within the immediate school community or the greater community. Students are involved in brainstorming ways that they can help meet the need, and plan the details of a project or event.
- **Action steps** are planned and carried out to meet the need, by students directly, to the extent appropriate for their stage of development.
- **Reflection** gives students the opportunity to talk and write about their experiences.

- **Demonstration** allows students to creatively show their peers, younger students, parents, or other members of the community what they did, why they did it, how they felt about it, and what they learned.

Randolph Academy is a public K-12 school designed to meet the needs of students with emotional and behavioral disabilities. Service learning projects have been a signature piece of the school program and an effective way to engage students who were previously non-compliant and oppositional in other school settings prior to enrollment.

Even the youngest students are engaged in service learning projects. For example, first and second grade students were taught about "random acts of kindness" and brainstormed ideas for how they could perform random acts of kindness within the school. The class came to agreement on a project that involved making hand painted clay ornaments, bedazzled with glitter and ribbon, to give as gifts to teachers and school staff. Attached to each ornament, a handwritten, colorful note included the staff member's name and a thank you for what they give to the school. The students delivered each ornament to every adult in the school community, practicing social skills as they expressed their gratitude face-to-face.

Another service learning project that is a long-standing tradition at Randolph Academy is a maple sugar shack that is operated by middle school science classes for several weeks in the spring. The project follows a unit of study on the plant life cycle. The culminating event involves students preparing and serving a pancake breakfast to senior citizens from the local community.

The connection of academic content to a real life need in the community is an important aspect of an effective service learning project. High school environmental science students served as data collectors for a river-keepers project. It was inspiring to see the sense of pride and accomplishment when the students presented to the board of education about their interactions with scientists in the community. Another science-based service learning project involved raising trout in tanks in the classroom, and then releasing the fish, under Department of Environmental Conservation supervision, into streams in the spring.

Watch a news report highlighting the efforts of some Randolph Academy students' Service Learning Project:
https://cutt.ly/Service Learning

Career and Technology Education (CTE) classes have offered "Manicures at the Manor," a project that involves cosmetology students providing manicures to senior citizens who live at a local nursing home. Over the years, many intergenerational friendships have developed, leading to a lasting personal bond. Not long ago, one high school student surprised her friend "Grandma Nellie" with a plate of homemade cookies. As a thank you, Grandma Nellie gave the high school student a small handkerchief. When the student shared the story with her teacher she said, "Grandma Nellie thinks I should carry this with me on my wedding day." Thus, service learning can create amazing heartwarming connections that compel students towards investment in the task because they are both giving and receiving through the process.

Strategy 53: Problem-Based Learning

In his book *World Class Learners: Educating Creative and Entrepreneurial Students*, author and associate dean Yong Zhao shares that the American education system should not be distracted by comparisons to countries like China's performance on standardized assessments but should foster students' entrepreneurial endeavors. He admits that the US does not fare well on standardized assessments when compared with other countries. Rather than focusing on standardized tests, Zhao says we should look at measures of entrepreneurial spirit, which include traits like "creativity, innovation, persistence, [and] risk taking,"[97] because the US far exceeds countries that have narrowed their curriculum to myopically focus on standardized testing measures. According to Zhao, curriculum would ideally be determined by the students, themselves, in support of problems that they identify which fuels an entrepreneurial drive.

With this in mind, Zhao speaks to the use of Project-Based Learning (PBL) as an approach that some have seen as the antidote to sit-and-get instruction. Unfortunately,

PBL is not a panacea. It's all too easy to create projects *for* students to complete (some would argue that these projects are often done by the parents). While they certainly are doing an activity, the learning can slip through the cracks. Though it is true that this type of PBL may lead to interest on the Engagement Continuum, this is not the type of PBL that will create absorption. Why not?

> In this model, PBL is used as a more effective way to reach prescribed content and skills. Consequently, the prescribed content and skills drive the project. The outcome is better understanding of the content or enhanced ability to apply the skills. The resulting products, if any, are only by products, of little consequence [to the student]…rarely are the products meant for an authentic audience, someone other than the teachers, the students, or their parents…Effectiveness of this model is often assessed by how well the students master the content or acquire the skills.[98]

Because the desired outcome is acquisition of the content or skills, it is the teacher (not the students) who controls what the students are able to do.

PBL that guarantees absorption would fall under the "Entrepreneurship Model" shown in Figure 12.1. That said, this level of freedom is often not possible in a traditional school's parameters, thus the "Mixed Model" is a reasonable place to start. The information shared here is a summary of the Mixed and Entrepreneurship Models of PBL described at length in the chapter, "Product-Oriented Learning" in *World Class Learners*.

Figure 12.1: Features of Three Different PBL Models[99]

PBL Model	Extended Outcome	Control	Setting
Academic Model	Academic content	Teacher-led	Primarily a single classroom
Mixed Model	Product within constraints of academic requirements	Teacher-student collaboration	Single or multiple classes, community
Entrepreneurship Model	Product	Student-led	School and Community

Read the Teacher's Guide to Project-Based Learning here
https://cutt.ly/PBL_Guide

With regard to the Mixed Model (MM), "externally prescribed content and skills, such as the state-mandated academic standards, are not ignored, but they are not starting points. The content and skills are not allowed to define, constrain, or guide the projects."[100] Since the content and skills still matter, the teacher or department are ultimately the decision makers about the project in the MM though they could gather student input. The role of the students in the MM is to "be creative and specialize in certain areas within the large project [and to]...provid[e] peer reviews of products."[101]

The MM is generally interdisciplinary and thus involves multiple teachers, is not bound to one class period per day, and may bleed into settings like a library or lab or even outside of the school like a business or museum. For the summative assessment, the guide, "Work that Matters: The Teacher's Guide to Project-Based Learning"[102] suggests evaluating:

1. Does the product meet or exceed the criteria we set at the start of the project?
2. Has the student developed the skills required for the execution of this project?
3. Has the student learned the curriculum content required for this project?

If you are ready for an even more engaging but also more challenging approach to PBL, consider the Entrepreneurship Model (EM). In this model, students learn content and skills through the creation of a product that appeals to customers outside of the school setting. For this reason, rather than thinking of EM PBLs as "project-based learning" think of it as *product-oriented learning*"[103] or POLs. Zhao says:

These POLs are conceived and developed by the students after they are able to convince the teacher to approve the project and, if needed, convince their peers to become partners. And for that they need a business plan, complete with documentations and analysis, and marketing strategies. The teacher, in this model, serves as the "venture capitalist," who helps decide if the project is feasible; the consultant, who provides suggestions and resources on demand; the motivator, who encourages at times of disappointment; the focus group, which provides feedback and critique on prototypes; and the partner, who provides complementary expertise and skills.[104]

In order to identify potential projects, the teacher may do a request for proposals or invite community members to share problems that they need assistance with.

Since EM POL is not linked to specific skills or content goals, it is generally not taught within the constraints of a course; thus, logistical considerations would be needed. For example, this could be an elective. Another example would be providing a set amount of time per day or during the week to allow students the time to work on their POL. In this case, think of a four-day instruction week with the fifth day devoted to time on the POL. Whatever the structure is, there needs to be a teacher available to serve the roles described above. In other words, though the students would have independent work time, they would not be abandoned.

The process for POLs is straightforward and follows the same steps that an entrepreneur would:[105]

1. Identify Needs
2. Come Up With an Idea
3. Assess Strengths and Resources
4. Convince Someone
5. Make the Product/Service
6. Market the Product
7. Post-Product Management and Maintenance

Strategy 54: Golden Lasso Moments

As a kid, author and instructional coach Michael Fisher loved superheroes, particularly ones that had their own television shows. He loved all the different powers that the different heroes had and at one time or another tried to emulate those powers: The Hulk's super strength, Superman's ability to fly, Batman's awesome gadgets, and Wonder Woman's Golden Lasso. He has several stories that involve rope, his younger brother, and unexpected doctor visits.

Michael often wondered what could be accomplished when there was power beyond the normal—when the freedom to be "more than" propelled humans into superhuman status. More than normal, more than capable, more than expected—all of these are pondered by all humans at some point, super or otherwise.

What does it take to be "more than?" What does it mean to go above and beyond? What are the benefits of engaging our own internal superheroes in order to accomplish extraordinary things? Almost a decade ago, Michael, with his co-author Janet Hale, explored the impact that engagement has on learning in their book *Upgrade Your Curriculum,* looking at distinct zones that represent the impact of low or high engagement with a learning task. Those zones are labeled: Conform, Outform, Reform, and Transform (see Figure 12.2).

Conform actions represented a low impact on both learning and engagement; actions that teachers took in their instructional practices that had very little meaning or connection for their students and ultimately resulted in little learning beyond exposure. With Outforms, though, there was a change to the level of engagement that onboarded students into the learning by changing the interest level but ultimately, had little effect on what was learned. In the Reform section, students lost some of the engagement but there was a greater impact on learning. Transform actions represented both a high impact on learning and high engagement for students.

Figure 12.2: Hale and Fisher's Impact Zones

	Impact on Engagement →	
Impact on Learning ↑	**Reform** • High Impact on Learning • Low Impact on Engagement	**Transform** • High Impact on Learning • High Impact on Engagement
	Conform • Low Impact on Learning • Low Impact on Engagement	**Outform** • Low Impact on Learning • High Impact on Engagement

That said, let's go back to superheroes. Many superheroes go through some sort of change or metamorphosis to transition into their heroic selves. As they TRANSFORM into their heroic self, they have specific skills and resources at-the-ready to accomplish extraordinary things. This transformation in superheroes is exactly the same kind of mindset we want learners to have. This transformation is the zone where learning is inevitable and students are so engaged that they want to stay in this bubble of awesome for as long as possible.

For Michael, the word for this heroic level of engagement is *compelled*. And the engagement here has to do with that which is compelling for a student, what Michael considers to be "Golden Lasso" moments. Wonder Woman's Golden Lasso was a tool that compelled others to tell the truth. They couldn't escape from the lasso's hold and they couldn't do anything different than what Wonder Woman was asking or suggesting of them. When students are so absorbed in the work they are doing that they are compelled to learn at their highest capacities, their learning is deeper, has a higher level of quality, and the products and performances that result are pretty amazing.

In the hierarchy of pedagogical practices, this is also called a "toward" state. Toward states have much to do with how learners feel about their learning. At the neurological level, the brain perceives what's happening and classifies it as good (students want to move *toward* it and engage) or bad (students want to move *away* from it and disengage).[106]

Learn more about flow in this short video:
https://cutt.ly/Flow-Theory

Some might also call this a state of flow. That state that we get into when everything comes together: the mood, the motivation, the resources, the support, the ongoing feedback, the constant creation, and the self-direction and self-governance to accomplish a task that is meaningful to us personally. That which is compelling to us keeps us in a deep state of learning and performance, unlike anything that is simply assigned and/or regurgitated. We are compelled, as if held by our own Golden Lasso, to do what we think matters the most.

That which is compelling is a specific form of engagement that we want learners to learn how to create and participate in themselves. But it takes practice. Teachers can create the conditions for Golden Lasso moments to occur and observe how kids ignite in those situations. This means a shift in pedagogy from low student autonomy with a tight structure controlled by the teacher, to a version of learning where students have the autonomy to make decisions about their learning and a looser structure within which to operate.

Golden Lasso Conditions

Let's take a look at what these Golden Lasso conditions might look like. Early on, Michael was interested in science. As young as five- or six-years-old, he was fascinated with biology and took all opportunities to observe and make sense of the world around him. In school, the learning was sanitized and alphabet-related when learning about animals, but at home, his family reinforced his knowledge-seeking with several key supports:

- His parents let him explore and discover.
- Michael's mother was a teacher and Michael was an early engager with texts, reading fluently by kindergarten.
- His grandmother gave him a high school biology text.
- As he got older, his teachers began to allow for his interests to overflow into the classroom in the form of sharing what he was discovering, presenting to the other students, and even creating school-based experiments to find what was beyond the text or other available resources.
- Michael's parents, teachers, counselors, and just about anyone who knew him helped seek out opportunities such as camps, school-based programs, or other science-related experiences for him to continue his learning.

Keeping Michael in this *transform* bubble where there was amazing learning and very high levels of engagement resulted in near-constant learning about scientific phenomena throughout school and throughout life. He now has an undergraduate degree in biology, a teaching credential in science, and he is still compelled daily to wonder, question, investigate, collect, observe, analyze, conclude, and share about science. Some very small moves by the adults and mentors that Michael had resulted in learning that was so compelling to him that he remains immersed in its hold even today.

Golden Lasso conditions can be created by simply giving kids an opportunity in the form of a prompt and the autonomy/permission to act on that prompt. When students come to adults with questions or obvious interests, it becomes an opportunity to launch them into compelling learning scenarios that could last for a moment or lifetime.

Prompts might include:

- What if you could _____?
- If I said yes to everything you're proposing, what might the result look like?
- What could you create if you had _____?
- What if you just did it yourself?
- What would it look like if you just decided to learn more about this on your own? What steps would you take?
- If you were in charge, what would you do?
- How can I help you make this happen?
- Who else do we need to involve to pull this off?
- Have you thought about how this might lead to an even bigger idea?
- If you did _____, could you monetize it? Is there an entrepreneurial opportunity here?
- What does success look like to you?
- If you figured _____ out, what would you do with that information?
- What resources do you need to keep the ideas flowing?
- Why not? Let's try it.

A teacher, mentor, or parent may even just suggest a greater content or interest level question that focuses the learning for the student or launches them into a deeper interest level in a topic.

Golden Lasso Example 1: Planting a Seed

Maeve is a student disconnected from school. Some of those disconnections are related to personal mental health issues that, while minimal, do have an impact on Maeve's ability to readily plug into learning scenarios. That said, Maeve loves to tell stories. Her grandmother encourages her to write down her stories. Maeve's grandmother is a professional development specialist who works with teachers and adult education. She talks often about Maeve and her stories with those she works with.

A colleague introduced Maeve's grandmother to the online self-publishing tool on Amazon's website, which she shared with Maeve. This prompted a change in Maeve to not only continue writing, but to create something that was longer and more involved than anything she had attempted before. Through her grandmother, she connected with other teachers and even some students to participate in cycles of feedback and revision that strengthened her stories and taught her much about the publishing process. Ultimately, Maeve used Amazon's publishing tool to publish her own book that is currently for sale on Amazon.

The conditions to create this Golden Lasso moment were simple. Her grandmother asked Maeve if she would like to publish her stories and then her grandmother supported her to realize the goal.

Golden Lasso Example 2: High School Students, Bats

At a high school in Land o' Lakes, Florida in 2014, a bat infestation prompted high school science teachers to reconsider parts of their curriculum. Faced with a rabies diagnosis for at least one dead bat, thousands that were infesting the area, and a lack of an effective coordinated response, the teachers turned to their students.

Their Golden Lasso prompt was along the lines of: If you were in charge, what would you do about the bats? Rather than marching through their already designed curricula, students were now being given the opportunity to come up with real solutions to a real problem. In the course of designing solutions, students learned a great deal about bats, their behaviors, and why they might be a nuisance or a niche in the ecosystem.

With support and guidance from their teachers, students decided to build bat boxes that would house the bats away from the school. They had to research what specific types of boxes would entice the bats to move in, how big the boxes had to be based on what they knew of the bats, and then construct the boxes and hang them in a place to encourage occupancy and decrease the opportunity for predation. In the course of learning about bats and their needs, students also discovered that by managing the bat population, they could also cut down on pesticide use because the bats, as insectivores, eat many of the nuisance bugs that the school had previously had to control with chemicals. Win-win.

Roping You In

Creating and supporting Golden Lasso moments teaches students several things that go well beyond content knowledge:

- Self-governance, i.e., who is controlling my actions and how do my actions improve the community in which I work and live?
- Self-reliance, i.e., I can do this, I can make my own decisions, and I know where to go if I do need help.
- That their interests matter to the learning.
- That they can reap the rewards of deep thinking about something they care about.
- That the adults around them will help them in their personalized endeavors to do great things.
- That what they want to learn about is worth exploring.

Golden Lasso moments feed our collective human needs for curiosity and exploration. *Having to learn* is far different than *being internally compelled to learn*. Paying attention to those wants and engaging with those curiosity-filled opportunities invites the deepest of engagement from our learners. This is much different than previous versions of schooling with authoritarian, "obey state" models that sought to normalize behaviors more than creating the conditions for igniting deep engagement and learning.

With years of practice, research, and analysis, we now know more about what it takes to help students learn to be deep thinkers and have a high degree of ownership and transfer in their learning experiences. Inviting these Transform Zones that foster flow states is critical to preparing our contemporary students for the ever-changing and dynamic world they will graduate into. These moments are critical to inviting that which is compelling to each individual student and using that to deepen the learning and upgrade the audience for their learning.

We create superheroes—Super Students—by creating the conditions for them to engage their own strengths and do extraordinary things rooted in what fascinates and intrigues them. Sometimes we have to be willing to break away from our controlled curriculum to create these opportunities. That does not mean abandoning the destination or the learning. Like the example with bats, allowing these moments to happen often means being willing to release control, increase trust, and invite spontaneity.

Strategy 55: FedEx Day

Imagine going to work and being told that you could work on whatever you wanted—you were not tethered to the curriculum or the standards. You were able to develop the thing that you have been thinking about forever but didn't have the time or permission to do. How would that make you feel? Now imagine that you're a student and instead of having to do the work that the teacher assigned, you were able to work on that thing that you have been wanting to do. How would that make you feel? Liberated? Inspired? Valued?

If you wanted to ship a package and guarantee delivery within 24 hours, you could go to FedEx. Using the concept of 24-hour delivery, Australian software company, Atlassian, is credited with the creation of professional FedEx days where for 24 hours employees are freed from the constraints of their normal work responsibilities and tasks and instead the employees are allowed to develop/work on their own ideas. At the end of the 24 hours, they share their projects with their colleagues. This can be done in teams or independently. When the day ends, there is a vote to see which project(s) was the best. This is called a FedEx Day.

FedEd Days do not just happen; they take careful planning and communication. Thus, while the creativity is confined to a specific 24-hour window, the planning for it is not. The following seventeen steps are directly quoted from the blog, www.Life-Long-Learners.com.[107]

1. Teachers should investigate the following web resources[iv] in order to gain a clearer perspective on the elements of a FedEx project:
    - "Reflection: The FedEx Project" (https://cutt.ly/FedExReflection)
    - "Innovation Day 2011" (https://cutt.ly/2011InnovationDay)
2. Discuss the FedEx project with students encouraging them to search for additional FedEx resources and ideas to share with the class.
3. Brainstorm possible projects and interests.
4. Determine the FedEx project day(s) and "delivery" schedule.
5. No marks will be assigned to this endeavour as the focus will be on learning, however some educators may wish to develop, with student input, a rubric for choosing FedEx "award winners."
6. Request "working titles" of projects by individuals and groups.
7. Although students may work individually, teachers may wish to encourage collaboration through a group endeavour. Each group, which may not exceed four members, must organize themselves so that all members contribute equally to the project.
8. Two possible strategies that teachers might use when reviewing group work are based on "score-card" submissions. Teachers might ask group members to complete a "score-card," similar to [the examples in Figure 12.3]. One technique recommends that each team (of two to four individuals) must submit a single team "score-card," which the members complete as a public, joint-venture,

---

[iv] Only two of four are listed here since the links for the other two no longer work.

indicating the agreed-upon effort percentage of each team member. An alternative strategy is to have each team member complete, in private, an individual "score-card" indicating how they considers the effort demonstrated by each team member (which must total 100%). Once this private, individual score-card is completed (and signed at the bottom by the student who is assessing all team-mates), it is submitted "in confidence" to the teacher. Lastly, some teachers might prefer to ask all groups to complete both a team and individual private "score-cards." If the sets of team and individual "score cards" could be duplicated on two different colours of paper, teachers might learn much from comparing the "score cards" results from the private, individual team members' percentages with the public, team-completed single "score-card."

Figure 12.3: FedEx Team and Individual Score Cards[108]

FedEx Project
TEAM SCORE-CARD

Each team is to discuss, complete ONE Team Score-Card, and submit it to the teacher.

Project Title: _____
_____

Delivery Date: _____

Members Name (Please print)   % Effort

#1: _____   _____
#2: _____   _____
#3: _____   _____
#4: _____   _____

Total Percentages must = 100%

FedEx Project
INDIVIDUAL SCORE-CARD

Project Title: _____
_____

Delivery Date: _____

Members Name (Please print)   % Effort

#1: _____   _____
#2: _____   _____
#3: _____   _____
#4: _____   _____

Total Percentages must = 100%

This FedEx Group Project "score-card" is submitted in confidence by:

_____

9. Provide help and direction in the weeks preceding the FedEx Day for students who are having difficulty deciding on a project topic. Help students get organized and on schedule as some will find the perceived "lack of direction" to be new and challenging. Facilitate goal setting so that all students are clear regarding what they hope to accomplish.

10. Determine how long each person or team will have to share their creations during the "delivery" celebration.
11. Begin the FedEx Day or Project and arrange to have all projects submitted at the agreed-upon deadline.
12. Facilitate project sharing during the "delivery" phase.
13. Establish a voting procedure so that all students complete rubrics on the projects of classmates.
14. Based on the completed rubrics, announce FedEx award winners.
15. Consider how students might be able to share their FedEx Projects on the web so that other students and teachers might benefit.
16. Ask students for feedback after they have had time to reflect on the process. In particular ask students to identify improvements that can be made.
17. Perhaps you might like to share ideas, resources or feedback with our readers about your FedEx Day by completing a "Comment" submission at the end of this blog post.

Alternate Use: The FedEx Strategy is one that can be used with teachers too, as shared in the introduction. The same site that outlined the 17 steps to use with students provides 14 steps to use with teachers.

Strategy 56: Room to Breathe

Erin Quinn and Tara Vandertoorn, Language Arts teachers, wanted to find a way to engage their Grade 8 students in literacy learning that welcomed them into a space that recognized texts as a way that human beings can find and create real meaning in the world. As they met at a coffee shop in their home of Calgary, Alberta, a few days before going back to school in August 2018, Tara and Erin talked about the perpetual "Kids these days!" complaints around the lack of writing kids do. They began to discuss how this perception is actually not true—young people engage in text consumption and creation more than ever before because they have a means to do so right in the palm of their hand. They talked about the sophisticated understanding of texts required to make a truly funny or satisfying TikTok video or Instagram story, and pondered how they might harness their teenaged students' innate knowledge of text consumption and creation and bring this into their classrooms. They acknowledged, too, that although students are already familiar with tools that allow them to create and consume, they would need a highly skilled toolkit in order to do this *critically*.

As they started to discuss the relationship between text interpretation and text creation, they landed on the idea that would transform learning in their classroom from that point on. Erin mentioned the common maxim that reading is like inhaling and writing is like exhaling, and their framework, Room to Breathe (R2B) was born. As they continued to brainstorm, Tara challenged the notion that it should be about reading and writing only, since their provincial curriculum asked them to engage students across the strands of reading, writing, listening, speaking, viewing, and representing. Their brainstorming developed into a fully fleshed-out approach to their entire year that positioned students as designers of their own learning, where students create their own projects in the strands of language arts, using conferencing and minilessons to build their own repertoire of critical and creative thinking tools.

How it Works

The Room to Breathe framework may seem overwhelming at first glance. Like all teachers, Erin and Tara were at first nervous about the idea of every student in the classroom working on a different project at once, with different deadlines, and different assessment criteria. That is why they created straightforward routines, processes, and tools to simplify this for both themselves and their students.

Erin and Tara began by familiarizing their students with the Language Arts strands—reading, writing, speaking, listening, viewing, and representing—and the associated learning outcomes from their local curriculum. They placed the students into small working groups and gave them all the outcomes, rewritten as "I can" statements, and cut them all up into strips.

The students first read the statements and, as a group, decided if it was an Inhale (text interpretation) or an Exhale (text creation). Each group had a large piece of chart paper titled with each of the Language Arts strands and they moved around their little strips of paper, sorting any relevant outcomes into their Language Art strands. As the groups rotated, they added to the work of the groups prior. The result of this work was two-fold. First, the students were able to clearly see which learning outcomes related to Inhaling versus those related to Exhaling. This was very clear with a great deal of class consensus. Secondly, they were also able to see that many outcomes related to many different strands, as there was a lot of crossover among strands. Erin and Tara purposefully set up the students to fail by asking them to do this. The students realized that an "I Can" statement such as "I can use strategies such as annotation, note-taking, paraphrasing, and making connections to previous learning to help me understand texts and keep track of my learning" couldn't be applied *only* to reading, because you can also paraphrase something you listen to or view. This collaborative work created a master document of "I Can" statements categorized by purpose (see Figure 12.4).

Figure 12.4: Room to Breathe "I Can" Statements

	Inhaling (Text Interpretation)	Check off when Included in a Room to Breathe task
	Goals & Reflection	
1	I can set, work towards, and track my progress towards goals in the interpretation of texts.	
2	I can reflect on my text interpretations, and express my preferences in what I like to read, view, and listen to, and give reasons why. I can change my mind, and explain why!	
	Choice	
3	I can choose texts to explore and explain why I chose them.	
4	I can use other peoples' suggestions and opinions to help me choose texts.	
5	I can choose a diversity of texts, not always sticking with what's familiar to me, and explore a wide variety of genres.	
	Tracking Understanding	
6	I can use strategies such as annotation, note-taking, paraphrasing, and making connections to previous learning to help me understand texts and keep track of my learning.	
7	I can record significant quotes from texts and record my interpretation of them.	
8	I can use tools to help me better understand texts.	
	Deepening Understanding	
9	I can explore various interpretations of a single text.	

10	I can make connections between my interpretation of a text and other texts, ideas, and information.	
11	I can use evidence from the text to support my interpretation.	
12	I can compare different texts and explore similarities and differences.	
13	I can explore how choices the author makes impacts the meaning created in a text.	
14	I can appreciate the artistry in a text.	
	Researching	
15	I can identify appropriate sources to find information on a specific topic.	
16	I can create a plan when researching a topic, and create a method for gathering and recording information.	
17	I can copy direct quotes from sources, and also paraphrase information in my own words and symbols.	
18	I can keep track of and credit the authors of the ideas I research.	
19	I can organize information in a variety of ways.	
20	I can evaluate my research, eliminating ideas that are not relevant, and identifying gaps in my research that still need to be filled.	
	Working with Others	
21	I can work with others to deepen my understanding of texts.	
22	I can use active listening techniques when working with peers.	
23	I can appreciate diversity by listening to and responding to others' ideas in a respectful way.	

	Exhaling (Text Creation)	Check off when Included in a Room to Breathe task
	Goals & Reflection	
1	I can set, work towards, and track my progress towards goals in the creation of texts.	
2	I can reflect on text creation, and express my preferences in what kinds of texts I like to create and why. I can change my mind, and explain why!	
	Make Choices	
3	I can explore different possibilities in text creation, weigh them, and make a decision, defending my choice.	
4	I can justify my choices for which genre I choose for a particular piece of text creation.	
	Experimentation	
5	I can experiment with different forms and genres, and make a plan going forward based on my experimentation.	
	Developing Ideas & Creating Texts	
6	I can create and maintain a bank of ideas for future text creation.	
7	I can craft texts that contain major and minor characters, and use techniques to develop these characters.	
8	I can create texts for a specific purpose or audience.	
	Enhancing Texts	
9	I can use tools to help improve my vocabulary, spelling, grammar, word choice, and conventions in my text creation.	
10	I can revise my texts, incorporating others' feedback and knowledge about effective texts.	
11	I can rewrite sections of my text to enhance meaning.	

12	I can use strategies that add artistry to texts, such as figurative language, playing with voice, and changing tone.	
13	I can use strategies that help me improve my spelling and grammar.	
14	I can use strategies that help me attend to capitalization and punctuation in my text creation.	
	Working with Others	
15	I can ask for feedback about texts I create in ways that will elicit specific and helpful feedback.	
16	I can use active listening techniques when working with peers.	
17	I can celebrate my own and others' accomplishments in text creation.	
18	I can monitor my language use and work towards using inclusive language.	
19	I can create texts with others, incorporating ideas from all members of the group to advance the text.	
20	I can work collaboratively by defining roles and responsibilities, negotiating to find the basis for agreement, setting objectives and time frames, and reviewing progress.	
21	I can set and uphold group norms for standards of work and behaviour.	

The next step was to provide students with a broad overview of the learning process. Room to Breathe requires students to exercise some independence in the routines that are a part of the work. For some students, this was a big adjustment with a steep learning curve. Tara and Erin spent a long time working through the routines step-by-step with their students. They spent a lot of time at the beginning of the year developing classroom norms to build a strong, trusting classroom community that valued academic risk-taking. This is an important step and is time well spent at the beginning of the year as it enables students to embrace the challenges present in a new way of learning.

312   The BIG Book of Engagement Strategies

Figure 12.5 is a flowchart students were given to help them as they got used to the process. One round of Room to Breathe is six assignments, one from each strand, grouped into three Inhale and Exhale pairs. Students self-design their own projects, using a planning sheet to help them do so. Students are not restricted in *what* they want to do for their project, but they must ensure they are addressing each "I can" statement at least once. One round takes about three months of school, with four or five hours allocated each week. Erin and Tara completed two rounds with their students over the course of the year, and had plenty of time left to attend to other classwork.

Figure 12.5: Room to Breathe Flowchart

To begin a project, students complete a planning sheet (see Figure 12.6). When completing their planning sheet, students choose 2-4 outcomes that they would focus on during that assignment. These are the outcomes upon which they will be assessed.

Figure 12.6: Planning Sheet

Room to Breathe   Name: _____

Plan it Out – Inhale (Text Interpretation)

Circle one:

Reading   Listening   Viewing

My task

What am I going to do?

My Goals

My goal is… (What I want to learn and get better at)
What do I need to learn to complete this task?
What "I can" statements am I developing while working on this task?

Pencil due date into your agenda. Add your due date to the classroom calendar.

_____   _____   _____
Student Signature   Teacher Signature   Parent Signature

Room to Breathe   Name: _____

Plan it Out – Exhale (Text Creation)

Circle one:

Writing   Speaking   Representing

My task

What am I going to do?

My Goals

My goal is… (What I want to learn and get better at)
What do I need to learn to complete this task?
What "I can" statements am I developing while working on this task?

Pencil due date into your agenda. Add your due date to the classroom calendar.

_____   _____   _____
   Student Signature   Teacher Signature   Parent Signature

At the end of two full rounds, each student must have checked off all of the learning outcomes from their "I Can" checklist. Even though a student is focusing on 2-4 specific outcomes per project, they are still working on many other outcomes incidentally. However, students are only assessed on the learning outcomes that they selected. Additionally, Tara and Erin continue to teach all of the outcomes through other classroom work.

Planning sheets are signed by the student and the parent. The student and the teacher then sit down together and have a learning conference. This is where Erin and Tara offer guidance to the student to ensure that the work they want to engage in is appropriately challenging and meaningful. These conversations are exciting for both the teacher and the student. They spitball ideas back and forth, and a student usually comes away from this collaborative conversation with an idea that's better than the one they came into the conference with.

One of the most challenging parts for the students in designing their own projects is ensuring that they involve complex forms of thinking. Erin and Tara's goal to support students in becoming more critical consumers and creators of media becomes important here. Students do not intuitively know when a project is critical and analytical and when it is not. To support students in this, Tara and Erin created a continuum of thinking document, loosely framed around Bloom's Taxonomy (see Figure 12.7). In their planning conversations with students, if students suggest something like, "I want to watch the new Spiderman movie, and then write a report about it," this continuum of thinking can help support a conversation so the student's inhale and exhale would become something like, "I want to compare the characters in the new Spiderman movie to Greek mythology, and then write a review critiquing the film's use of character archetypes."

In this initial conversation, students are also supported in setting reasonable deadlines for their work based on the complexity of the task they have selected. The due date for the task is also the student's next conference date. To manage as many due dates as there are students in the classroom, Erin and Tara have the students write their due dates on a big classroom calendar. Once the Inhale has been approved, the teacher then signs the planning sheet and the work begins.

Figure 12.7: Continuum of Thinking

A Continuum of Thinking in Room to Breathe

Continuum of Thinking ↓

Remember
- Summarizing a topic you researched or a text you read/viewed/listened to.
- Literal retelling of a plot or event.
- Listing items from the text.
- Identify characters, plots, ideas, concepts.

Understand
- Plot summary with personal connections.
- Paraphrase.
- Comparing two texts.
- Contrasting two texts.
- Identify figurative language.
- Interpret and explain characters' qualities and motivations, connecting to concrete evidence from a text.

Apply/Analysis
- Opinion with general reference to the text.
- Analysis with general reference to the text.
- Explain the effect of figurative language on the "reader."

Evaluate
- Analysis with specific and detailed references to the text that leads logically to a personal opinion.
- Support an interpretation of the text with specific evidence from the text.
- Evaluate gathered information and create an interpretation (you + text = meaning).
- Discuss how figurative language is used to create meaning.

Create
- Apply your detailed and specific analysis to your exhale creation.
- Demonstrate evidence of why you made the specific choices that you made.
- Reflect on how you have created meaning in your exhale.
- Present your interpretation of your inhale in a purposeful way to create new meaning.
- Use figurative language to enhance meaning in your exhale.
- Consider your audience, and find ways to delight, inspire, motivate, and inform them.

After the first Inhale planning sheet has been approved, the conferencing process begins and is repeated for each subsequent strand. The teaching and assessment process for R2B are heavily dependent on student-teacher conferencing. The student completes their Inhale or Exhale assignment, reflects on their outcomes, and completes the planning sheet for their next Inhale or Exhale project. For example, a student begins their first Inhale by listening to a *Radiolab* podcast and taking notes on the interview techniques the hosts of the podcast use. Before the due date, the student completes a planning sheet for their first Exhale, which is to create their own podcast about rap music, and demonstrate the interview skills they noticed in the *Radiolab* podcast. When it's time for their scheduled conference, the student brings the notes from the *Radiolab* podcast, other evidence of the "I Can" statements they had selected, and the planning sheet for their next Exhale. During this conference, the student and teacher are able to discuss the student's work relative to the learning outcomes they selected on their planning sheet. Together they discuss where the student was successful and identify what the student's next steps will be for learning in the student's next project. Together, they collaborate to decide on a grade for the work based on the outcomes demonstrated. They then review the next planning sheet and the teacher signs off, and the students starts again. This process repeats as the students work their way through all six strands.

During conferences, targeted learning needs are identified and instruction is provided in the form of "mini-lessons." These short, 5-10 minute lessons target specific skills that are directly relevant to the work currently being done in the classroom. Sometimes they are relevant for all students, such as how to correctly cite a source, and sometimes they are useful to only a small group, like how to annotate song lyrics. In some cases, they are delivered during the conference to an individual student, such as the case where one student wanted to know the traits of a Petrarchan sonnet in order to write his own hip-hop-inspired sonnet. Depending on the needs of the group of students, mini-lessons may be repeated several times throughout the full round of Room to Breathe, since something that was not important learning for a student in October might become really important in December as they're working on a different project. A student should walk away from a mini-lesson with a new skill or knowledge that they will immediately use and apply.

Another important teaching tool for students is the use of mentor texts. Inspired by Allison Marchetti and Rebekah O'Dell's books on mentor texts and literary analysis and their website https://movingwriters.org/, one lesson all students participate in is how to find and analyze a mentor text. In the previous example of listening to an episode of the *Radiolab* podcast, the student used the podcast as a mentor text; the purpose was to learn from a professional author or creator in a specific genre and apply techniques they used in creating their own text. Students become adept at using publications like *Teen Vogue*, *The Ringer*, and *Rolling Stone* to notice how real writers format their text, write about movies and music, and provide evidence and examples to support their claims. This process is often very enlightening to students as they notice how professional writers follow, and break, the "rules" of good writing.

At the end of each Exhale, students publish their work to their grade level blog. This is an essential step because Erin and Tara want their students to create work for an authentic audience. The blog is also shared with parents. Time is set aside every few weeks to let students explore the blog to read and comment on their classmates' work. Ideas for new projects often emerge from this exploration time. Students are also encouraged to publish their work to other authentic audiences, and some have submitted writing to contests and open calls for publications.

The Principles

Several principles underlie the Room to Breathe approach that Erin and Tara have created. These principles highlight how Room to Breathe leads to significant student engagement and are factors in what creates the conditions for students to become absorbed in their learning.

1. **Principle 1: Literacy is multimodal and multilayered.** A truly generous definition of *text* understands that texts are much more than just books. Embracing the kinds of multimodal and multimedia texts that students engage with on a daily basis brings relevance to their learning. Literacy no longer means just reading books and a few poems from a regimented syllabus or antiquated canon. Students today are constantly engaging with a wide variety of texts and supporting 21st-century learners has to include accessing 21st-century texts.

2. **Principle 2: Student choice and ownership leads to authentic text creation.** This is where the possibility for students to move into absorbed engagement truly lies. When students accept the invitation to create projects that hone in on their interests, fascinations, and ideas, students will be more likely to become absorbed by what they're doing. Tara and Erin have seen this happen time and time again. Students focus on a topic they love, and create a truly innovative project that involves deeply and critically considering the ideas they want to explore. And when teachers let go of the need to direct the learning and are willing to embrace the ambiguity of not knowing

what the students will do, then student engagement thrives. In Room to Breathe, students are not given the option to simply comply. Because it is completely student-directed, the student is the one deciding the parameters of the work they will do. In no situation are they completing work just because the teacher told them to.

3. **Principle 3: All students need time to practice in order to succeed.** In Room to Breathe, students are constantly practicing the analysis and interpretation of texts across the strands and developing creative and innovative ways to share their own meaning and analysis with the world. All students, no matter where they begin this journey, need practice in order to do this. Room to Breathe meets each student where they are and the student and teacher, together, determine the next steps in learning. Practice and growth are continuous.

4. **Principle 4: Assessment *is* teaching, so teaching happens at school with students.** Assessment occurs with the students in conferences. Erin and Tara talk to the students about what they've done, what they've learned, what they're proud of, and what their next steps are. This conversation shifts assessment away from being evaluative and more about using feedback to drive learning forward. The role of assessment in student engagement cannot be overstated. Assessment has historically been used as a tool to encourage compliance. In order for students to move away from an understanding of assessment as evaluative (in other words, they do the work to receive the consequence of a good grade), and towards being formative (they do the work in order to grow and learn), Erin and Tara focus on carefully and deliberately building a culture of trust in their classrooms. The trust they build with their students is what enables them to have truly open and honest conversations with students about their next steps in learning, and help them understand that *everyone* has next steps in their learning.

5. **Principle 5: Every kid gets what they need.** The instruction that happens in Room to Breathe is "just-in-time" instruction that gives students lessons that are immediately relevant and applicable to their work. No student wastes time receiving instruction on something that is not immediately relevant to their work. Students are then able to apply their new learning immediately to the work at hand, increasing the likeliness that these lessons will be transferable.

6. **Principle 6: Students need an authentic audience to learn from and create for.**
Through Room to Breathe's use of mentor texts, students begin to understand that the best teachers exist everywhere around them. They come to know that texts that other people have created and published can be helpful in understanding how texts work and give them ideas for their own work.

When students have a broader audience beyond the teacher and publish their work for others, students can move beyond the compliant phase of engagement. Conversations with students when planning a new project often went something like this:

> Student: "I'm going to make a poster about the kind of irony in *The Office*."
>
> Teacher: "Why?"
>
> Student: "Well… to show the kinds of irony."
>
> Teacher: "Who is this poster for?"
>
> Student: "Well, you."
>
> Teacher: "I already know about the forms of irony. Who really needs to know this? Why? And how will you reach them?"

At this point, the student goes back to the drawing board, sometimes independently and sometimes collaboratively with Erin or Tara, and figures out who really wants to know about irony in *The Office*. Students then create a method of communication that truly reaches this audience.

Conclusion

Room to Breathe has sparked students to create truly remarkable projects rooted in students' passions and interests, like a rewriting of the final episode of *How I Met Your Mother* to provide a more satisfying conclusion, a critical analysis of a Childish Gambino album, an Instagram account reflecting the character arc of the protagonist in *Where'd You Go, Bernadette?* or creating a podcast developing a narrative analysis of a favorite hockey team's most recent win. Students have told Tara and Erin how important Room to Breathe was in their success, teaching them how to cast a critical eye on the media they consume, and develop a greater appreciation for what it means to create for others. Most importantly, Erin and Tara repeatedly heard feedback from the students that they *loved* the work they were doing. Learning in this way felt fun, important, and relevant to who they were as people and what goals they had in their own learning. This is where true engagement thrives.

Chapter Summary

This chapter was about moving someone from the point of interest to absorption by creating long-term tasks typically known as "projects." The notion of assigning projects to students is not special or uncommon. What makes these projects absorbing is that they are student-driven. This chapter started by sharing pitfalls that are easy to fall into when creating projects *for* students. Projects *by* students require the students to be the creators and to focus on what they want to learn. This makes these projects compelling and impactful beyond the unit or course; this also makes these projects figuratively messy. Teachers who dare to support projects like this will have students learning how to be connected to an audience outside of the school and students who are not just adept at receiving feedback, but students who asking for it. Students working on absorbing projects tap into both topics that are absorbing to them and also beliefs, skills, and/or people who they find absorbing.

Looking for even more strategies to
EXPLORE PROJECTS?
Please visit my website, www.LyonsLetters.com/learnmore, for print and digital recommendations including books, websites, videos, and more!

Thank you again to Lori DeCarlo for contributing Service Learning Projects, Michael Fisher for contributing Golden Lasso Moments, and Erin Quinn and Tara Vandertoorn for contributing Room to Breath—three strategies included in this chapter.

Reflection Prompts

1. In your own words, what is the problem with most problem-based learning tasks?

2. Think of a project that you have assigned in the past. How can you modify it so that it is more student-driven?

3. Write about a time when you were compelled to learn. What was the topic and what conditions made the learning compelling?

4. Name one thing you could do tomorrow based on what you learned from this chapter.

5. Tweet me @LyonsLetters to share an idea for a future reading or digital resource I should share on www.lyonsletters.com that would help someone who is interested become absorbed.

Persistent Questions

1. What have you done so far regarding the three challenge questions from Chapter 1?

    a. **Three:** Find at least three people with whom to share your learning.

    b. **Two:** Find at least two ideas that change you.

    c. **One:** Apply at least one idea from your reading.

    _____
    _____
    _____

2. What have you learned so far, and how will you use it?

    _____
    _____
    _____

Section V: Conclusion

Chapter 13 is the last chapter and brings to a close The BIG Book of Engagement Strategies. *It has been a long journey from the beginning to end, and the hope is that not only was the journey worth it, but that you are changed as a result. What's more, that you're ready, willing, and able to take what you have read and see what it looks like in your school.*

Chapter 13

Do It

"Do it now. Sometimes later becomes never."
~ Unknown

Recognizing Your Thinking Before You Read…

- Reread the quote at the top of this page and reflect on a time when you thought you would take action but waited. What impact did waiting have?

  _____
  _____
  _____

- How has your understanding of engagement changed as a result of reading this book?

  _____
  _____
  _____

- Now that all is said and done, what have you learned? What will you do?

  _____
  _____
  _____

Let's End at the Very Beginning

As you read in Chapter 1 and saw at the end of every chapter in the book, I invited you to read with a purpose. As a reminder, there were three action-oriented purposes:

- **THREE**: Before you read, identify at least three people with whom you will share ideas you're having as a result of your reading. It doesn't matter who you will share your ideas; it just matters that you will share.
- **TWO**: As you're reading, find at least two ideas that change you…it may be because you are surprised or unsure or validated. It doesn't matter why you change; you're just noting the change.
- **ONE**: When you're done reading, apply at least one idea. Don't limit yourself to a professional application; it could just as easily be a personal one. The point is that you do more than just read and think about engagement—it's that you take what you've read and thought and do something with it.

How'd you do? What have you learned, and what will you do about it? It's not enough to change your thinking—your actions need to change too.

One Bite at a Time

Think of something that you love to eat like pizza, cookies, a burger, or even watermelon. Unless you're in some type of eating contest, you would never want to shove the food you love whole into your mouth all at once. Instead, we enjoy the process of eating the foods we love bite by bite. This is the approach I recommend regarding trying out the strategies in this book—they are not meant to be devoured in one grand attempt because most will take time to decide what it will look like in *your* school with the people (adults and children) *you* work with. Even trying just one of these strategies to the point of feeling like it is one that you have internalized and personalized will take time, patience, and practice. To make the process of implementation enjoyable, here are some strategies on how to digest the strategies shared in this book.

- **Start Small:** Find a strategy that sounds fairly easy to do and do it. You'll feel great about putting something into action.

- **Don't Be a Hero:** Try one strategy at a time. Get familiar, comfortable, and good at that strategy and then add another.
- **Ask for Help:** Find someone who you trust to be a great thought-partner with you. Pick that person's brain to come up with ideas on how to implement a strategy that you want to try.
- **Hold Yourself Accountable:** Find someone who you trust to be a great accountability-partner for you. Ask that person to help to hold you accountable for trying out a strategy.
- **Celebrate:** Even if what you tried bombed, celebrate that you tried! You cannot expect the people you work with (students or adults) to feel like it's safe to take risks if you do not. This doesn't mean you won't succeed, just that you should celebrate the risk no matter what the result is.
- **Focus on the Learning:** One of the goals for using any strategy is to achieve better outcomes—in the case of the strategies in this book, those better outcomes would be increased levels of engagement. Another goal is to be reflective on the impact of the strategy. For this second reason, as you embark on putting these strategies into action, remember to focus on what you are learning as a result of the impact of the strategy.
- **Personalize:** The strategies in this book are meant to be a springboard into increasing engagement and not meant to be a scientific manual in how to achieve this end. In other words, if you want to alter these strategies, GO FOR IT! Teaching is certainly a science, but it is also an art. Be creative and make the strategy yours!
- **Ask Around:** I have already said it, but it bears repeating, "Everyone has at least one strategy to increase engagement. That means if you are ever stuck, all you need to do it talk with people you already know and trust. They will be able to give you the inspiration you need."
- **Give Back:** I know that you have a great strategy that you use to increase engagement. Please let others know about it so you can help them to help others. That includes me! Please contact me at lyonsletters@outlook.com with a great engagement strategy. I'd love to learn from you!

- **Visit www.LyonsLetters.com**: In addition to the resources already linked on my website that you might find helpful, as I get suggestions for books, videos, articles, websites, and strategies, the website grows. Please subscribe when you're there so you can get updates.

You Did It!

In the book, *The Archer,* Paulo Coelho wrote an allegory about a man, Tetsuya, who worked as a carpenter, but was once a famous archer. The boy working for Tetsuya had no idea of his archery talents, and upon discovering this secret asks Tetsuya to teach him to how to be a great archer himself. In response, Tetsuya tells the boy,

> "I will teach you all the necessary rules, but I can do no more than that. If you understand what I tell you, you can use those teachings as you wish. Now, a few minutes ago, you called me master. What is a master? I would say that he is not someone who teaches something, but someone who inspires the student to do his best to discover a knowledge he already has in his soul."[109]

Engagement is not difficult to understand, but that doesn't mean it is easy to create in schools. Even so, you have both the ability and knowledge. You have always had this in your soul. You are the master now so inspire your students to do their best and discover the knowledge they already have in their souls.

If you set a goal to finish this book, this is a time of celebration. You did it! With over fifty strategies, reading this book from start to finish is certainly an accomplishment. However, just like moving from non-compliance to compliance is worthy of celebration but not satisfaction, that is how I hope you're feeling now. Reading *The BIG Book of Engagement Strategies* is important, but not nearly as important as trying out what you are taking away from the book. It's time to set a new goal and to ask yourself now that you you're done reading, what will you start doing?

References

Chapter 1

[1] Lyon, H. (2020). *Engagement is not a unicorn (it's a narwhal): Mind-changing theory and strategies that will create real engagement* (p. 166). Alexandria, VA: EduMatch.

[2] Rothman, D. (Producer). (2020, May 24). CBS Sunday morning [Television series episode].

[3] Miller, Ronald. (2017) *Building a story brand: Clarify your message so customers will listen* (p. 77). New York, NY: HarperCollins Leadership.

Chapter 2

[4] Pink, D. H. (2009). *Drive: The surprising truth about what motivates us*. New York, NY: Riverhead Books.

[5] Yeager, D. S., & Walton, G. M. (2011). Social-psychological interventions in education. *Review of Educational Research, 81*(2), 267-301. doi:10.3102/0034654311405999

[6] Making sure each child is known. (2017, October 27). Retrieved October 24, 2020, from https://www.edutopia.org/video/making-sure-each-child-known

[7] Making sure each child is known. (2017, October 27). Retrieved from https://www.edutopia.org/video/making-sure-each-child-known

[8] Zacarian, D., Alvarez-Ortis, L., & Haynes, J. (2017). *Teaching to strengths: Supporting students living with trauma, violence, and chronic stress* (p. 42). Alexandria, VA: ASCD.

[9] Wright, J. (n.d.). How to: Manage problem behaviors: check-in/check-out. Retrieved from https://www.interventioncentral.org/node/970770

[10] McIvor, T., & Ross, B. (2016, August 09). Check in check out video tutorial: Educational behavior intervention. Retrieved from https://www.youtube.com/watch?v=vP7GJ72UxsA

[11] Vorrath, H. H., Brendtro, L. K. (2011). *Positive peer culture*. New Brunswick, NJ: Aldine Transaction.

[12] Durlak, J. A., Weissberg, R. P., Dymnicki, A. B., Taylor, R. D., & Schellinger, K. (2011). The impact of enhancing students' social and emotional learning: A meta-analysis of school-based universal interventions. *Child Development*, 82.

[13] Martin, J. E. (2017, August 11). Affirming and advancing SEL: The evidence is here. Retrieved October 12, 2020, from https://medium.com/@act/affirming-and-advancing-sel-the-evidence-is-here-3f33319062d1

Chapter 3

[14] Pearson, G. (2011, October 09). African famine: "I see you." Retrieved from http://www.huffingtonpost.ca/glen-pearson/africa-famine_b_922063.html

[15] Pearson, G. (2011, October 09). African famine: "I see you." Retrieved from http://www.huffingtonpost.ca/glen-pearson/africa-famine_b_922063.html

[16] Richardson, J. (1999, August/September). Norms put the 'golden rule' into practice for groups. *Tools for Schools*. Retrieved from https://learningforward.org/docs/tools-for-learning-schools/tools8-99.pdf?sfvrsn=2

[17] What we do. (n.d.). Retrieved March 21, 2021, from http://www.annefrankproject.com/what-we-do

Chapter 4

[18] List of unsolved problems in physics. (2020, September 14). Retrieved September 27, 2020, from https://en.wikipedia.org/wiki/List_of_unsolved_problems_in_physics

[19] Taleb, N. N. (2018). *Skin in the game: Hidden asymmetries in daily life*. New York: Random House.

[20] Tzapinar. (2012, February 26). Benjamin Zander - Work (How to give an A). Retrieved from https://www.youtube.com/watch?v=qTKEBygQic0

[21] Lyon, H. (2020). *Engagement is not a unicorn (it's a narwhal): Mind-changing theory and strategies that will create real engagement* (p. 75). Alexandria, VA: EduMatch.

Chapter 5

[22] Chand, S. R. (2016). *Who's holding your ladder?: Selecting your leaders, leaderships most critical decision* (p. 46). New Kensington, PA: Whitaker House.

[23] @KellysEdu. (2016, April 19). "Swimmer, shark spotter or flag pole holder?! Sue Meyes asks 'how do you react to change?' #tdsbEd #growthmindset" [Twitter Post]. Retrieved from https://twitter.com/kellysedu/status/722439529450356737?lang=en

[24] Sivers, D. (2010, February). How to start a movement. Retrieved from https://www.ted.com/talks/derek_sivers_how_to_start_a_movement?language=en

[25] Belshaw, D. (2009, October 23). Learning objectives: The basics. Retrieved from http://dougbelshaw.com/blog/2009/10/23/learning-objectives-the-basics/

[26] Animation. (2017, November 28). Retrieved from http://usscouts.org/usscouts/mb/mb158.asp

[27] Animal helpers.pdf. (n.d.). Retrieved from https://docs.google.com/file/d/0B6ggdlXxWNQ-Z1pzc19OVzJYUW8/edit

[28] Gold, J., & Gibson, A. (2018, August 16). Reading aloud to build comprehension. Retrieved October 13, 2020, from https://www.readingrockets.org/article/reading-aloud-build-comprehension

[29] Kozlowski, M. (2020, June 21). Audiobook trends and statistics for 2020. Retrieved October 13, 2020, from https://goodereader.com/blog/audiobooks/audiobook-trends-and-statistics-for-2020

[30] Kozlowski, M. (2020, June 21). Audiobook trends and statistics for 2020. Retrieved October 13, 2020, from https://goodereader.com/blog/audiobooks/audiobook-trends-and-statistics-for-2020

Chapter 6

[31] Lyon, H. (2020). *Engagement is not a unicorn (it's a narwhal): Mind-changing theory and strategies that will create real engagement* (pp. 143-144). Alexandria, VA: EduMatch.

[32] Marzano, R. J. (2003). *What works in schools: translating research into action*. Alexandria, VA: ASCD.

[33] Alrubail, R. (2015, December 17). The power of peer feedback. Retrieved from https://www.edutopia.org/discussion/power-peer-feedback

[34] Sackstein, S. (2017). *Peer feedback in the classroom: Empowering students to be the experts* (p. 14). Alexandria, VA: ASCD.

[35] Teachers observing teachers: A professional development tool for every school. (n.d.). Retrieved from https://www.educationworld.com/a_admin/admin/admin297.shtml

[36] Chaffey, D. (2020, October 19). Golden circle model: Sinek's theory value proposition: Start with why. Retrieved October 24, 2020, from https://www.smartinsights.com/digital-marketing-strategy/online-value-proposition/start-with-why-creating-a-value-proposition-with-the-golden-circle-model/

[37] Lima, C. (2014, March 03). Simon Sinek - Start with why - TED Talk Short Edited. Retrieved from https://www.youtube.com/watch?v=IPYeCltXpxw

[38] Chaffey, D. (2020, October 19). Golden circle model: Sinek's theory value proposition: Start with why. Retrieved October 24, 2020, from https://www.smartinsights.com/digital-marketing-strategy/online-value-proposition/start-with-why-creating-a-value-proposition-with-the-golden-circle-model/

[39] Rasmussen, A. (2016, January 6). Starting with why. Retrieved from https://threeteacherstalk.com/2016/01/06/starting-with-why/

[40] Fradkin, A. (2016, November 21). Exploring wonder and the NGSS with Paul Andersen. Retrieved from https://www.legendsoflearning.com/blog/exploring-ngss-paul-andersen/

[41] What is Phenomena-based learning? (n.d.). Retrieved from https://twigeducation.com/blog/what-is-phenomena-based-learning/

[42] NGSS EQuIP rubric: Using phenomena. (n.d.). Retrieved from https://www.teachingchannel.org/video/using-phenomena-achieve

[43] NGSS EQuIP rubric: Using phenomena. (n.d.). Retrieved from https://www.teachingchannel.org/video/using-phenomena-achieve

[44] Using phenomena in NGSS-designed lessons and units. (2016, September). Retrieved from https://www.nextgenscience.org/sites/default/files/Using Phenomena in NGSS.pdf

[45] Encouraging academic conversations with talk moves. (2018, November 16). Retrieved October 17, 2020, from https://www.edutopia.org/video/encouraging-academic-conversations-talk-moves

[46] Encouraging academic conversations with talk moves. (2018, November 16). Retrieved October 17, 2020, from https://www.edutopia.org/video/encouraging-academic-conversations-talk-moves

[47] (2020, June 26). What is the QFT? Retrieved November 04, 2020, from https://rightquestion.org/what-is-the-qft/

[48] (2020, June 26). What is the QFT? Retrieved November 04, 2020, from https://rightquestion.org/what-is-the-qft/

[49] Liljedahl P. (2016). Building thinking classrooms: Conditions for problem-solving. In: Felmer P., Pehkonen E., Kilpatrick J. (eds) *Posing and solving mathematical problems. research in mathematics education.* Springer, Cham. https://doi.org/10.1007/978-3-319-28023-3_21

[50] Zimmerman, A. (2018, November 13). "Number talks" to grow mathematical minds. Retrieved October 05, 2020, from https://www.scholastic.com/teachers/blog-posts/alycia-zimmerman/number-talks-grow-mathematical-minds/

[51] Nsta. (2020). *Science and engineering practices*. NGSS@NSTA. https://ngss.nsta.org/practicesfull.aspx

[52] APPENDIX F – science and engineering practices in the NGSS. (2013, April). Retrieved October 18, 2020, from https://www.nextgenscience.org/sites/default/files/resource/files/Appendix%20F%20%20Science%20and%20Engineering%20Practices%20in%20the%20NGSS%20-%20FINAL%20060513.pdf

[53] Marzano, R. J., Pickering, D. J., & Pollock, J. E. (2001). *Classroom instruction that works: Research-based strategies for increasing student achievement* (p. 4). Boston, MA: Pearson Education.

[54] Marzano, R. J., Pickering, D. J., & Pollock, J. E. (2001). *Classroom instruction that works: Research-based strategies for increasing student achievement* (p. 7). Boston, MA: Pearson Education.

[55] Hogle, P. (2016, December 20). Forgetting helps you remember: Why spaced learning works. *Learning Solutions Magazine.* https://learningsolutionsmag.com/articles/2168/forgetting-helps-you-remember-why-spaced-learning-works.

[56] Why your students aren't really learning and how you can help. (2019, February 12). Retrieved January 30, 2021, from https://thecttl.wordpress.com/2019/02/07/why-your-students-arent-really-learning-and-how-you-can-help/

[57] Briggs, S. (2015, July 20). Why straight-a students haven't learned as much as you think. Retrieved January 30, 2021, from https://www.opencolleges.edu.au/informed/features/why-straight-a-students-havent-learned-as-much-as-you-think/

[58] Frank, T. (2020, July 17). How to remember more of what you learn with spaced repetition. Retrieved January 30, 2021, from https://collegeinfogeek.com/spaced-repetition-memory-technique/

[59] Tunga, H. (2017, September 06). Exploring new frameworks to train leaders? You want to see this one! Retrieved February 03, 2021, from https://www.trainers-toolbox.com/exploring-new-frameworks-to-train-leaders-you-want-to-see-this-one/

Chapter 7

[60] DuFour, R., DuFour, R. B., Eaker, R. E., Many, T. W., & Mattos, M. (2016). *Learning by doing: A handbook for professional learning communities at work* (p. 164). Bloomington, IN: Solution Tree Press.

[61] DuFour, R., DuFour, R. B., Eaker, R. E., Many, T. W., & Mattos, M. (2016). *Learning by doing: A handbook for professional learning communities at work* (p. 168). Bloomington, IN: Solution Tree Press.

[62] Wright, J. (n.d.). RTI in a time of staff cuts: Ideas to provide quality interventions with less... Retrieved from https://www.interventioncentral.org/response_to_intervention_rti_staff_cuts

[63] Scherer, M. (2012). Perspectives / Finessing Feedback. *Educational Leadership,70*(1), 7.

[64] Wan, T. (2018, July 23). 'When' does learning happen best? Dan Pink on the science behind timing and education - EdSurge News. Retrieved from https://www.edsurge.com/news/2018-01-02-when-does-learning-happen-best-dan-pink-on-the-science-behind-timing-and-education

[65] Dueck, Myron. (2014). *Grading smarter not harder: Assessment strategies that motivate kids and help them learn* (p. 65). Alexandra, VA: ASCD.

[66] Garcia, K. (n.d.). Flipped classroom. Retrieved from http://texascomputerscience.weebly.com/flipped-classroom.html

[67] Willis, J. (2016, December 07). Using brain breaks to restore students' focus. Retrieved October 18, 2020, from https://www.edutopia.org/article/brain-breaks-restore-student-focus-judy-willis

[68] Willis, J. (2016, December 07). Using brain breaks to restore students' focus. Retrieved October 18, 2020, from https://www.edutopia.org/article/brain-breaks-restore-student-focus-judy-willis

[69] Posey, A. (2019). *Engage the brain: How to design for learning that taps into the power of emotion* (p. 60). Alexandria, Virginia: ASCD.

Chapter 8

[70] Grant, A. (2019, April 02). Stop asking kids what they want to be when they grow up. Retrieved October 15, 2020, from https://www.nytimes.com/2019/04/01/smarter-living/stop-asking-kids-what-they-want-to-be-when-they-grow-up.html

[71] Nottingham, J. (2017). *The learning challenge: How to guide your students through the learning pit to achieve deeper understanding* (p. xvii). Thousand Oaks, CA: Corwin.

[72] Free graphics. (2020, August 06). Retrieved October 18, 2020, from https://www.challenginglearning.com/learning-pit/free-graphics/

Chapter 9

[73] Schmittou, D. (2020, October). Heather Lyon reminds us all that engagement is not a unicorn. It is real and it is possible. Retrieved October 18, 2020, from https://www.youtube.com/watch?v=8GCCqruuDjg&t=7s

[74] Schmittou, D. (2020, October). Heather Lyon reminds us all that engagement is not a unicorn. It is real and it is possible. Retrieved October 18, 2020, from https://www.youtube.com/watch?v=8GCCqruuDjg&t=7s

[75] McTighe, J., & Wiggins, G. (2012). Understanding by design framework. Retrieved from https://www.ascd.org/ASCD/pdf/siteASCD/publications/UbD_WhitePaper0312.pdf

[76] Adams, N. (n.d.). *Presentation on theme: "UbD: Stages of Backward Design"*. Slide Player. https://slideplayer.com/slide/16298748/.

[77] Clear, J. (2018). *Atomic habits: an easy & proven way to build good habits & break bad ones*. United States: Penguin Publishing Group.

[78] Schinske, J., & Tanner, K. (2014). Teaching more by grading less (or differently). *CBE—Life Sciences Education, 13*(2), p. 161. doi:10.1187/cbe.cbe-14-03-0054

[79] Brookhart, S. M. (2017). How to Give Effective Feedback to Your Students (p. 6). Alexadria, VA: ASCD.

[80] Hehir, J. (Director). (2020, May 17). Episode X [Television series episode]. In *The last dance*. ESPN.

Chapter 10

[81] Lyon, H. (2020). *Engagement is not a unicorn (it's a narwhal): Mind-changing theory and strategies that will create real engagement* (p. 89). Alexandria, VA: EduMatch.

[82] Greene, J. P., Kisida, B., & Bowen, D. H. (2018, September 17). The educational value of field trips. Retrieved from https://www.educationnext.org/the-educational-value-of-field-trips/

[83] Greene, J. P., Kisida, B., & Bowen, D. H. (2018, September 17). The educational value of field trips. Retrieved from https://www.educationnext.org/the-educational-value-of-field-trips/

[84] The benefits of learning through field trips. (2016, January 09). Retrieved from https://www.teachthought.com/learning/the-benefits-of-learning-through-field-trips/

[85] Mandel, S. (n.d.). Why use virtual field trips? Retrieved from http://www.phschool.com/eteach/professional_development/virtual_field_trips/essay.html

[86] Pang, A. S. (2018). *Rest: Why you get more done when you work less* (p. 94). New York, NY: Basic Books.

[87] Cannon, L. (2011, February 24). Tech companies host internships for middle schoolers. Retrieved from https://www.inc.com/articles/201102/george-haines-tech-companies-host-internships-for-kids.html

[88] Scheffer, J., Wong, L., & Aher, G. (2018, October 23). Student-run genius bar: The facilitator's guide. Retrieved from https://www.iste.org/explore/articleDetail?articleid=499&utm_campaign=EdTekHub Lead Generation&utm_source=hs_email&utm_medium=email&utm_content=67220631&_hsenc=p2ANqtz-84ARXnOnndQEHsQRsA7siqE9HZP_T8CR7fInVlx31FnQVF-qJWz2nSTMEM_6bxe91Vp0D_74nQE7YS0pk3UENbpQRaCg&_hsmi=67221397

Chapter 11

[89] Lizingham, C. (2020, February 19). There's a reason why potato chips are so addictive. Retrieved October 22, 2020, from https://www.eatthis.com/this-why-its-so-hard-stop-eating-chips/

[90] Gladwell, M. (2007). *Blink: The power of thinking without thinking* (p. 160). New York, NY: Little, Brown.

[91] Gladwell, M. (2007). *Blink: The power of thinking without thinking* (p. 162). New York, NY: Little, Brown.

[92] Burgess, D. (2012). *Teach like a pirate: Increase student engagement, boost your creativity, and transform your life as an educator.* San Diego, CA: Dave Burgess Consulting.

[93] Burgess, D. (2012). *Teach like a pirate: Increase student engagement, boost your creativity, and transform your life as an educator* (pp. 83, 89, 95, 111). San Diego, CA: Dave Burgess Consulting.

[94] Cherry, K. (2019, October 07). How does self-determination theory explain motivation? Retrieved November 07, 2020, from https://www.verywellmind.com/what-is-self-determination-theory-2795387

Chapter 12

[95] Berman, S., Schumer, S. (1998). *Service learning for the multiple intelligences classroom* (pp. xxii-xxiii). Andover, MA: SAGE Publications.

[96] Arnold, H., Elias, M. J. (2006). *The educator's guide to emotional intelligence and academic achievement: Social-emotional learning in the classroom.* Thousand Oaks, CA: SAGE Publications.

[97] Zhao, Y. (2012). *World class learners: Educating creative and entrepreneurial students* (p. 94). Thousand Oaks, CA: Corwin Press, a Joint Publication with the National Association of elementary School Principals.

[98] Zhao, Y. (2012). *World class learners: Educating creative and entrepreneurial students* (pp. 199-200). Thousand Oaks, CA: Corwin Press, a Joint Publication with the National Association of elementary School Principals.

[99] Zhao, Y. (2012). *World class learners: Educating creative and entrepreneurial students* (p. 199). Thousand Oaks, CA: Corwin Press, a Joint Publication with the National Association of elementary School Principals.

[100] Zhao, Y. (2012). *World class learners: Educating creative and entrepreneurial students* (p. 201). Thousand Oaks, CA: Corwin Press, a Joint Publication with the National Association of elementary School Principals.

[101] Zhao, Y. (2012). *World class learners: Educating creative and entrepreneurial students* (p. 201). Thousand Oaks, CA: Corwin Press, a Joint Publication with the National Association of elementary School Principals.

[102] Patton, A., & Robin, J. (2012, February). Work that matters - Innovation Unit. Retrieved from https://www.innovationunit.org/wp-content/uploads/2017/04/Work-That-Matters-Teachers-Guide-to-Project-based-Learning.pdf

[103] Zhao, Y. (2012). *World class learners: Educating creative and entrepreneurial students* (p. 204). Thousand Oaks, CA: Corwin Press, a Joint Publication with the National Association of elementary School Principals.

[104] Zhao, Y. (2012). *World class learners: Educating creative and entrepreneurial students* (p. 203). Thousand Oaks, CA: Corwin Press, a Joint Publication with the National Association of elementary School Principals.

[105] Zhao, Y. (2012). *World class learners: Educating creative and entrepreneurial students* (pp. 205-208). Thousand Oaks, CA: Corwin Press, a Joint Publication with the National Association of elementary School Principals.

[106] Zmuda, A., Alcock, M., Fisher, M. L. (2017). *The quest for learning: How to maximize student engagement.* United States: Solution Tree.

[107] Dan Pink recommends a 'FedEx day' for students and teachers. (2011, June 3). Retrieved from http://life-long-learners.com/dan-pink-recommends-a-fedex-day-for-students-and-teachers/

[108] Dan Pink Recommends a 'FedEx day' for Students and Teachers. (2011, June 3). Retrieved from http://life-long-learners.com/dan-pink-recommends-a-fedex-day-for-students-and-teachers/

[109] Coehlo, Paulo. (2020). *The archer* (p. 11). (M. Jull Costa, Trans.) New York, NY: Knopf.